GW01018215

THE ART NOUVEAU POSTER

François Mathey, self-portrait

First of all thank you to my friend Nicholas Lowry, President of Swann Galleries in New York, with whom I organised the first modernist posters sales in 2000. Over the years we have gathered a unique set of images from this period which has made this book possible.

And thank you to a well-established and always hungry team: Nicolas Guichard, Anne Trinh, Thierry Sarfis and Olivier Cabon, tireless once they are refuelled.

Frances Lincoln Limited
www.franceslincoln.com

The Art Nouveau Poster

Translation by Stewart Spencer

First Frances Lincoln edition 2015

First published as 'L'Affiche Art Nouveau' by Editions Hazan, Paris, 2015

A catalogue record for this book is available from the British Library.

978-0-7112-3718-6

Design Thierry Sarfis, execution/direction Olivier Cabon, Thotm
Production Claire Hostalier, éditions Hazan
Printed and bound by Stamperia Artistica, Trofarello (TO), Italy

1 2 3 4 5 6 7 8 9

THE ART NOUVEAU POSTER

ALAIN WEILL

FRANCES LINCOLN LIMITED
PUBLISHERS

CONTENTS

CHAP BOOK

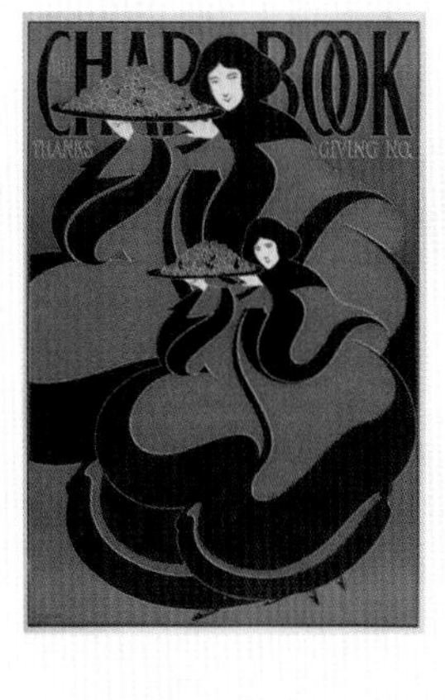

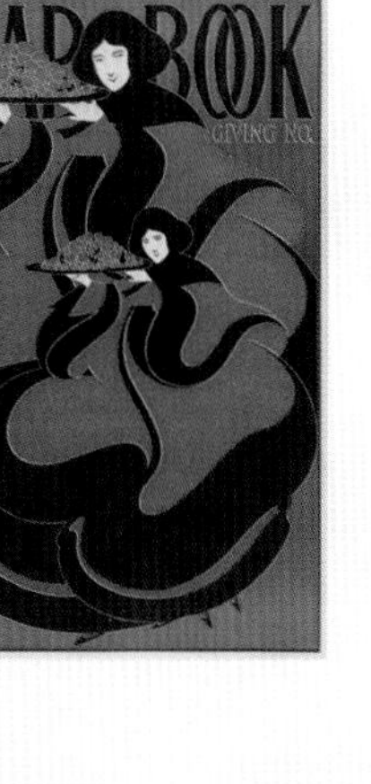

CAFFÈ
COSTINA'S COFFEE Co
(ITALY)

HANA KVAPILOVÁ
RECITACE

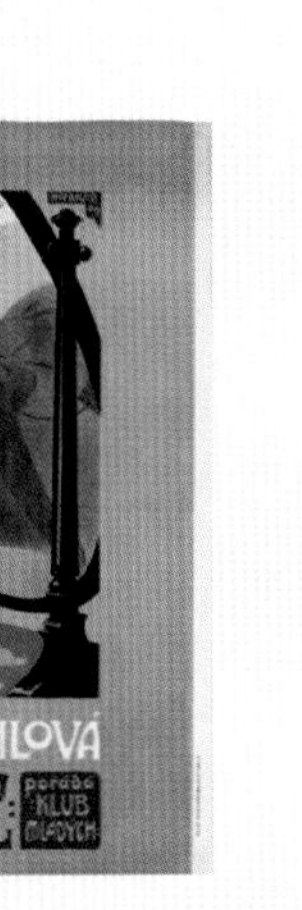

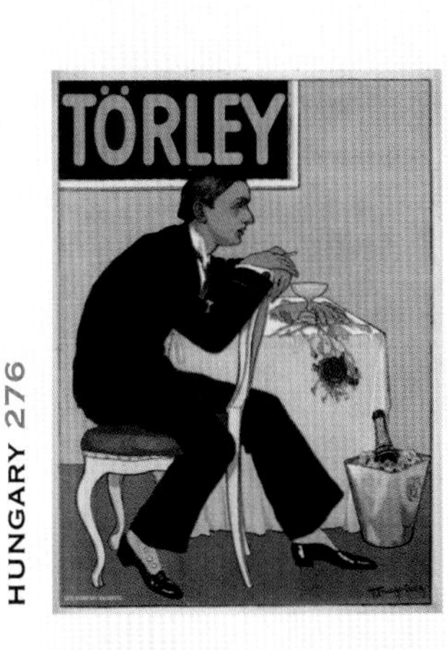
TÖRLEY

TUTKI
DO PAPIEROSÓW
RADOM
KRAKÓW
M.PASCHALSKI

M.S KOBBS SÖHER
GÖTEBORG
ÄKTA THEER

COLOUR POSTERS: AT HOME WITH THE DAUBERS

I don't get it – I just don't get making a fool of yourself at exhibitions and not giving a shit about getting a stiff neck by ogling dirty linen in gilt frames.

Instead of a load of old cobblers like this, let's suppose we're outside in the street, pissing against a wall, out for a stroll with a friend or going back to the daily grind before rushing back to the hovel we call home where, without putting ourselves out, we can see posters, not that sickening drivel produced by phonies who are two a penny. No, colour posters that show simple down-to-earth folks, animals, flowers and trees, as in pictures painted in oils.

It's like an open-air exhibition that lasts all year round and that's free for all to admire wherever they happen to be.

Sometimes the young lads who make them really know their stuff, but still these posters aren't trying to be fancy and aren't placed behind glass or exhibited by some precious collector whose name means nothing to us. They may be taken down at a moment's notice and others pasted in their place. And so on. The posters couldn't give a damn. And that's good. It's art, for God's sake, it's stunning, it's a blend of life and art with no tricks to it within the grasp of all decent men and women.

It has to be said that among these posters are some that have no reason to give themselves airs and graces – those, for example, that are by Guillaume, Bac, Choubrac, Balluriau, Lefèvre, Silva, Gray, Métivet, Sinet, Toché, Truchet, Bourgeois, Noury, Lunel and the rest of them. Some of them aren't too bad, but none of them really cuts the mustard.

But the looniest of them all – as is only right and proper – are those that beat the drum for pseudo-patriotic shit – parties, books and plays. There's nothing funny about that.

If an artist has any brains in his noddle, he couldn't care less about his country but just thinks it's a load of old nonsense. If he has to paint soldiers, he doesn't miss a trick but sticks the amazing gobs of drunkards, scoundrels and wastrels on bullion-fringe epaulettes (they need to look realistic!) and he ignores the foot-sloggers' nasty looks that say a lot about the discipline's incompetence and about such a filthy profession's ability to turn people into morons.

What then? The only people who can draw jingoistic posters like these are scatter-brained artists scarcely capable of creating the outlines of a pile of cow-dung or of smearing ointment on the arse of a mangy cur.

To hell with all these poor duffers! Let's turn instead to all those fine fellows who can make a decent fist of it.

When it comes to posters, Chéret has certainly produced a damned lot. There is no way that they can all be listed. His most recent are OLYMPIA, SAXOLÉINE and PANTOMIMES LUMINEUSES. The women in his posters are all very buxom; they wiggle their arses, stick out their breasts and laugh like little tarts; they have turned-up noses, tousled hair, feathered bonnets and togs that billow in the breeze. There's also a collection of wide-eyed, wide-mouthed brats. But no black for him, no shadows or outlines. Everything is whiplash curves, everything is chock full of flamboyant colours – it's as explosive as dynamite and as fresh as a field of daisies.

That Lautrec's got a hell of a nerve, and no mistake. No half measures, the way he draws, or the way he colours either. Great flat dollops of white, black and red and simplified forms – that's all there is to it. He's got them off to a tee, those gaga old capitalists, completely past it, sitting at tables with clever little tarts drooling over them and trying to make them fork up. There's LA GOULUE, REINE DE JOIE, LE DIVAN JAPONAIS, and two bars that are called Braunt's. That's all he's done in the

Félix Fénéon by Henri Martin

poster line, but what's so fantastic is the single-minded way he does it, the bare-faced cheek of it, the humour. It's one in the eye for all those halfwits who can never bear to taste anything stronger than a marshmallow.

Willette has designed hardly any posters at all, but when he comes up with the goods, it's really grown-up: L'ÉLYSÉE-MONTMARTRE, L'ENFANT PRODIGUE and, most recently, a new one for an exhibition at the Champ-de-Mars that shows a buxom farmer's wife tilling the soil with a musical plough drawn by children that are as good as gold.

Grasset has designed some ten or so posters coloured by a grid of close-set lines. His most recent are LES TAPIS DE LA PLACE CLICHY (a camel, an Arab and a commercial traveller), LE CHOCOLAT MEXICAIN and L'ENCRE MARQUET.

There follows a list of ten or so other fellows, each of whom has produced a couple of posters, all of which are really quite wonderful.

Gausson (a ballerina holding up a sheet);

Luce (the bawling young Mévisto* togged out in a black Pierrot costume);

Ibels (the same Mévisto observing a labourer breaking the hard ground with his pickaxe, together with a private killing time and a prole lighting his pipe);

Bonnard (FRANCE-CHAMPAGNE, stylish wisps of black on pink, white and pale yellow);

Steinlen (VERNET-LES-BAINS); Denis (LA DÉPÊCHE DE TOULOUSE); Forain (LES ARTS DE LA FEMME); Aman-Jean (LA ROSE-CROIX).

Three others whose posters I should very much like to see wiped clean are Lucien and Georges Pissarro and Vuillard.

Don't be mad, comrades, at seeing me list the names of the sharks who commissioned the posters in question. It sure as hell isn't to offer them free publicity but to indicate as quickly as possible the leading lights that I've been talking about.

Also, I have an idea at the back of my head that I want to submit to you now.

These posters are stunning – why not make use of them from time to time?

If they've been in place for only a short time, if it's raining cats and dogs or if they're stuck to cardboard, there's a good chance you can unglue them, for heaven's sake – only watch out for the cops.

Once you're back home, what on earth's to be done with them?

Wash them under plenty of cold water, hang them out to dry over a broom handle or by using some bits of string, patch up any tears and Bob's your uncle, you can then pin your easy kill on the wall of your pad where, needless to add, your bastard landlord has allowed the wallpaper to crumble away.

A Lautrec or a Chéret at home – it certainly brightens up the place.

It creates a riot of colour and brings a sense of fun to your digs.

Sure! Posters really add style.

And so you can grab a painting at a knock-down price more chic than the daubings that are the delight of the arseholes from high society.

And now, let's be off to see the colour of a bottle of light wine at the bar opposite.

Félix Fénéon, *Le Père peinard*, 30 April 1893

* Mévisto was the stage name of Auguste-Marie Wisteaux, an actor at the Théâtre Libre and a childhood friend of the theatre's owner, André Antoine.

Louis Abel-Truchet, 1900, detail

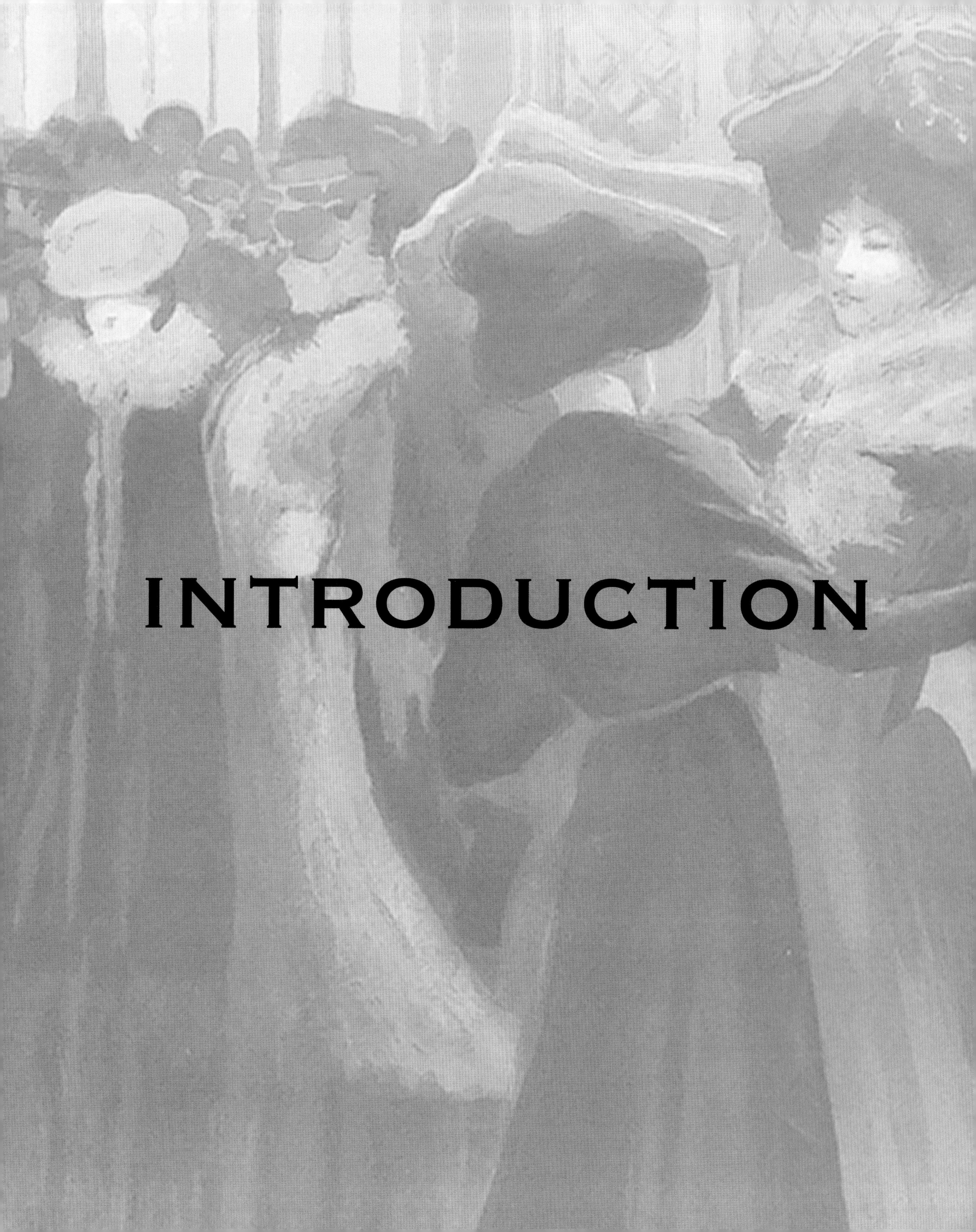

INTRODUCTION

Félix Vallotton, *c.*1896

For my opening gambit I have chosen a particularly brilliant text by a critic and visionary pioneer. Félix Fénéon was the anarchist assistant editor of *La Revue blanche* before taking over the running of the Bernheim Gallery, where he was one of the first to understand Primitivism. In his article for *Le Père peinard* he uses an exuberant and wholly appropriate argot to describe the discovery of street posters by someone of an inquisitive frame of mind.

Art nouveau was a vast movement that essentially evolved in Europe and, to a lesser extent, in the United States in the second half of the nineteenth century and was a reaction to the prevailing lack of creativity in the decorative arts, in which the dominant forms were pastiche and academicism.

Art nouveau was not a part of the theory of successive '-isms', while its name, often the result of chance, differed from country to country.

Octave Maus and Edmond Picard were the first to describe themselves as 'believers in the new art', a phrase they used in the journal *L'Art moderne* that they published in Brussels from 1881 onwards. In France, L'Art Nouveau was the name of the gallery that Samuel Bing opened in Paris in 1895,[1] while in Germany it was the magazine *Jugend*, established in 1896, that gave the movement its name: Jugendstil. The term Secession was also used in both Germany and Austria. In Barcelona people spoke of '*modernismo*', in Italy of the Stile Liberty[2] and in the United States of the Tiffany Style. In France commentators of an ironic frame of mind christened it the '*style nouille*' – literally, the 'noodle style'. The German equivalent was *tenia belga*, or Belgian tapeworm. For the Goncourt Brothers, it was the 'Yachting Club Style', a term that requires no further comment, just as is the case with the surprising '*os de mouton*', or 'sheep bone' style.

Jean Prouvé, who was the son of the principal of the École de Nancy and, after 1945, a proponent of a more functional approach to the arts, summed up the idea perfectly when he wrote that art nouveau was not so much a style as the desire for a style based on three key words: new, young and modern.

The world's first International Exhibition was held in London in 1851. If we ignore the magnificent Crystal Palace that was built to house the exhibits, its contents caused bewilderment, Dickens, for example, complaining that 'I don't say "there is nothing in it" – there's too much.'

Historicism and pastiche were the dominant styles at this time, tolling the death knell of the decorative arts. The British were the first to stage a recovery, when William Morris founded his Arts & Crafts movement and championed the return of the pre-Renaissance artisan. Morris's disciple, John Ruskin,

Gisbert Combaz, 1899

1. It is interesting to note that the two Parisian kingpins of this fashion were both German, Bing himself and his alter ego, Julius Meier-Graefe, who created the Maison Moderne.
2. The name is derived from that of Arthur Liberty, an English dealer in *objets d'art* from India and Japan who also manufactured printed and dyed fabrics and opened a shop in Paris.

‘WE NEED ONLY LOOK AT WILLIAM MORRIS – THIS MAN HAS PRODUCED BOOKS THAT ARE READABLE AND OBJECTS THAT CAN BE USED’
HENRI DE TOULOUSE-LAUTREC, letter to his friend Henri Nocq

Koloman Moser, 1898-1899

helped in no small way to promote the movement’s theories, but whereas those theories enjoyed a very real success in the world of the book, the movement inevitably withered as a result of its refusal to embrace industrialization. As the French writer Roger Marx has written, ‘they lost their way in the night of the past in their attempts to light up the future’.[3] In spite of this, there is no doubt that it was Morris who triggered these new developments. Octave Mirbeau may not have been one of Morris’s most outspoken detractors, but he was still indignant at this state of affairs: ‘Is it not ridiculous that anyone wanting to acquire a pretty fabric, for example, or a tastefully worked brass object or a piece of furniture that is not a heavy and stupid copy of earlier forms should have to go looking for it in England where, encouraged by William Morris, an extremely interesting movement involving an artistic decorative renaissance is growing more distinctive by the day and aspiring to ever greater perfection in the process?’[4] The underlying principle of art nouveau remained the same: the rejection of all attempts to distinguish between the major and the minor arts and a refusal to countenance the historicist pastiche with any degree of equanimity.

Eugène Viollet-le-Duc struck an equally rebellious note: ‘It is barbaric to reproduce a Greek temple in Paris or London, since any attempt to transplant such a monument to a different setting and to imitate it there betrays an ignorance of the principle that caused it to be built in the first place.’ An entire generation rose up in revolt. In 1888, the Nabis pleaded for the abolition of the dividing line between painting and decoration, and ten years later the inaugural number of *Ver Sacrum* (Sacred Spring), the official journal of the Vienna Secession, announced that ‘We know no difference between “great art” and “intimate art”, between art for the rich and art for the poor’.[5]

3. Roger Marx, *Les Maîtres de l’affiche 1896–1900*, Chêne, Paris, 1978. The five volumes that make up *Les Maîtres de l’affiche* were originally published in Paris between 1896 and 1900. An English translation of Marx’s introductory matter, reproducing all 240 images, was published by Academy Editions of London in 1977.
4. Octave Mirbeau, illustrated supplement to *Le Journal*, 29 April 1893
5. Anon., ‘Weshalb wir eine Zeitschrift herausgeben’, *Ver Sacrum*, 1 (Jan. 1898), 6.

Henry van de Velde struck a ribald note: 'The bourgeoisie has reduced the role of art to a sense of ownership. We exhaust ourselves trying to laugh in spite of ourselves in a setting marked by ennui.' And Jean Prouvé, writing in 1983, described the art of 1900 as 'an attempt to break down the traditional barriers between the different genres, to modify the existing frames of existence and to open up the way to a new social conscience'.[6]

The spirit of this generation lived on in the Bauhaus and in what Prouvé termed '*stylisme*'. In the event it was the word 'design' that carried the day. And yet, however spectacular this attempt to breathe new life into the decorative arts, it remained the preserve of an enlightened and spendthrift bourgeoisie that followed in the wake of every fleeting fashion.

Fritz Dannenberg, 1896

Although still in its earliest infancy, the poster was about to enjoy a golden age, profiting from the progress that had been made in printing and in France's economic growth. Paris was the capital of luxury and pleasure and as such it drew young artists from all over the world. Between the two Universal Exhibitions of 1889 and 1900, the decorative arts triumphed and, at their centre, the poster became increasingly successful. In this it was helped by a specifically French development in the form of a law that came into force on 29 July 1881, allowing posters to be stuck to any object and to any site that was not specifically excluded. Such tolerance was unique.

The poster could not have developed as it did without a revolution in colour printing bound up with the discovery of Japanese art, more especially the *ukiyo-e* engravings and the vogue that these enjoyed.

The Hokusai Manga that Félix Bracquemond bought in 1856 served as a model for a generation, while London, Paris and, indeed, the whole of Europe witnessed an invasion of orientalism: the Paris shop La Porte Chinoise opened its doors in the early 1860s; and the enthusiasm on the part of collectors such as the Goncourt Brothers, Philippe Burty and Théodore Duret was equalled only by that of Manet, Degas and Pissarro. As we have already noted, Samuel Bing opened his gallery L'Art Nouveau in 1895, having previously published *Le Japon artistique* between 1888 and 1891.

As André Mellerio observed in his seminal study in 1898, 'the first thing that strikes one about the development of the coloured lithograph is not just the number of artists who have taken an interest in it, but also their diversity'.[7]

What is true of the print and engraving is equally true of the poster, which likewise attracted talented young artists of the succeeding generation.[8]

6. In *Le Livre des Expositions Universelles*, Éditions des Arts Décoratifs, Paris, 1983.
7. André Mellerio, *La Lithographie originale en couleurs*, L'Estampe et l'Affiche, Paris, 1898.
8. The work was also published by the journal *L'Estampe et l'Affiche*.

Mellerio also explains what was so modern about Jules Chéret: 'If, with regard to the current movement, we were asked to define the line of demarcation which, once crossed, allowed the chromolithograph to enter the world of art, we would have no hesitation in locating it in the work of Chéret. Chéret breathed new life into the poster. Indeed, he may even be said to have created it for the modern world, not only producing an oeuvre all of his own but exerting a widespread influence. [...] Artistic inspiration was wedded in advance to technology and found direct expression in his chosen method of execution.'[9]

The artists who signed up to the movement revealed an astonishing stylistic diversity. And to this variety must be added the particular characteristics of the countries from which they hailed. As the German art historian Gerhard Bott noted in 1977, 'by Jugendstil, every artist meant his own individual style'.[10]

Even so, we may list a number of major lines of development.

The first of these lines is the one associated with the interest in the Middle Ages evinced by William Morris and by the leader of the Pre-Raphaelites, Dante Gabriel Rossetti. (The group's name speaks for itself.) Their aim was to rediscover the freedom of medieval artisans and to revive the gestural language of those craftsmen who had built the Gothic cathedrals of Europe.

According to Eugène Grasset, 'the Renaissance was an ill-fated period'. It was necessary in his eyes 'to study the Middle Ages and derive from it the common sense that was to be found in everything at that time. We then need to set to work with the same common sense and the same sense of freedom. And yet here too, it would be wrong to copy medieval art and to seek to introduce it in that way into modern life.'

Grasset was on a knife edge here, but he averted the danger by providing a sense of direction: 'We shall find in nature all of the elements that we could possibly desire.' In advancing this view, he was echoing the members of the École de Nancy, including Émile Gallé, who in 1892 had argued that 'Our roots are in the depths of the forest, on the banks of springs and on the mossy grass.' He will also have been thinking of the architect Victor Horta, who three years later advocated a naturalist but structural approach to art: 'Let us abandon the leaf and the flower but retain the stem.'

In both Paris and Nancy, the French variety of art nouveau tended to embrace floral motifs, exerting a considerable influence on Italy and Spain, inspiring the Anglo-Saxon nations and establishing schools throughout Eastern Europe and even as far afield as Russia and Japan.

9. Mellerio, *La Lithographie* (note 7).
10. Gerhard Bott, *Jugendstil (Europalia 77)*, Palais des Beaux-Arts, Brussels, 1977, p.14.

Maxime Dethomas, 1897

Frédéric-Auguste Cazals, 1894

The other major source of inspiration was the Japanese engraving in the *ukiyo-e* tradition, which opened up a new field to the most daring forms of composition, spelling the end of symmetry, of a frontal perspective and of relief, all of which were abandoned in favour of outlines and solid colours.

Among the most spectacular examples of this approach are the posters of Toulouse-Lautrec and the Nabis. The demand for posters grew, and the numerous illustrated magazines of the period saw their illustrators turn to poster

'WE ARE CERTAINLY NOT CLAIMING TO INVENT AN ART, FOR SUCH A THING IS IMPOSSIBLE, BUT SHALL CONTENT OURSELVES WITH LEADING THE WAY BY ABANDONING ALL COPIES OF THE ORNAMENTS FROM ANOTHER AGE.' EUGÈNE GRASSET

Anonymous

art. Even artists who normally worked at the easel occasionally turned their hand to posters. The result was a mosaic of cosmopolitan talents that placed itself in the service of advertising: Alphonse Mucha was Czech, Grasset and Théophile-Alexandre Steinlen were Swiss, Georges de Feure was Dutch and Manuel Orazi was Italian, to name only a handful of poster artists of the period.

French printers were the first to equip themselves with large lithographic presses and to take on qualified staff who worked under the benevolent eye of the censor. With Montmartre and its bars and nightclubs providing a touch of insolence that was taken up throughout the rest of Europe – suffice it to mention Els Quatre Gats (The Four Cats) in Barcelona and Die Elf Scharfrichter (The Eleven Executioners) in Munich – Paris may legitimately be described as the citadel of art nouveau. And yet it was Brussels that was the movement's capital.

Brussels' geographical position has always ensured that it has been a veritable hub of activity, and this, coupled with what were once rich reserves in terms of its mines and industries, to say nothing of its colonial presence, meant that it was also a meeting place for all who believed in art nouveau, a point proclaimed by Octave Maus and Edmond Picard when they established Les XX in 1883. 'Enforcing no aesthetic outlook and imposing no interdictions,' they turned Brussels into a centre of European creativity, while mounting 'a constant rear-guard action against academicism'. Les XX remained a force to be reckoned with until disbanded in 1893, when it was replaced by La Libre Esthétique. The new group continued to operate until 1914, offering a range of concerts, lectures and exhibitions.

The list of invited guests is impressive,[11] while art societies flourished. Horta was commissioned to design the Maison du People, one of art nouveau's rare contributions to the social life of a nation. Meanwhile, Van de Velde drew up plans for his revolutionary Villa Bloemenwerf and the banker Adolphe Stoclet invited the Viennese Secessionist architect Josef Hoffmann to design a villa for him and his family, the Palais Stoclet.

The Paris–Brussels axis influenced the whole of Europe, although each country developed its own specific features and evolved at its own particular pace. But the movement's floral style was trivialized, leading to its decline. Its death knell was sounded by the Universal Exhibition of 1900, and from then on it was Germany and, later, Austria that led the revival.

Bismarck may have brought about the unification of Germany, but the country remained a federation of small states, each of them proud of its Academy of Fine Arts, where the Hellenistic and historicist pastiche held uncontested sway. But a younger generation aware of all that was unfolding in Paris rose up in revolt, triggering a series of secessionist movements. The first to be established was in Munich – the traditional capital of the fine arts – in 1893, its creation heralded by a poster by Franz von Stuck, who tried his hand at a modern typeface while retaining the inevitable profile of Minerva. It is not in the artistic and literary journal *Jugend*, which unwittingly gave its name to the movement, that we should look for the revolution that was taking place in the arts at this time but in the satirical weekly *Simplicissimus*, which was likewise founded in 1896. Thomas Theodor Heine designed the red bulldog and the poster for the Munich cabaret Die Elf Scharfrichter that depicts the magazine's team of writers and editors in their entirety. The Lex Heinze governing censorship in the Reich meant that Heine spent time in one of Kaiser Wilhelm's prisons.

In Berlin the local Secession was relatively timid and changed very little, the main exception being the magazine *Pan*. The anarcho-Communist Erich Mühsam wrote mockingly that 'Paris lives, Berlin functions'. The other centres of the Secessionist movement in Germany were Dresden, Hamburg and, above all, Darmstadt and Weimar. The young grand duke of Hessen, Ernst Ludwig, was Queen Victoria's grandson and as a result maintained privileged contacts with Great Britain, most notably with Charles Robert Ashbee, who in 1888 founded the School and Guild of Handicraft. Ernst Ludwig decided to build an Artists' Colony in Darmstadt from the ground up and in 1899 invited the Austro-Hungarian architect Joseph Maria Olbrich

11. Guests included Chéret, Toulouse-Lautrec, Walter Crane, James McNeill Whistler, James Ensor, Fernand Khnopff, Théophile-Alexandre Steinlen, Félicien Rops, Auguste Renoir, Maurice Denis, Paul Gauguin, Claude Monet, Odilon Redon, Rodin, Georges Seurat, Alfred Sisley, Jan Toorop, Vincent van Gogh, Henry van de Velde and Théo van Rysselberghe.

Thomas Theodor Heine, 1896

to work on the project. In turn Olbrich was joined by other modernist designers, including Peter Behrens and Hans Christiansen. The grand duke's aim was to forge a link between the cause of art and the development of Hessen, his typically German vision involving the concept of a total work of art – Wagner's idea of the *Gesamtkunstwerk* – that would emerge from the fruitful encounter of artists with representatives of trade and industry. The Mathildenhöhe Artists' Colony opened in 1901 with a seminal exhibition, *Ein Dokument deutscher Kunst* (A Document of German Art), that was promoted by an elongated poster designed by Behrens and depicting a hieratic woman from which every whiplash curve was studiously exorcised. Olbrich's poster for the exhibition was similar to one he had already designed for Vienna and presented a perspective ending in a building constructed from decorative, geometric elements, a typically Viennese design. The demands of historical truth require us to point out that the good people of Darmstadt were left profoundly unimpressed by these developments.

Joseph Maria Olbrich, 1901

For the *Kunst im Handwerk* exhibition that was held in Munich that same year and that celebrated the arts and crafts, Bruno Paul designed two wading birds in delicately outlined flat tones, marking the end of the historicist allegory.

In his capacity as advisor to Grand Duke Wilhelm Ernst of Saxe-Weimar-Eisenach, Count Harry Kessler invited Harry van de Velde to open a school of decorative arts in Weimar, and although the grand duke himself soon lost interest in the project, the Grand-Ducal Saxon Schools of Art and Arts and Crafts became a melting pot for years to come. It was thanks to the initiative of the architect Hermann Muthesius, who introduced the ideas of the British Arts & Crafts movement to Germany, that the Deutscher Werkbund was established in Munich in 1907, marking another important stage in the evolution of design.

The Werkbund brought together avant-garde figures in architecture and the decorative arts and the cream of German industry, producing tangible results in the form of projects that included the long-term partnership between Behrens and the head of AEG, Emil Rathenau.

There was an often lively debate. Muthesius, for example, was all in favour of standardization, whereas Henry van de Velde was just as vigorously opposed to the idea. Before leaving Germany in 1917, the latter designated Walter Gropius as his successor. By now everything was in place for the creation of the Bauhaus: the grandiose social project of which art nouveau had been dreaming was finally on track. As early as 1907 Eugène Grasset had sought in vain to promote such a project: 'Artists have restricted themselves to copying, tracing and casting their ideas into a working mould. [...] The solution to this state of affairs will be found in the use of the machine, a use better understood than hitherto, because at present we are merely being obstinate in our attempts to hand over to the machine what was once produced by manual labour.'[12]

Austria-Hungary had been weakened by its defeat at the hands of Prussia at Königgrätz in 1866 and by the stock market crash of 1873 as well as being undermined by bureaucratic routine – pilloried as 'Kakanien' by Robert Musil in *The Man without Qualities.*[13] As his interminable reign drew slowly to an end, the Austro-Hungarian Kaiser, Franz Joseph, treated himself to one final firework display.

Vienna was teeming with talented artists in every area of creative endeavour, all of them supported by a well-to-do and enlightened bourgeoisie.[14] In 1897 a group of seven architects led by Otto Wagner joined forces with dissident members of the Vienna Künstlerhaus and founded the journal *Ver Sacrum* (Sacred Spring). Gustav Klimt became their leader.

Things now moved very quickly. The inaugural exhibition was announced by means of a poster designed by Klimt and depicting Minerva watching Theseus's encounter with the Minotaur, the style still Hellenistically correct. The censor's only warning shot concerned Theseus's genitalia, which had to be covered up. In spite of this, Klimt triumphed, and the exhibition allowed the Viennese to discover Rodin, Khnopff and Whistler, followed in 1900 by van de Velde, the Maison Moderne, the Glasgow School and Ashbee.

Events continued to move with astonishing speed, and in 1898, for the second exhibition, Olbrich designed the Secession building. Having failed to obtain a professorship at the School of Applied Arts, he left Vienna for Darmstadt. It was not long before the school's staff included Josef Hoffmann, Koloman Moser and Alfred Roller. Within the shortest possible space of time the modernists were in charge of the institution's teaching programme.

In 1900 the Pavilion designed by Jacob and Joseph Kohn was enthusiastically acclaimed at that year's Universal Exhibition, for the Secessionists were able to rely on an avant-garde industrial technique dominated by Thonet Frères and the Kohn Brothers that allowed the mass production of bentwood items at a very reasonable cost. One notable example of this style was the Café Museum in Vienna, a building designed in 1899 by Adolf Loos, who was later to proclaim the death of ornament. It was furnished with bentwood chairs by Thonet Frères. Four years later, in 1903, came another spectacular advance,

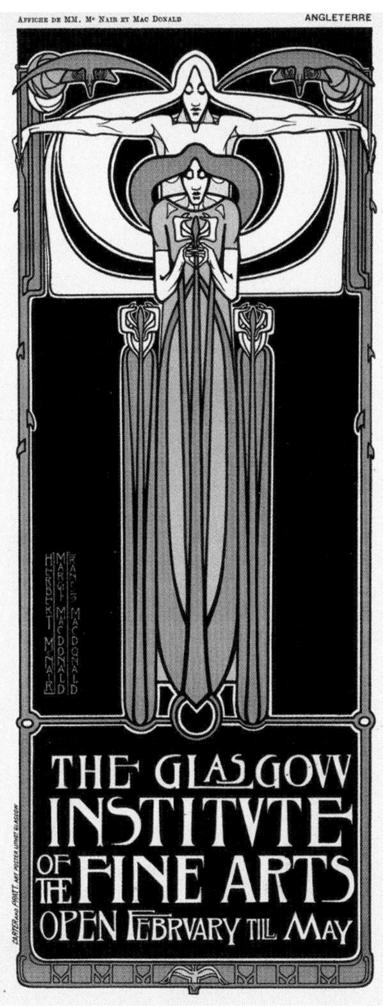

Frances McDonald and Herbert McNair, 1895

12. Eugène Grasset in a lecture given to the Union Centrale des Arts Décoratifs in 1907.
13. Robert Musil, *The Man Without Qualities*, trans. Sophie Wilkins and Burton Pike, Picador, London, 1995.
14. Josef Hoffmann, Leo Putz, Olbrich, Adolf Karpellus, Maximilian Kurzweil and Koloman Moser.

'THAT WHICH CAN SERVE BUT A SINGLE PERSON IS VERY CLOSE TO SERVING NO ONE.' HENRI VAN DE VELDE

Josef Hoffmann, 1905

when Hoffmann and Kolo Moser founded the Wiener Werkstätte and applied themselves to every branch of the decorative arts. The forms promoted by the Werkstätte were original and stripped of ornamentation, their rare motifs being geometrical in design, proclaiming a revolution that even spread to fashion. The decorations in the Cabaret Fledermaus that opened in 1907 were entirely the work of Hoffmann.[15] The whole of the bar was covered with a patchwork of ceramic tiles produced by the Wiener Werkstätte, while Hoffmann also designed the furniture, which leads us on to the graphic arts. While Charles Frederick Worth and Jacques Doucet were dressing the wealthy in Paris, the Wiener Werkstätte was also taking an interest in fashion, creating fabrics and patterns that were entirely original and that are found in some of Klimt's portraits of the members of the Austrian bourgeoisie. Such designs helped the Wiener Werkstätte to survive until the 1920s.

In less than two years floral designs had practically disappeared, and the numerous posters produced to publicize the forty-nine exhibitions of the Secession provide a veritable conspectus of the possibilities inherent in the graphic arts at this time. Decorative abstraction soon came to dominate through the use of repeated motifs – we may even risk using the words 'kinetic' and 'psychedelic' to describe a typography that mocked the very idea of legibility. These quasi-incestuous exercises in typography were the work of Moser, Roller, Ferdinand Andri, Ernst Eck and Richard Harlfinger.

Oskar Kokoschka arrived on the scene in 1908 with a style recognizable by its bright colours and bold outlines. A pupil of Bertold Löffler, he was already moving in the direction of Expressionism, a movement that also numbered among its members Egon Schiele, who exhibited at the Secession in 1918, the final year of his life.

To all of these posters we may add those of another group, the Hagenbund, and others associated with particular cultural venues such as the Cabaret Fledermaus. None of them had any discernible effect on advertising but provided designs well summed up by the term 'joyful apocalypse', the subtitle

15. The title is a nod in the direction of Johann Strauß's operetta, which sums up to perfection the decadent atmosphere in Vienna in the 1870s.
16. This is the subtitle of the retrospective exhibition catalogue, *Vienne, 1880–1938*, ed. Nicole Ouvrard and published by Éditions Centre Pompidou in 1986.

of a retrospective exhibition held at the Centre Georges Pompidou in 1986.[16]

Most of the students who trained in Vienna and who include Ernst Deutsch-Dryden and Julius Klinger soon moved on to Munich or Berlin, where the final pre-war revolution unfolded.

The geographical proximity of Munich and Vienna meant that there was a constant exchange of ideas between them. To cite only one particularly notable example, the entire team of Die Elf Scharfrichter headed by the singer Marya Delvard left Munich to work at the Cabaret Fledermaus in the Austrian capital.

The young artists of a new generation could follow the burgeoning growth of Jugendstil, while also profiting from a modern system of education.

In Munich, Ludwig Hohlwein is a perfect example of the sort of teacher that the Jugendstil movement was able to produce: having studied architecture in Munich, he visited Paris, London and Vienna, before starting to work as an interior designer inspired by the Arts & Crafts movement and by the Glasgow School. His designs reflect his ability to assimilate all of these different influences, notably that of the Beggarstaff Brothers. He quickly made a name for himself as Bavaria's leading poster designer, and it was in order to provide a counterweight that Franz Paul Glass, Friedrich Heubner, Carl Moos, Emil Preetorius, Max Schwarzer and Valentin Zietara formed the group Die Sechs.

Unlike Munich, Berlin initially had nothing that might have entitled it to play a historic role in the development of the poster. Apart from the advertisement pillars dotted around the city, there were few places where posters could be displayed, and what posters were produced were relatively small in format.

Although Berlin was already a vast industrial and commercial capital, it required the encounter between the self-taught Lucian Bernhard, who came to Berlin to work with Edmund Edel, and Ernst Growald, who ran the Hollerbaum & Schmidt print works, before Berlin was able to forge its own style with the *Sachplakat*, or object poster, in which the advertised object stood out against a uniform background, while the name of the firm was reproduced in an extra-bold typeface. Apart from Edel and Paul Scheurich, Growald also signed up a number of refugees from Vienna and Munich, namely, Deutsch-Dryden, Klinger and Hans Rudi Erdt. The Berlin School established a pragmatic style that finally did away with the floral style's excesses and with Vienna's graphic exaggerations.

Anonymous, *c.* 1900

Fritz Helmuth Ehmcke, 1914

Jean Peské, 1898, detail

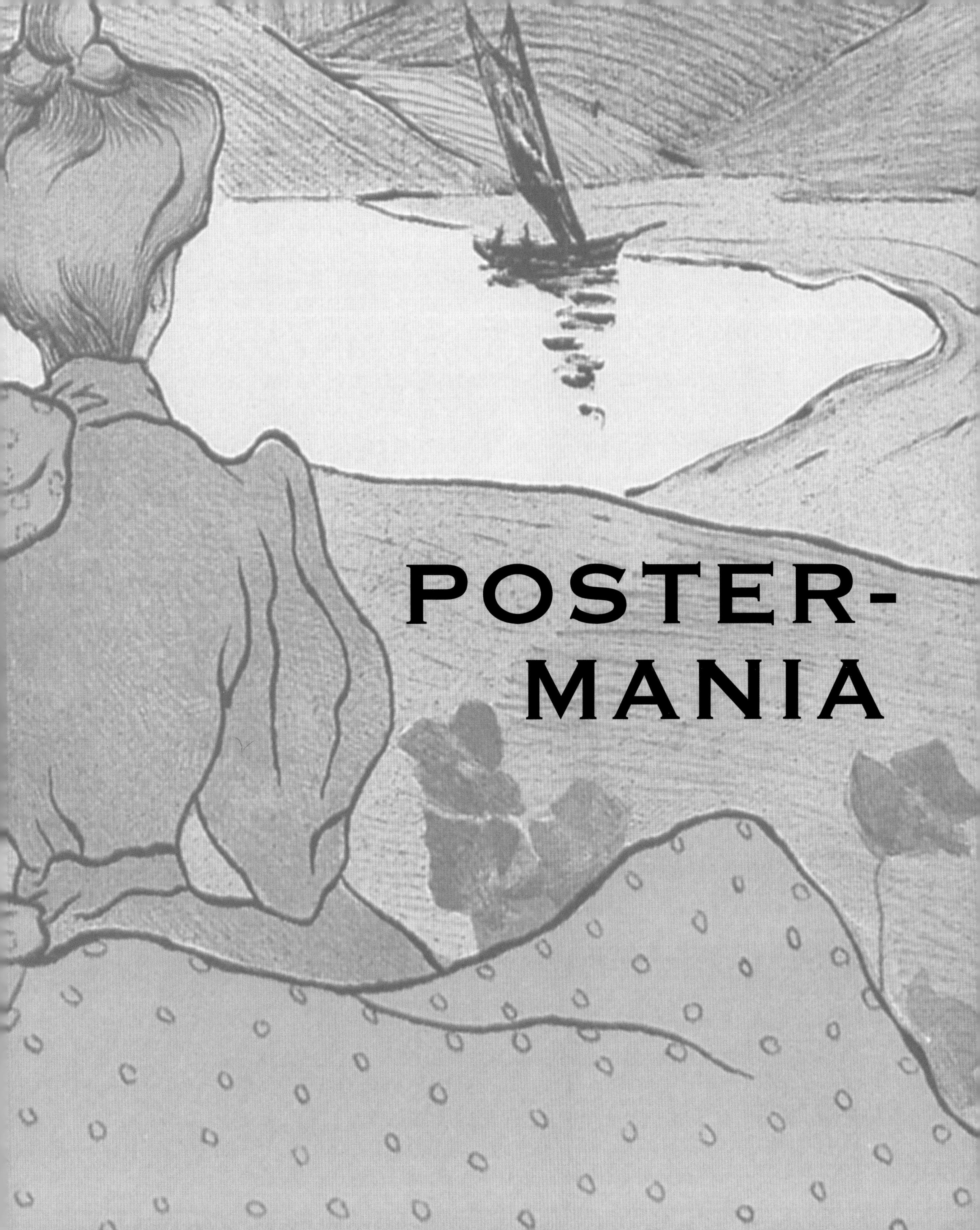

POSTER-
MANIA

EXPOSITION
D'AFFICHES
Françaises
&
Etrangères
—
Modernes
&
Retrospectives
—
ARTISTIQUES
ENTRÉE
1 Fr
AU CIRQUE DE REIMS
Du 7 au 17 Novembre
1896
Lithographie MATOT-BRAINE. Reims

Kalas, 1896

Ernest Maindron by Jules Chéret

Jules Chéret (drawing from 1891)

Vignette by Félix Vallotton

If tens of thousands of posters have survived time's brutal distraint, it is because collectors intervened to divert them from their primary function and because many were produced specifically with those collectors in mind. In the second half of the nineteenth century members of the middle classes became avid, not to say obsessive, collectors, the tremendous interest in the arts of China and especially Japan fuelling a revival of the art of engraving. Once Jules Chéret had given it a real artistic value, the poster became the new madness of the age.

A number of pioneers understood this at a very early date. At their head was Ernest Maindron, the secretary of the Academy of Sciences. If Chéret may be hailed as the father of the poster, Maindron is the father of poster aficionados.

Published in 1886, Maindron's book *Les Affiches illustrées* was the first study to be devoted to the subject[1] and was written to celebrate the achievements of Chéret, who was also treated to a lengthy study in Henri Beraldi's *Les Graveurs du XIXe siècle*, which catalogued no fewer than 950 posters, all of them, of course, from the writer's own collection. 'Today', Beraldi announced, 'it is the poster that brings joy to the lover of engravings and so we need to catalogue them much as we would catalogue engravings and etchings. And why not?'[2] A number of bookshops were starting to sell posters, and the exhibition that the indefatigable Maindron organized as part of the 1889 Universal Exhibition in Paris proved to be a triumph. They was recognized as a valid art form, Chéret received the Legion of Honour and the fashion for posters was launched.

In his second volume, *Les Affiches illustrées, 1886–1895*, Maindron could clearly see which way the wind was blowing and wrote, presciently, that 'We have unwittingly opened up the way for dealers. [...] By multiplying in number, the collector has created a new industry and has allowed an exigent factor to enter his life, a factor that can only disturb his serenity. All that our streets no longer have to show is offered to all-comers at inflated prices by dealers' portfolios of engravings and in the display windows of bookshops.'[3]

1. Ernest Maindron, *Les Affiches illustrées*, H. Launette, Paris, 1886, p.1.
2. Henri Beraldi, *Les Graveurs du XIXe siècle: Guide de l'amateur d'estampes modernes*, 12 vols, Librairie L. Conquet, Paris, 1885–92, esp. 4 (1886), 170 and 176. Beraldi's section on Chéret may be found on pp.168–203 of volume 4.
3. Ernest Maindron, *Les Affiches illustrées, 1886–1895*, G. Boudet, Paris, 1896, p.3.

Henri-Gabriel Ibels, 1894

James Ensor, 1898

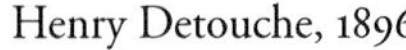

Henry Detouche, 1896

Arsène Herbinier, 1899

Frédéric-Auguste Cazals, 1894, Verlaine and Mauréas

Perre Roche, 1896

Armand Rassenfosse, 1896

Henri de Toulouse-Lautrec, 1895

Jean Peské, 1898

In 1891 Octave Uzanne coined the word *affichomanie* – a mania for posters. That year Edmond Sagot published his first catalogue featuring 2,333 items, of which 567 were by Chéret. Some 254 predated 1869 and, being extremely rare, had already been sold at correspondingly high prices – around fifty francs apiece – whereas the most recent ones by Chéret and others started at two francs and rarely commanded more than ten.[4]

Another interesting point is that Sagot, who knew exactly where he was going, devoted only 132 items to commerce and industry, in the process eliminating many anonymous posters and ones produced by small and often provincial printers. Toulouse-Lautrec was a brilliant exception. The Imprimerie Cassan ordered a poster from Mucha, who influenced two local artists, Jane Atché and Arthur Foäche, while the newspaper *La Dépêche* called on the services of both Maurice Denis and Lautrec.

Soon, Sagot could no longer be ignored, and in a way that may seem surprising, commerce began to influence the production of an article that a priori could not be sold. Collectors and those who commissioned the posters were often the same people. Jules Roques, the owner of *Le Courrier français*, was a friend of Chéret and not only commissioned posters from him but published them as supplements to his newspaper, reproducing them in a smaller format. Maurice Fenaille, the owner of the Saxoléine company that made safety oil for gas lamps, likewise invited him to undertake design work.

4. By way of comparison, it is worth pointing out that at this date admission to the Moulin de la Galette cost 1.5 francs; a meal at the Ermitage tavern was 3 francs; a third-class return ticket from Paris to Dieppe and back was 6 francs; a year's subscription to the illustrated humorous weekly *Le Rire* was 8 francs.

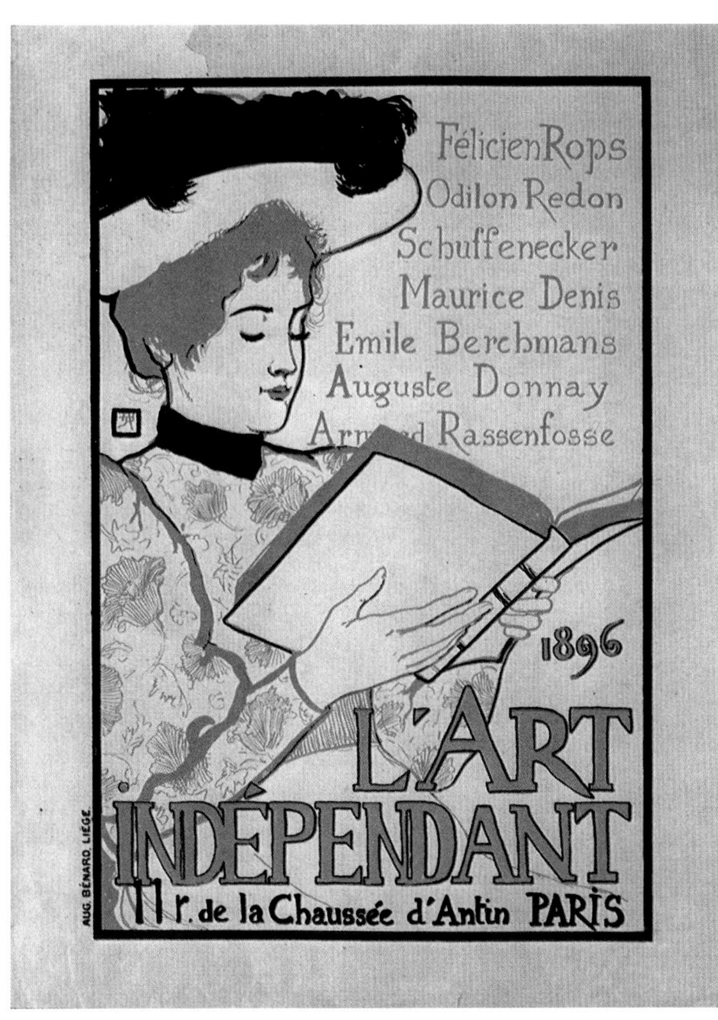

Armand Rassenfosse, 1896

Georges Lemmen, 1910

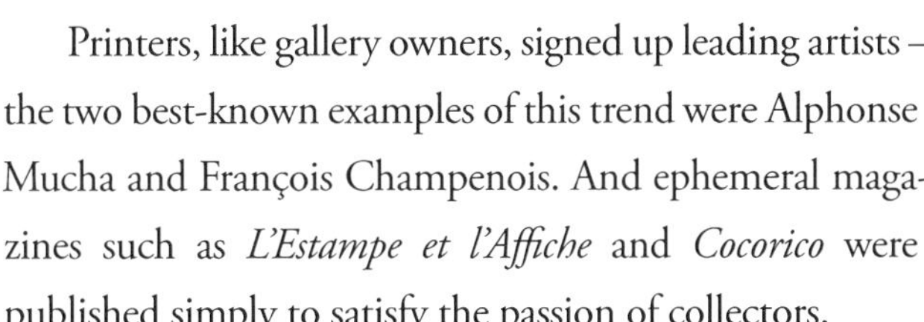

Printers, like gallery owners, signed up leading artists – the two best-known examples of this trend were Alphonse Mucha and François Champenois. And ephemeral magazines such as *L'Estampe et l'Affiche* and *Cocorico* were published simply to satisfy the passion of collectors.

'Our designers have followed this movement, and they have been right to do so. Many of them now have an accredited agent, who sells proof engravings, letter-proofs, first- and second-quality posters, posters printed in limited editions, posters bearing their author's signature and even numbered posters.'[5] Vast amounts of money could be made in this way, the client, the artist and the gallery owner all taking a share of the jackpot.

Even more successful was *La Plume*, an arts journal which under the direction of Léon Deschamps published probing articles, sold limited-edition posters and, above all, produced a prestigious series of posters for the Salon des Cent that was held in the journal's offices in the Rue Bonaparte.[6]

There were also ever more dealers: Sagot, Arnould and Pierrefort commanded the top end of the market and issued catalogues, but many bookshops, including Vannier, Sapin and Brunox, also turned their hand to publishing, as did dealers in prints such as Victor Prouté, Henri Petiet and Ambroise Vollard. Even a second-hand bookseller, Le Père Didier, commissioned a poster.

Within its own lifetime the art poster already had its own pantheon in the form of *Les Maîtres de l'affiche*, which was published by Chaix in five volumes between 1896 and 1900, each of which had a substantial print-run

5. Maindron was certainly thinking of Sagot and his catalogue entry 426b.
6. We should also mention *La Critique*, which was run by Georges Bans, who also issued a series of posters, including ones designed by Gustave Jossot, Frédéric-Auguste Cazals, Léon Lebègue and Misti.

P. H. Lobel, 1897

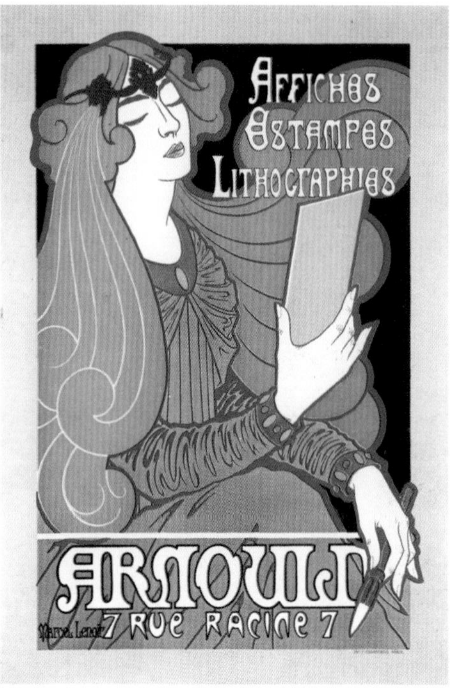

Marcel Lenoir

Gaston Noury

and an introduction by Roger Marx. A quarter of the plates were by Chéret – we are never better served than by ourselves.

But who were these fans of poster art and what was the strange business that they transacted? All collectors seem to have shared a similar profile, namely, well-to-do members of the middle class afflicted by a condition that might be called collectionitis. Georges Pochet, who in 1902 donated six thousand posters and other documents to the Musée des Arts Décoratifs, was a leading figure in what was then the highly lucrative business of selling bottles of perfume. He was also an habitué of the Théâtre Libre and Le Chat Noir. And he collected practically everything. Alexandre Henriot owned a company that made champagne and was president of the Reims Art Society,[7] where he exhibited his collection in 1896, illustrating it with a catalogue listing no fewer than 1,690 items. Unfortunately the collection went up in smoke during the German bombardment of the city in 1914. Gustave Dutailly was the mayor of Chaumont and also represented the town in the Chambre des Députés. He donated his collection to the town. This collection was rediscovered in the late 1980s and triggered a number of international conventions in the graphic arts. A poster lover in Nancy, René Wiener, gave his collection to the Musée Lorrain in 1939.

There were – and remain – many ways of collecting posters. After all, not everyone can have the same sort of friendly relations as those that Chéret had with Dutailly. Chéret generously gave Dutailly a series of posters, and the latter responded by donating twenty francs to the workers' emergency fund at the Imprimerie Chaix.[8] The least expensive option was to roam the streets at night, following a bill-sticker and removing the poster before the glue had had time to set. A journalist may find good copy in anecdotes like this, but the operation was complicated and, in practical terms, a messy one since the poster then had to be washed. A more cunning approach was to bribe the bill-sticker and buy the poster from him. This type of misappropriation was so common that bill-stickers were followed by inspectors to check that the poster had

7. The exhibition was held at the Cirque de Rheims, which adopted the historical form of the city's name, rather than its modern version, Reims.

8. It is perhaps ironical that when the workers at the Imprimerie Chaix went on strike in May 1968, they sold rolls of Chéret's posters as a way of funding their movement: large numbers of these posters still existed at this date.

9. Paul Prouté, the doyen of dealers in engravings, clearly remembered 'visits from bill-stickers coming to extend their weekends and shorten their working day'.

Grün's posters carried the notice 'This poster may not be sold or given away'

Ramón Casas, 1899

been properly positioned.[9] For posters by Grün, which were especially desirable, Chaix printed a note: 'Anyone found in possession of this poster will be prosecuted.' Chaix was not joking. But collectors could also bide their time – and they were clearly not lacking in the patience needed to gratify their passion – and write to the artists in question, the latter being reluctant to turn down a chance to earn some extra income, to which end they asked their printers to provide them with proof copies of their posters. Foremost among this group was Toulouse-Lautrec, whom we find writing to an unidentified correspondent in 1896: 'I beg leave to inform you that I have some Aube posters at your disposal, stamped impressions, at M. Ancourt's at a price of 50 francs for 50.'[10]

On 2 December 1896 he wrote to the Belgian publisher Edmond Deman: 'Thanks for the paper. I haven't tried it yet. I have had a Lender proof sent to you. For you 30 francs, for the public 50 francs. This vulgar detail is simply to make sure you don't let it go for less.'[11]

10. Henri de Toulouse-Lautrec, *Correspondance*, ed. Herbert D. Schimmel, Gallimard, Paris, 1991, p.307; Engl. trans. *The Letters of Henri Toulouse-Lautrec*, ed. Herbert D. Schimmel, Oxford University Press, New York, 1991, p.298.

11. Ibid., p.308; Engl. trans., p.298.

12. See the impassioned study by Nicholas-Henri Zmelty, *L'Affiche illustrée au temps de l'affichomanie (1889–1905)*, Mare & Martin, Paris, 2014.

13. Mucha's heirs still owned huge quantities of the large-format *Job* in the 1970s.

The foregoing gives an idea of the various forms of trafficking that were available. It was also possible to go knocking on an advertiser's door. A letter written by Clément Cycles to Sagot on 1 March 1895, for example, provides more information on this question: 'In view of the large number of requests for posters, we have taken the decision to sell them to collectors for ten francs each. It will therefore be more than enough if you pay 2.50 francs. You will find in the packet eleven posters rather than ten – the eleventh is for organizing the deal.' Clearly prices had risen considerably since 1891.

This is not the place to expatiate at any length on this subject.[12] It is, however, worth noting that in general Sagot ordered in batches of ten or twenty but was clearly able to restock. Even so, he ordered 900 copies of Mucha's poster for Imprimerie Cassan Fils.[13] Sagot was also at the very heart of a business that was currently undergoing a process of internationalization and was in contact with Utrillo & Rialp in Barcelona, who supplied him with 200 copies of one of Ramón Casas's posters for Anis del Mono – possibly by way

Paul Berthon, 1898

Pierre Bonnard, 1894

William Henry Bradley, 1895

of an exchange deal since the Spanish publishers were themselves selling posters. Sagot also invited his clients to subscribe to *Pèl y Ploma*. Finally, in 1895, a court case that can only be described as Byzantine in its complexity saw Sarah Bernhardt and the printing firm of Lemercier on opposite sides of the courtroom, when 4,000 posters were ordered but only 3,450 were delivered. Lemercier was found guilty, although his punishment was nugatory. When we recall that when the Théâtre Sarah Bernhardt was taken over by the city of Paris and hundreds of these posters were found in the roof timbers, we can only start to dream . . .

The print-runs of posters extended from 500 copies to 10,000, the last-named record set by Steinlen's poster for Vingeanne Sterilized Milk now in the Archives Verneau. But these figures do not include possible reprints. We may also be right in suspecting that a considerable number of posters never saw any glue, unless it was that of the person mounting the poster on card.[14]

Charles Hiatt was right to note that 'The collecting of pictorial posters needs nothing more than a little heroism'.[15] It also made the fortune of a new class of professionals: the craftsmen who created the means to display such objects, including revolving display stands, entire pieces of furniture and sophisticated cabinets.[16]

The imagination of poster enthusiasts knew no bounds, and some, such as Roger Braun,[17] were particularly badly affected: Braun built an entire theatre in his library, recreating his favourite posters by means of painted backdrops and actors judiciously chosen and costumed. In this way he reconstructed the Reims exhibition poster of Ernest Kalas, Maurice Réalier-Dumas's posters for Mumm Champagne and Blandy Madeira, Steinlen's poster for Mothu & Doria and Lucien Lefèvre's poster for Jacquot Shoe Polish. 'Finally the curtain came down, and our apprehension vanished when we heard the delighted applause elicited by the climactic final tableau, which showed Harlequin eating madeira grapes, the bill-sticker brushing Mothu's clothes, Doria asking for a light from a bottle of Jacques Mumm champagne and Pierrot declaring his love to a

14. See the *New York Tribune*, 18 Aug. 1901. Clients had no thought of buying the magazine that was being advertised: they wanted only the poster.
15. Charles Hiatt, *Picture Posters*, G. Bell, London, 1895, p.366.
16. When Julius Paul's collection, which had been stolen by the National Socialists, was bought by the Albertina at a much-reduced price, the display cabinets cost more than the posters.
17. Braun's extensive collection was donated to the Musée des Arts Décoratifs in 1941.
18. Excerpt from a letter from Braun to Henriot cited by Alain Weill, *L'Affichomanie: Collectionneurs d'affiches – Affiches de collection, 1880–1900*, Musée de l'Affiche, Paris, [1980], p.6. Henriot was keen to return to 'more serious' things: 'When shall I see you to bring our dealings up to date and talk about the latest masterpieces that have sprung up in every quarter?'

romantic bookshop that seemed deeply moved by the gesture, and so on.'[18]

This by no means exhausts the list of collectors, who were extremely numerous. The Besnard Collection was dispersed on Florence Camard's advice at several auctions in Orléans, starting in 1977 – Besnard had collected hundreds of items. I too auctioned off several of these collections, including one owned by a particularly wealthy woman from Versailles, and I saw several others pass into the hands of rivals. In particular, the Jules Adeline Collection that had belonged to the critic of the *Journal des arts* was sold at three auctions in Joigny in 2009.

Each country has had its own major collectors whose names have gone down in history. Members of the poster's church militant, they played a significant role in disseminating the art poster by organizing exhibitions and in many cases by donating their collections to museums.[19]

One of the earliest societies to be established was the Société Belge des Affichophiles, which published a monthly bulletin, *L'Affiche artistique*. Its secretary was Léon Grell, who was a friend of Max Elskamp and a leading figure on the Belgian arts scene,[20] maintaining links with his counterparts throughout the whole of Europe. In Barcelona one of the leading poster lovers was the precocious collector and polymorph Lluís Plandiura i Pou who came from a family of sugar producers and who was barely twenty when he began collecting posters. He was in contact not only with Léon Grell but also with Ferdinando Salce in Treviso[21] and with Charles Bolton, Ned Arden Flood and J.M. Spark in New York. It was Spark who supplied the needs of European collectors.[22] Posters were on sale at Brentano's, C.S. Pratt, Meyer Bros and Gustave P. Fressel.[23]

From his base in Moscow, the critic and historian Pavel Ettinger sought out posters from Central Europe that he then sold on to Plandiura. Many letters passed between them, swapping items, arranging sales and even organizing loans for exhibitions, including two that Plandiura curated in Barcelona in 1901 and 1903.

19. Wilhelmine Germany deserves credit for opening museums of the decorative arts and for endowing them with sufficient funds to establish collections of graphic works. Justus Brinckmann at the Museum für Kunst und Gewerbe in Hamburg and Friedrich Deneken at the Kaiser-Wilhelm-Museum in Krefeld assembled remarkable collections of posters. According to the catalogue for the exhibition *Belle Époque à l'affiche, 1885–1914* at the Musée des Beaux-Arts in Strasbourg in 1981 (p.4), 1,400 posters were acquired between 1892 and 1896 thanks to a grant from the Sengenwald Bequest.
20. He donated his extensive collection to the town of Antwerp in 1914.
21. After collecting posters for sixty years, Nando Salce gave his extraordinary hoard of posters to his native Treviso in 1962.
22. The same is true of the Catalan dealer Lluis Bartrina, who exported Catalan posters, advertising them in the pages of *L'Estampe et l'Affiche*.
23. The small periodical for North American collectors, *Poster Lore*, reckoned there were 6,000 collectors in the United States and a further 1,000 in Canada.

Maurice Réalier-Dumas, 1895

Maurice Réalier-Dumas, *L'Affiche vécue*, 1895

Charles E. Dawson

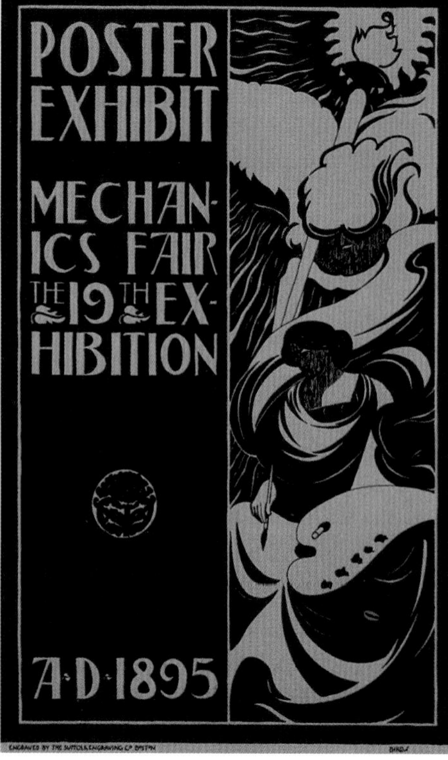

Elisha Brown Bird, 1895

Mosnar Yendis, 1897

Plandiura then sold the exhibits immediately afterwards to the city of Barcelona.

Alexandre de Riquer was another poster lover who often visited Paris and travelled the length and breadth of Europe, collecting posters in a more logical way. His collection, too, was bought by the city of Barcelona.[24]

Spark was the principal intermediary between Europe and the United States, and in 1908 he welcomed a young Jew from Berlin who had come to pursue his studies in dentistry. The youth – Hans Sachs – had fallen in love with the art poster in 1898, when a friend of his father in Paris sent him three of Mucha's posters of Sarah Bernhardt and he began a collection that he completed during visits to Vienna, Switzerland and Italy.

Spark advised him to buy American posters but as a true collector refused to open his address book to him. In spite of this, the youth made the acquaintance of the only German collector of any renown, Walter von Zur Westen.[25] The leading poster collector in Germany, Hans Sachs, had founded the Verein der Plakat-Freunde (Society of Poster Lovers) in 1905 as a forum for meetings and the exchange of ideas, but Zur Westen struck a discouraging note, claiming that the whole of the poster movement was dying, which was indeed true. 'Even the Belgian Society of Poster Lovers has died after only a brief existence, and the same is true – in spite of its interesting articles – of the English illustrated magazine *The Poster*.'[26] Sachs was unimpressed. His initial membership of 100 rose to 10,000 thanks to the publication of his magazine *Das Plakat*, which appeared between 1910 and 1924 and which remains our most important documentary source of the poster art of this period. His collection of 12,300 posters – all of them ingeniously classified, labelled and stored – was impounded by the National Socialists when he left for the United States in 1938. Declared destroyed in an air raid, it was exhumed for an exhibition in Berlin and finally handed back to Sachs's heirs in 2012 (some 5,000 posters had survived), only to be auctioned off in three separate sales organized by Guernsey's of New York in January 2013.

24. It was advertised in *L'Estampe et l'Affiche*.

25. Walter von Zur Westen is also the author of a two-volume study, *Berlins graphische Gelegenheitskunst*, Otto von Holten, Berlin, 1912.

26. Plandiura sold his collection to the city of Barcelona after exhibiting it in 1901 and 1903.

'WELL! YOU COLLECT THAT – BUT IT'S FOUND ON EVERY WALL.' ALEXANDRE DEMEURE DE BEAUMONT

Hans Sachs in his studio

John Hassall, 1902

By a curious coincidence an Austrian collection has recently resurfaced at Swann Galleries in New York. As was the case in Germany, the poster was slow to make an appearance in Austria. Ottokar Maschka, himself a collector and the author of the standard study of the subject, noted that it was 'impossible to purchase posters in any major arts institution' and that 'the art poster continues to be little appreciated'. Julius Paul, a major distributor of cigarette papers, began his collection in 1895. When he died in 1937, his nephew, in order to escape from Austria, was required to sell the collection in dubious circumstances. The collection passed to the Albertina Museum in Vienna, where it remained until 2008, when it was handed back to Paul's heirs and sold at auction by Swann Galleries in 2013.

By 1895–6 exhibitions made possible by what one might term the Collectors' International were opening all over the world. The London exhibition of 1894 was organized by the collector and entrepreneur Edward Bella. In 1895 the Pratt Institute of Brooklyn held an exhibition that spawned others all over the United States. And by 1896 Vienna, Dresden, Brussels and Reims – to name only four – had followed suit. By 1897 Moscow and St Petersburg had also joined the list.

In every country, books, articles in arts journals and specialist journals that for the most part led very brief lives informed and comforted collectors.[27]

Competitions reflected the mania for posters, stimulating public interest not so much with posters

27. A more or less complete list appears in the catalogue edited by the author and published by the Musée de l'Affiche in 1980, *L'Affichomanie: Collectionneurs d'affiches – Affiches de collection, 1880–1900*.

Anonymous, 1898

France	The two studies by Ernest Maindron and, among journals, *Les Affiches étrangères*, *Le Courrier français* and *La Plume*. *Cocorico* and *L'Estampe et l'Affiche* lasted no more than three years, while *Les Maîtres de l'affiche* survived from 1896 to 1900.
Belgium	The study by Alexandre Demeure de Beaumont, *L'Affiche illustrée*, is the standard textbook on the subject, but there were also numerous journals such as *L'Affiche artistique*.
Spain	Two journals: *Pél y ploma* and *Luzen*.
Italy	*Emporium* and articles by Vittorio Piar.
Germany	Two studies, *Das moderne Plakat* by Jean Louis Sponsel (1897) and *Das moderne Plakat am Ende des 19. Jahrhunderts* by Walter von Zur Westen (1914), the second of which offers an account of the rise of the German poster. Articles appeared in *Deutsche Kunst und Dekoration* and, above all, *Das Plakat* from 1910.
United States	Scribner's *The Modern Poster*, *Posters in Miniature*, *Scribner's Magazine* and three ephemeral titles, *The Poster*, *Bradley His Book* and *The Inland Printer*.
Great Britain	Charles Hiatt's *Picture Posters*, numerous articles in *The Studio* and small specialist publications such as *The Poster*, which survived for only two years.

J. Courvoisier, 1913

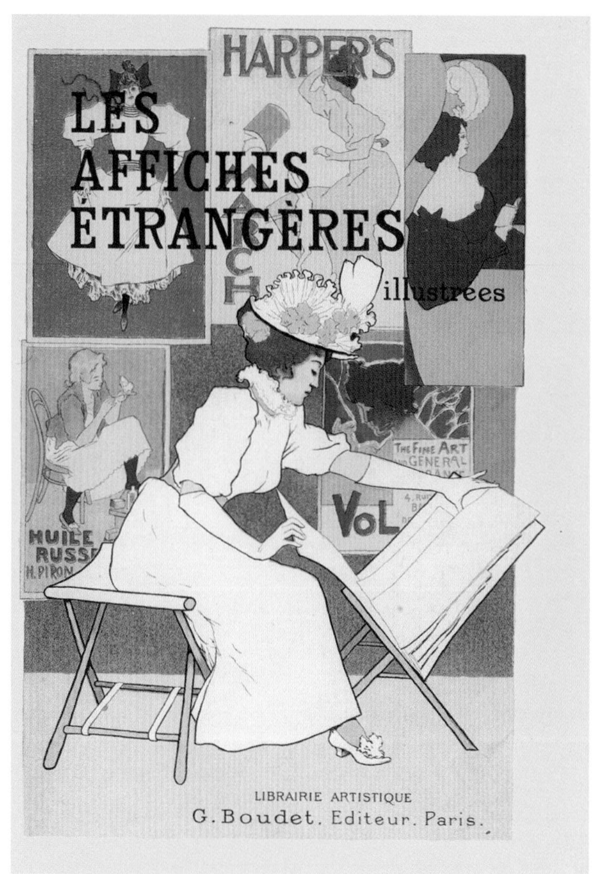

Armand Rassenfosse, 1897

as such as with a choice and in the process scoring an indirect hit.

Bi-Borax went the furthest in this regard, printing a poster in which the eight projects that had been selected were submitted to a public vote. The entries in the Byrrh Competition were exhibited at the Galerie Georges Petit.

A reduced-size copy of the poster designed by the finalists, *La Lune à 100 mètres* (The Moon at 100 Yards), was published by *L'Éclair*.

We may limit ourselves to two examples that gave rise to much discussion. In 1896 the American periodical *The Century Magazine* ran a competition to promote the publication of a life of Napoleon, demonstrating a particular snobbishness by appointing a Parisian jury made up of well-known academic painters. The competition generated considerable publicity as the prize was awarded to Lucien Métivet. A furious Toulouse-Lautrec published his own design, which he paid for out of his own pocket.[28] The result is easy to understand since Métivet's poster is a classic and certainly more graphic than Lautrec's.

The fashion for competitions was launched.

The competition designed to promote an Argentinian product, Cigarillos Paris, may seem strange inasmuch as art posters did not exist at all in Argentina. The firm's owner, Manuel Malaguida, was Catalan and a typical example of an industrialist who had been won over to the cause of the art poster.[29] His first competition was held in 1900 and was intended in the main for Spanish artists. Clearly satisfied with the result, he published a poster depicting the winners. A second competition was international in scope. The prizes ranged from $6,000 to 22,000 gold francs, a considerable sum at that time. There was an enthusiastic response. The two first prizes both went to Italians, Aleardo Villa and Leopoldo Metlicovitz, while the third prize was awarded to Ramón Casas, an old hand at this kind of competition.[30]

It is no doubt a unique case in the history of art that a handful of collectors were able to undermine an entire

28. The competition was organized by the Galerie Boussot & Valadon. Lautrec probably entered because the director of the gallery, Maurice Joyant, was a friend of his.

29. See Eliseo Trenc in Francesc M. Quilez (ed.), *El Cartell Modern*, Museu Nacional d'Art de Catalunya, Barcelona, 2007, p.258.

30. He won the first prize in the Anis del Mono Competition in 1897 and the second prize in the Cordoniu Champagne Competition in 1898.

Fernand-Louis Gottlob, 1898

Elisha Brown Bird, 1896

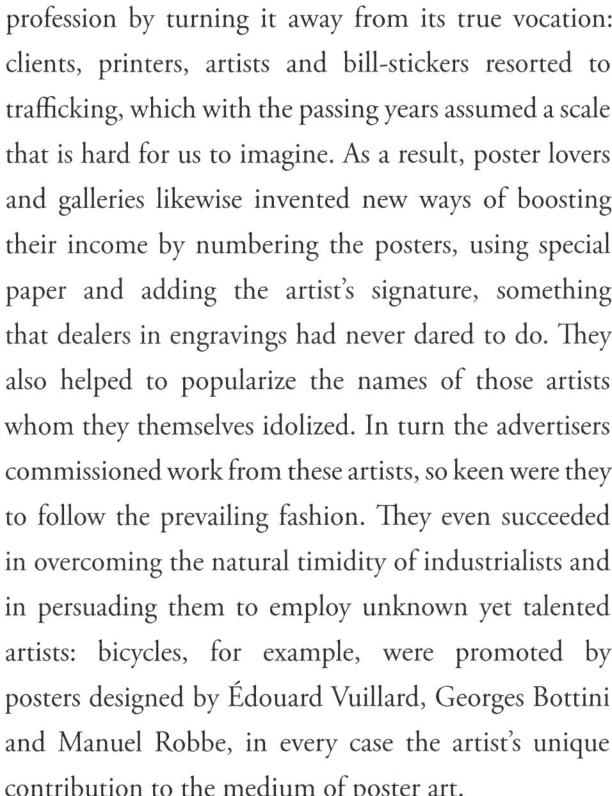

profession by turning it away from its true vocation: clients, printers, artists and bill-stickers resorted to trafficking, which with the passing years assumed a scale that is hard for us to imagine. As a result, poster lovers and galleries likewise invented new ways of boosting their income by numbering the posters, using special paper and adding the artist's signature, something that dealers in engravings had never dared to do. They also helped to popularize the names of those artists whom they themselves idolized. In turn the advertisers commissioned work from these artists, so keen were they to follow the prevailing fashion. They even succeeded in overcoming the natural timidity of industrialists and in persuading them to employ unknown yet talented artists: bicycles, for example, were promoted by posters designed by Édouard Vuillard, Georges Bottini and Manuel Robbe, in every case the artist's unique contribution to the medium of poster art.

In supporting art nouveau as a movement and in promoting poster art as a novel art form, these collectors helped to accelerate the spread of a new graphic art. Starting out from a type of commercial poster that could no longer luxuriate in mediocrity, they unwittingly set in train a development that was to lead to the birth of graphic design over the course of the twentieth century.

By various untoward turns of events, their collections finally enriched the holdings of the museums of the decorative arts that were then in the process of being built. And while these collections may all have been similar, since this was a sign of the taste of the time, they remain invaluable witnesses to their time precisely because of their taste.

As the mania for posters reached its peak, so magazine posters and dealers spread throughout the towns and cities of Europe and further afield. Posters quickly became big business, without, however, proving particularly successful as a form of publicity. They did little to promote the sale of the books and magazines that they were in fact intended to encourage.[31] ♣

31. See Nancy Finlay, 'American Posters and Publishing in the 1890s', *American Art Posters of the 1890s*, ed. David W. Kiehl, Metropolitan Museum of Art, New York, 1988, pp.45–56, esp. p.51.

THE CHAP BOOK: A REAL FAKE POSTER?

On 14 November 1895 Toulouse-Lautrec wrote to Léon Deschamps to inform him that he had 'received from *La Plume* the sum of two hundred francs for reproduction rights to a poster in folio size, *The Chap Book*.'[1] This poster was hand-pulled by Chaix, the firm that had already printed a number of the artist's other posters, including *Caudieux* and *Babylone d'Allemagne*. One hundred copies were run off but without any mention of the printer's name. Some were numbered. The work in question was a print.

The poster, conversely, mentions Chaix's print works, the type of ink used (Lorilleux) and the 'Affiches Artistiques' of *La Plume*. Toulouse-Lautrec's letter is badly worded but it leaves us in no doubt that the artist did not have a hand in the print and above all that the reproduction had not been foreseen.

It is, indeed, a strange poster. We know that Toulouse-Lautrec designed another small poster measuring 48 x 35.5cm/19 x 14in for an American firm, The Ault & Wiborg Company ('Makers of Fine Printing and Lithographic Inks'). It is his only known zincograph. He designed all the plates and provided instructions on how it should be printed. The copies were run off in America.

The Chap-Book was an ephemeral magazine published by Stone & Kimball and, in keeping with contemporary fashion, it reproduced a number of posters, the best of which were the work of William Bradley. All were accurately catalogued, collected and conserved by American museums and galleries. None includes the piece attributed to Toulouse-Lautrec. And none is in a horizontal format, which in any case made it impractical to display in bookshops. Moreover, none of the specialist journals and numerous works by Anglo-Saxon writers that were published at that time mentions Lautrec's poster, which would undoubtedly have caused a sensation, inviting both admirers and detractors. American writers invariably mentioned the work of French artists, reserving their particular praise for Eugène Grasset, who produced a number of posters which, as *La Plume* pointed out in a special number on the illustrated poster, were printed in America. Métivet, who, as we have noted, won *The Century Magazine*'s competition for *A New Life of Napoleon* (Toulouse-Lautrec was one of the losers in this competition), had his poster printed and, as was the case with Louis-Maurice Boutet de Monvel, his design was also the subject of critical comment. In his excellent study *American Poster Renaissance*, Victor Margolin writes that 'There is no record that the poster was displayed in America, but it may have been used to promote the sale of *The Chap-Book* in Paris'.[2] This is, of course, economically inconceivable.

This total silence is puzzling, as is the reference to the 'Affiches Artistiques' of *La Plume* in place of the name of the publisher. We know that the print was sold in Paris, notably by *La Plume*, which is bizarre, to say the least. It is undoubtedly a genuine Lautrec. But is it a genuine poster? No doubt it was a poster designed especially for lovers of poster art.

The question to which we shall likely never find an answer concerns whatever agreement may have been reached between Léon Deschamps on the one hand and Stone & Kimball on the other. ❧

1. *Toulouse-Lautrec: Correspondance* (note 12), p.292; Engl. trans., p.283 (letter from Henri Toulouse-Lautrec to Léon Deschamps, 14 Nov. 1895).
2. Victor Margolin, *American Poster Renaissance*, Castle Books, New York, 1975, p.31.

Henri de Toulouse-Lautrec, 1895

Paul Berthon, detail

THE DECORATIVE PANEL

Alphonse Mucha

It seems to have been the English Pre-Raphaelite painter Dante Gabriel Rossetti who first had the idea of creating four decorative panels on the subject of the four seasons. Conceived in London in 1869, the idea eventually led nowhere.

It was again Jules Chéret who proved to be a pioneer in this regard, for, according to the *Chronique des arts et de la curiosité*, 'Monsieur Jules Chéret has just had the felicitous idea of applying the resources of his art to decorating our apartments. [...] If successful, this experiment may resemble the posters in the streets by shaking us out of our old-fashioned habits concerning our interiors. [...] The four panels can be framed and glazed and form veritable paintings that are uniquely cheerful in character.'[1] This report certainly puts things in perspective, for what strikes us today as banal was clearly somthing new in the early 1890s. In practice we are dealing here with four lithographed panels representing mime, music, dance and comedy that Chéret designed for Maison Pattey, a wallpaper dealer at 16 Boulevard Montmartre in Paris. Two hundred copies were hand-pulled in seven or eight colours on special paper.

The critical response was enthusiastic, and rightly so.[2] Chéret had never felt so comfortable in the medium and, above all, he had never produced such rich and complex designs. Even so, they remained unique in his output. Was the middle-class market not ready for him? Was the price of the panels too high? Whatever the answer, he designed no more panels until *La Fileuse* (The Spinner) and *La Dentellière* (The Lace Maker) for the 1900 Paris Universal Exhibition.

Other publishers were interested in mining this rich seam, but they preferred to focus their activities on smaller areas. Their aim was not to distribute their products to the largest possible market but to concentrate on projects similar to the albums published by Marty and Vollard.

1. *La Chronique des arts et de la curiosité*, 12 Dec. 1891.
2. See Gabriel Mourey's article in *Le Courrier français*, 6 Dec. 1891.

Alphonse Mucha

'IT IS THROUGH UNDRESSING THAT HE DRESSES'

RENÉ DUBREUIL, LA PLUME

Jules Chéret, *La Pantomime*, 1891

Jules Chéret, *La Comédie*, 1891

Jules Chéret, *La Danse*, 1891

Jules Chéret, *La Musique*, 1891

Élisabeth Sonrel, 1901

Alphonse Mucha

Alphonse Mucha

Gaspar Camps

One such project was Charles Verneau's set of 'mural prints' in 1894, a plan welcomed by Ernest Maindron but compromised by an incoherent choice of artists – Eugène Ogé designed two panels alongside Steinlen and Adolphe Willette. But yet again the project led nowhere.

Within four years, however, the situation had changed. Collectors were now snapping up posters and having them framed in order to display them at home. Why not extend the range of images available while retaining the same artists and the same basic design, with a female sitter and a floral background? Champenois presumably decided that because posters were often too big, he should produce prints conceived in terms of interior design.

Swept along by the insatiable thirst of the contemporary bourgeoisie, printers and publishers devised a new concept that proved tremendously successful. Why burden oneself with large formats? Why misappropriate posters, whose publicity aspect might well put off a bourgeois audience? Instead, printers and publishers decided to enlarge their client base beyond collectors while retaining the most successful artists and their money-spinning designs. They would produce designs suitable for interior decoration. This, too, was an idea almost certainly thought up by Champenois.[3]

Champenois was already a major printer specializing in chromolithographs that advertised biscuits, tea and chocolate in the form of publicity brochures and posters but also postcards, menus, labels and even chromolithographs on metal sheeting. He worked for some of the leading brands, including his principal client, the biscuit manufacturer Lefèvre-Utile. Following a court case with his former partner Lemercier, he was lucky to win back both Sarah Bernhardt and Alphonse Mucha and lost no time in signing a contract with the latter which worked very much to his own advantage.

Initially Mucha was much taken by the idea of designing decorative panels: 'I was happy to be involved in an art designed for the people and not for the salons. It was good value, within the reach of everyone, and found a place for itself not only with well-to-do milieus but also

3. See Daniel Bordet, *Les cent plus belles images de Champenois imprimeur*, Dabecom, La Ferté-Bernard, 2004.

Georges Privat-Livemont

Georges Privat-Livemont

Paul Berthon

Louis Abel-Truchet, 1900

Eugène Grasset, *La Morphinomane*, 1897

with poorer families.'[4] Champenois proved a real terror: for example, a project for a calendar, *Zodiac*, in 1896 exists in nine variants (new ones are being discovered all the time), one of them without the text, another as a tear-off calendar that was used by his sales representatives. There followed a design titled *Champenois* and intended for domestic display and another for his friends at *La Plume*. Otherwise, commercial considerations were paramount, including designs for the Bagnolet Soap Factory, for the Imprimerie Ducros, for the Cachou Lajaunie breath freshener and for the Grande Maison de Blanc in Brussels.

That same year – 1896 – also saw the launch of a new type of product in the form of a decorative panel that was neither a print in terms of its format and limited print-run nor the sort of reproduction of an academic painting that was printed in its thousands. Rather, it was an original creation. This experimental work was called *The Seasons* and comprised four panels that proved so startlingly successful that Champenois produced a smaller version that he sold to advertisers. The following year Mucha was commissioned to design a further series of panels on the same theme, which led him in turn to extend his field of endeavour to jewellery and other arts.

For those potential purchasers with less room at their disposal, Champenois went on to produce panels in pairs: Byzantine heads in a square design and *Dawn* and *Dusk* in a horizontal format. These works could be printed on various surfaces, including Japanese vellum and satin, in limited editions and in formats as small as a postcard. His imagination was boundless, and it is easy to see why, after working for him for five years, Mucha, who was keen to devote himself to painting, left for New York.

Of course, Champenois had anticipated this development, and one of his sales representatives' catalogues reflects the fact that alongside Mucha's florid art nouveau style, he was also employing Gaspar Camps from Barcelona, Élisabeth Sonrel, Luigi Rossi and many others, enabling him to cater for every taste.

The fashion spread like wildfire, and many artists turned their hand to it.[5] Eugène Grasset was one, albeit with a radically different vision and an eye-catching imagination: *La Morphinomane* (The Morphine Addict) and *La Vitrioleuse* (The Acid Thrower) both date from 1894 and both are quite terrifying. He then joined forces with his publisher, Malherbe, to design ten lithographs depicting women's faces surrounded by flowers or fruit and titled *Temptation*, *Danger*, *Jealousy*, *Coldness* and so on, all of them extraordinary and singularly serious images. His crowning achievements both date from 1900: *L'Éventail* (Woman with a Fan) and *L'Ombrelle* (The Parasol). His disciple Paul-Émile Berthon threw himself into the medium in 1897, depicting women playing medieval instruments and also producing flower portraits, all of them in pastel shades ranging from yellow to brown. A prolific artist, Berthon went on to paint landscapes and portraits of sovereigns.

Georges Privat-Livemont might have been expected to seize such an opportunity, but nothing could have been further from the truth. His contribution to the medium is limited to a little gem, *La Vague* (The Wave), together with two women, one of them painting, the other working as a sculptor, and, finally, some flowers and cherubs lacking in any real interest.

The decorative panel disappeared from the scene as quickly as it had appeared.

This is as good a place as any to mention some of the initiatives on the margins of our subject.

We begin with the Union for Moral Action, an organization with a particular loathing of posters and one that took exception to the way in which they were licensed, seeing in poster art an incitement to debauchery. It persuaded Pierre Puvis de Chavannes, the highly respected president of the Société des Beaux-Arts and, moreover, an extremely interesting artist in his own right, to grant the society permission to reproduce one of his frescoes from the Panthéon, *St Genevieve as a Child at Prayer*, which it did at great expense, producing large-scale reproductions that proved, however, largely ineffectual.

Another rather short-lived initiative typical of the high ideals of the age was supported – like the

4. In a series of cards published by Albert Bergeret in Nancy and entitled *La Journée de la midinette* (The Daily Round of the Young Dressmaker). On the wall of the dressmaker's room is one of Mucha's decorative panels. These were sold at two to three francs each, placing them within the financial reach of a very large public.

5. Even so, the market did not swallow everything. Firmin Bouisset had become famous thanks to his daughter advertising Menier Chocolate. He designed a poster for the Salon des Cent depicting a young girl seen in profile and set against an art nouveau floral background. He later produced some decorative panels based on the same design, but their rarity suggests that they did not sell very well.

Louis Abel-Truchet, 1900

Eugène Grasset

Gaspar Camps

poster itself – by Roger Marx in his book *L'Art social* (1913), arguing that the art in question should return to basics in the form of panels felt to exert a healthy influence on young flaxen-haired members of society. Heywood Sumner adopted a similar approach in Great Britain using imagery drawn from the Bible and from agriculture, successfully exhibited at the Libre Esthétique in Brussels in 1894. Money was made available, and Étienne Moreau-Nélaton for Larousse and Clémentine-Hélène Dufau for Paul Ollendorff hurled themselves into the breach, for all that that breach remained open for only a short space of time. Clémentine-Hélène Dufau also designed the poster for the exhibition that was devoted to the subject, while posters by Hugo d'Alesi advertising the French provinces were also used. ☙

Clémentine-Hélène Dufau

Alexandre de Riquer, *Spring*

Alexandre de Riquer, *Summer*

Alexandre de Riquer, *Autumn*

Alexandre de Riquer, *Winter*

Alexandre de Riquer, finally, produced his own version of the four seasons for the Parisian publishing house of Pierrefort. A letter that Pierrefort wrote to de Riquer in 1899 is full of fascinating information:

Dear Sir,

Forgive me for having taken so long to write to you, but I was keen to let you know that everything is proceeding smoothly. I encountered various difficulties, above all with regard to the paper, which I was unable to find in the size that you wanted. I asked a manufacturer, who will provide paper exactly similar to the one used by Mucha for his animated Flowers. It is a cream-coloured paper that will support a large number of colours.

As far as the number of colours is concerned, I merely hinted at these and referred to your advice. A good printer would undoubtedly be able to reproduce everything using six colours. But to be on the safe side, we have settled on seven.

The artist responsible for the lithographic process is not only skilled in the use of colour but is also an excellent designer. He admires your panels very much and will do everything in his power to reproduce them properly. I have additionally agreed to keep an unflinching eye on this process myself. We shall experiment, something that is not easy, given the size of the lithographic stones.

I now come to the question of payment.

To judge by your letter of 23 July [18]99 – and without invalidating our earlier arrangements – it seems that you prefer a fixed sale of your panels for a sum less than you might have received if you had sold them all, a sum that I agree would have been uncertain, and so I would suggest that I buy your *Seasons* panels for the sum of 2,000 francs payable as follows: 500 francs on 10 September; 500 francs on 10 October; 500 francs on 10 November; and 500 francs on 10 December 1899. These sums will be remitted to you by the Crédit Lyonnais. Or you can draw a bill of exchange on me if you prefer. The final settlement will be made, therefore, before the end of the year.

In all likelihood, the panels cannot go on sale for another two and a half months, since I am keen to display them all at the same time. It would be desirable, then, if the article in *Le Studio* did not appear until November.

I am at present preparing an album of exclusively decorative plates. It contains sketches by de Feure, Mucha, Lorant-Heilbronn, George Auriol, Berchmans and Privat-Livemont. We want to publish only choice pieces signed by a small number of artists. The album will contain thirty or so plates. I'd be happy to number you among our contributors.

To conclude and to return to your *Seasons* panels, I hope you will allow me to make an observation and at the same time to leave you to decide whether or not it is a reasonable one. Do you not think that the *Winter* panel – which I have to admit I find very beautiful – stands a little apart from the others by dint of its subject matter? Let me explain. *Spring*, *Summer* and *Autumn* are personified as voluptuous Ladies. Does *Winter* necessarily have to evoke sadness and indigence both as a decorative subject and as a theme of artistic expression? I think that among the Fairies and Princesses who, in my eyes, represent the seasons, there could be a Lady with magnificent clothes who would be the Frost Princess. She might be picking corollas of ice among the leaves of ivy. Beside her, either serving as an embellishment on her dress or in the form of a sheaf spilling over in her arms, there might be an abundance of Christmas roses. The princess's head might be bowed or she might be depicted in profile looking right. She would appear in an undulating snow-covered landscape shrouded in a blue veil. The sun would be on the point of setting on the horizon in a pink, yellowish, purple, violet, blue, greenish and grey sky in which the first stars would be starting to appear. A final ray of sunlight would strike her, causing the ice pendants decorating her hair and clothing to sparkle and glitter like precious stones. At her feet, the cracks in the ice on a frozen stream whose green translucency the viewer may be able to admire would grow iridescent with prism-like tones. To one side the branches of trees would be weighed down with wisps of snow. Lit by the setting sun, the snow would appear pink and violet and seem to blossom into life. In the undulations in the snow, which would start at the frozen stream and melt with the blue and rose-pink hillsides, we might see the footprints of birds in which the light would play. Stalactites would hang from the branches before falling to the ground, forming the strings of a harp to which robins would cling, or else there might be a frozen waterfall rising up at one side of the scene and forming the pipes of an organ that would sparkle in places. (On re-reading this, I find this fiendishly complicated.)

I seem to be writing literature (and what literature!), I've got carried away, but – at the risk of making you smile – I wanted to prove to myself that it is possible to evoke extremely colourful subjects to depict winter, while also recalling the three other panels in terms of their composition and colours.

You can do whatever you like with this observation of mine. As I have already said, the *Winter* that you sent me is very good; but, in the event of your following up my idea, I shall keep it for a further series of panels that would be simpler in design and more realistic and might comprise only two or three panels.

I look forward to reading your response. I am, Sir, your most obedient servant, E. Pierrefort.[1] ♣

1. Apart from his enthusiasm for undiluted symbolism, Pierrefort also tells us that he was planning to use seven colours and that he had found a good lithographer – neither de Riquer nor Mucha and their cohorts would stoop to this aspect of the lithographic process. The fee of 2,000 francs was very high. The letter also shows us that Pierrefort was planning an ambitious album for the following year.

Maurice Marodon, detail

THE LITTLE QUEEN

Georges A. Bottini, 1897

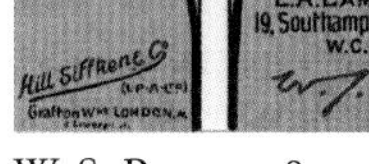

W. S. Rogers, 1899

Anonymous

Georges Gaudy, 1898

The 1890s were not only the golden age of the poster, they also witnessed the triumphant ascendancy of the bicycle. Both quantitatively and qualitatively, sales publicity was largely dominated by a product which in the space of only ten years had ceased to be a luxury and become a popular consumer item.

The figures speak for themselves: in Paris 200 exhibitors presented 613 machines at the 1894 Salon du Cycle that was held at the Salle Wagram, whereas by 1895 there were 350 exhibitors with 820 models. In the United States there were twenty-seven bicycle manufacturers in 1890, employing 1,800 workers. Within a decade there were 312 employing 17,000.

The bicycle initially appealed to a middle-class market fanatical about this embodiment of modern life. Uniquely inquisitive as he was, Henri de Toulouse-Lautrec used to meet his friend Tristan Bernard at the Buffalo Velodrome near the Porte Maillot in Paris. Bernard was the track's director, and cycle races were the latest fashion. In turn this encouraged Toulouse-Lautrec to produce his only truly commercial poster: *The Simpson Chain*. Alfred Jarry was immensely proud of his bicycle. It may be added that in 1891–2 a licence obtainable from their local police station was needed by all who wanted to cycle in Paris.

A bicycle was expensive. Top-of-the-range models had their own showrooms in the Quartier des Ternes between the Avenue de Wagram and the Avenue de la Grande-Armée. Aware that their products were aimed at a chic clientele, manufacturers knew they could appeal to artists who were admired by a limited group of initiates. Bicycle-mania went hand in hand with poster-mania. For an aperitif that was clearly aimed at the small world of the bicycle, Édouard Vuillard conceived a highly esoteric evocation of a velodrome, even if *Bécane* remained unique in his output. Georges Bottini, who frequented the city's American bars, dreamt up an elegant little jewel of a poster for Médinger Cycles, but he too made no further contribution to the medium, much as Manuel Robbe produced no more cycling posters after a couple of striking examples for Plasson Cycles.[1] Jean-Louis Forain was in charge of promoting the second Salon du Cycle. His poster shows two young women cyclists dressed according to the latest fashion in cycling – cycling was also one of the first manifestations of the women's liberation movement.

1. In the United States, the top end of the market was dominated by William H. Bradley, who produced designs for Victor Bicycles, and Edward Penfield, who designed posters for Orient Cycles, The Northampton Cycle and Stearns Cycles. In 1896 Columbia Cycles organized a competition that was won by Maxfield Parrish.

'THIS LITTLE MULE THAT YOU LEAD BY THE EARS AND DRIVE FORWARD BY KICKING IT WITH YOUR FEET.' ALFRED JARRY

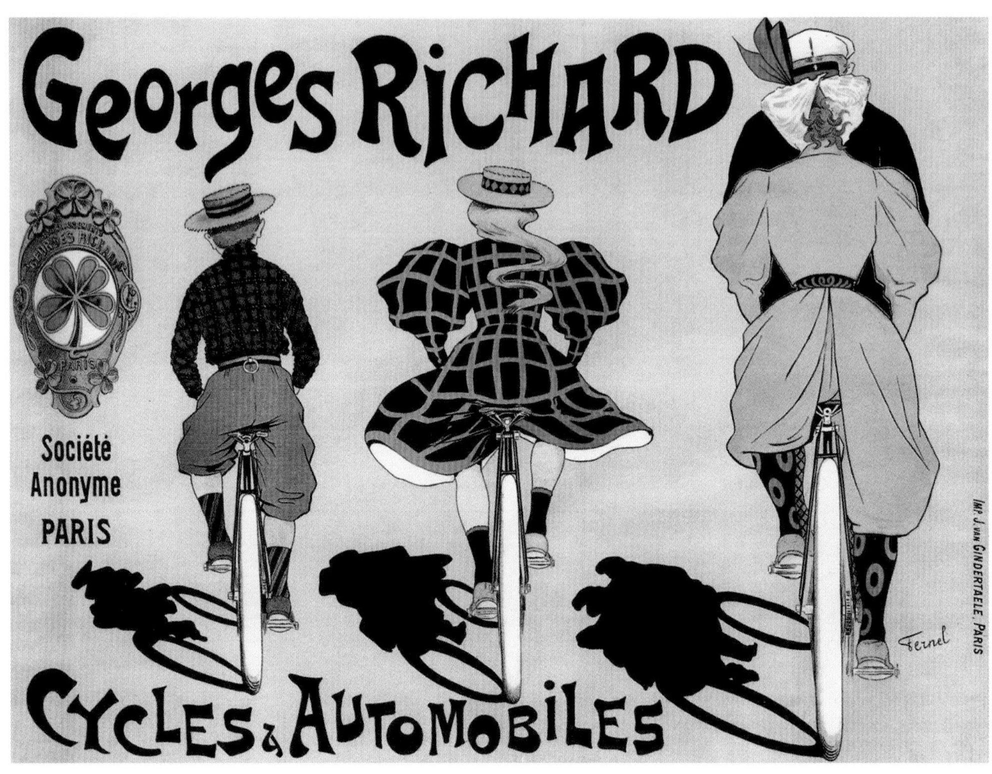

Fernand Fernel, 1896

Henri Thiriet, 1897

F. W. Ramsdell, *c.* 1899

William Henry Bradley, 1896

Henriette Bressier, *c.* 1900

Arthur Foäche, *c.* 1900

Wilhio

Manuel Robbe, 1897

Maurice Marodon

By suggesting that the corset had been abandoned, bloomers and short jackets were the first visible signs of this latest development. In many fashionable posters, women were no longer depicted as idealized creatures but as forerunners of the later suffragettes.

With the increased number of French, British and American makes, posters appeared in their hundreds. Metal frames and the Dunlop inner tube had existed since the early 1890s, but to these features were now added the free wheel, dials and efficient brakes. In turn poster artists rivalled the bicycle's designers with an imagination that easily turned to eccentricity, creating designs that covered the whole range of styles that were fashionable at that time.

Brand names that had the financial means to do so but which were unwilling to take any risks appealed to the leading poster designers, Chéret, Grasset and Mucha. It was for Perfecta Cycles that Mucha created one of his masterpieces. What is particularly astonishing is the number of times that the major advertisers changed their style: Clément and Gladiator were capable of switching abruptly from banal ornamentation to the most florid art nouveau and even to the sort of kitsch designs in which Pal (Jean de Paléologue) specialized. After a while La Française used only the leading French cycling champions. The supremacy of Parisian artists and printers meant that it was in the French capital that foreign manufacturers, too, produced their posters.

So as not to bore the reader, we will list only a handful of major trends. We have already mentioned elegantly dressed women, but there were also women, more or less undressed, whose role extended from allegory to sensualist kitsch, to say nothing of other depictions of elegant encounters, humorous scenes such as the wife running off on the eve of her wedding and the praise of speed. And there were also, of course, military men (the army was a major client), politicians and crowned heads of state. There were also the most insane emanations of the most florid style, nods in the

Pal

Pal

'IF YOU WANT TO, LET'S DREAM WHAT IS GOOD!
MY TANDEM HAS WHEEL-RIMS OF WOOD
AND TWO TYRES THAT NEVER GO FLAT.
IT'S ROUXEL & DUBOIS! FANCY THAT!'

ALPHONSE ALLAIS

Lunel, *c.* 1894

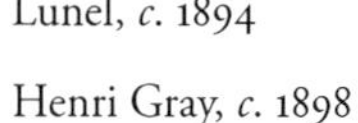

Henri Gray, *c.* 1898

Henri Gray, 1899

Anonymous, 1905

Pal, 1895

Arthus

Henri Gray, *c.* 1897

direction of historicism and posters depicting all of the nations of the earth, not to mention a joyful menagerie of animals and even women in space.

This prodigious kaleidoscope of designs was a specifically French phenomenon: with rare exceptions such as the delightful poster designed by W.S. Rogers[2] for the Stanley Cycles Show, British posters were anonymous, which was almost always synonymous with mediocrity. And the same was true of the United States, where Strobridge was the main printer, while in Austria the market was dominated by Weiner. In Germany Fritz Rehm designed a number of fine posters for Victoria Cycles, whereas in Belgium Georges Gaudy was a true specialist drawing fashionable women and their machines from every conceivable angle. Two countries in which the bicycle enjoyed tremendous popularity were Denmark and the Netherlands, but whereas posters were little used to advertise cycling in the former, they made at least a tentative start in the latter, where laudable work was done by Johann Georg Van Caspel for Hinde-Rywielen and by F.G. Schlette for the leading firm of Fongers. ❧

2. Rogers also collected posters. Published by Greening & Co. in London in 1901, his *Book of the Poster* remains a mine of information.

Jean-Louis Forain, 1894

Edward Penfield, 1896

Victor Mignot, 1897

Henri de Toulouse-Lautrec, 1892, detail

FRANCE

Jules Chéret, 1879

'THANK YOU TO CHÉRET.'
RAOUL CERTAT, LA PLUME

By the late Romantic period in France art posters were advertising the publishing trade and the world of opera, with the poster gaining a reputation as a typically French cultural phenomenon. The finest lithographers of the day – Paul Gavarni, Henri Monnier, Tony Johannot, Auguste Raffet and many others who have since then fallen into neglect, including Bertall (the trade name of Charles Albert d'Arnoux) and Alexandre Calame – designed posters that could be admired in display cabinets in bookshops and that were intended for collectors who subscribed to works sold in instalments: this was the heyday of the popular edition. For technical reasons, most were in black and white.[1]

Two legendary posters – Honoré Daumier's of the warehouses at Ivry and Édouard Manet's for Champfleury's book about cats – are in fact lithographs glued to a letterpress background and belong to the medium's prehistory.

1. Some – especially those advertising operas – introduced colour, often using stencilling, revealing an exceptional degree of skill.
2. See Marc Martin's excellent study, *Les Pionniers de la publicité*, Nouveau Monde, Paris, 2012. Figures are taken from this volume.
3. Their sizes are demi-colombier (40 x 60cm/15.75 x 23.62in) or quarter-colombier (30 x 30cm/11.81 x 11.81in). The latter is barely a poster at all.

By combining all that we know about registration rights (posters were subject to stamp duty), the holdings of the Bibliothèque Nationale and the handful of surviving professional records, we can form an idea of exactly what was involved in bill-sticking.[2]

Paris and its environs accounted for around 50 per cent of all the posters produced and displayed in France. Posters for public spectacles accounted for 63 per cent of the total, while 80 per cent were in a smaller format that generally allowed them to be displayed on advertising pillars.[3] Both the shows themselves and the printing works were grouped together in an area known as 'Tout-Paris'. Starting out from the Seine, this area followed the grand boulevards from the Madeleine to the Bastille. The area was covered by 300 posters. Valuable evidence survives to indicate exactly how and where these posters were displayed. 'In 1876, 300 of Chéret's posters for

Édouard Manet, 1868

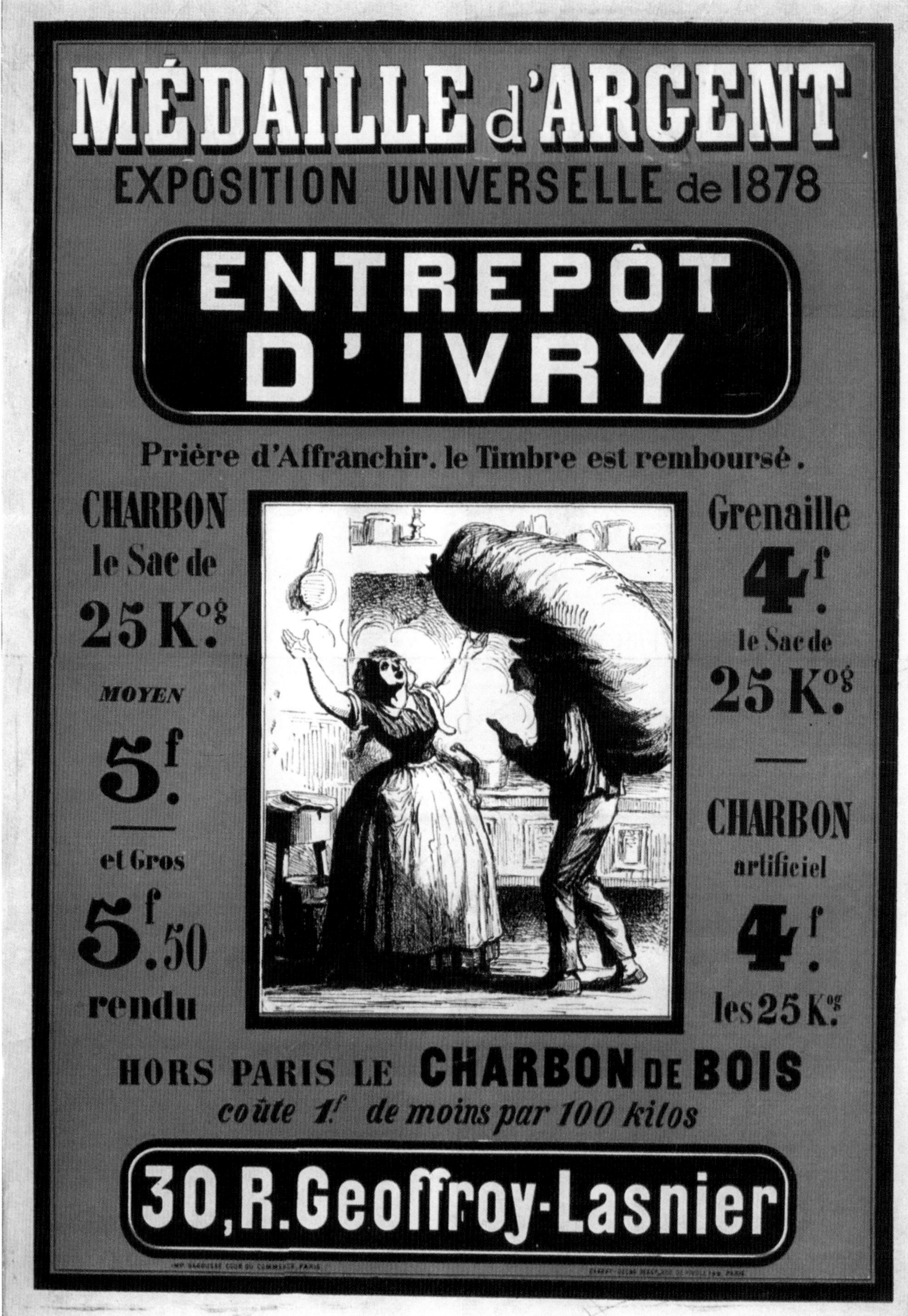

Honoré Daumier, 1878

L'Homme-Femme Soprano at the Concert-Promenade de L'Horloge were posted throughout central Paris. On 14 May 1894, 117 posters advertising Brunin at the Café des Ambassadeurs were distributed. Of these, eleven were displayed at the Opéra. On 27 January 1879 the La Ruche café-concert – a humble establishment on the Place du Château d'Eau – asked the bill-sticker Monsieur Drouart to distribute 200 posters advertising its revue *Tant va la Ruche à l'o* "throughout Tout-Paris". Of these, 150 were to be posted on reserved hoardings, while the remaining fifty were to be fly-posted.' These three examples indicate not only the importance of advertising for the cafés-concerts of the period but also the modest means employed: a few handfuls of posters were enough to draw audiences from all over Paris.'[4] According to their copyright notice, half of these posters were printed by Charles and Émile Lévy. The former identified his products as 'American Posters', the latter as 'French Posters'.[5]

4. See Alain Weill (ed.), *Le Café-Concert 1870–1914*, UCAD, Paris, 1977.

5. In the light of the number of posters produced by Chéret and the Frères Choubrac, we may well question the efficiency of this system.

Everything changed within the space of twenty years. Of the twenty-one printing houses listed in 1880, only three still existed by 1900. Charles and Émile Lévy had gone, although Chaix guaranteed a third of their production, including the work of Jules Chéret and his stable of young disciples. Others who disappeared include Champenois with his star, Alphonse Mucha, and Paul Dupont, who had Pal under contract. These three alone represented 50 per cent of all the posters produced. If we add Camis, with his prestigious team of Firmin Bouisset, Nicolas Tamagno and Albert Guillaume, and Bourgerie, both of whom specialized in advertising for commerce and industry, we may conclude that the other members of the profession, who may have been qualitatively just as remarkable and who included Malherbe and Verneau, still lagged far behind them.

The main reason for this development may be found in the law of 29 July 1881 that removed all restrictions on bill-sticking, leading to a free-for-all, with the City of Paris, the Poor Law Administration and the French Railways all inviting tenders from eager advertisers. Large companies were formed, including Bonnard-Bidault and Dufayel, with the sole purpose of covering the city in posters, either on walls and fences or displayed on panels reserved for that purpose, guaranteeing that they would be maintained and preserved.

Henceforth regarded as a viable medium, the poster attracted commerce and industry as well as tourism. The larger sizes – double-colombier and bigger – had made up 20 per cent of the total in 1880. By 1900 this figure had risen to 46 per cent.

Gustave Jossot, 1897

Pal, *c.* 1895

JULES CHÉRET

Jules Chéret, 1899

As noted in the Introduction, Chéret was undeniably the father of the poster and hailed as such by his contemporaries. This son of a printer served his apprenticeship as a lithographer but was essentially self-taught as a poster artist, attending evening classes and spending his Sundays at the Louvre. He found a sponsor in the person of the parfumier Eugène Rimmel, for whom he designed a number of labels. He also accompanied Rimmel on his travels and in that way got to know the work of his god, Giovanni Battista Tiepolo, in Venice. Rimmel additionally lent him the money to open his own studio in 1866. Chéret's success story was typical of the second half of the nineteenth century, when men of talent who were hard-working and ambitious were able to rise up the professional ladder with prodigious speed. Chéret soon forged links with major clients, all of whom believed in the new medium and who placed their faith in his talent: they include Maurice Fenaille, who commissioned posters for two of his company's products, Saxoléine and Benzomoteur; Auguste-Arthur Géraudel, a pharmacist who invented the pastilles and purgatives that bore his name; the impresario Charles Zidler; and Jules Roques, the owner of *Le Courrier français*, who was so enthusiastic about Chéret's work that he did much to promote it.[1] Chéret sold his studio to Chaix, the biggest Parisian printer, in 1881 but stayed on as a company director. This marked the culmination of his career, while also acknowledging the place that the poster had by now begun to play in the field of the fine arts.

In 1886, Henri Beraldi devoted a lengthy article to Chéret in the fourth volume of his *Les Graveurs du XIXe siècle*, appending a list of no fewer than 950 posters. In 1889 a retrospective of Chéret's work was shown at the Palais de l'Industrie at that year's Paris Universal Exhibition. The following year he was awarded the Légion d'Honneur for 'creating a new industry of art since 1866 by applying art to commercial and industrial printing'. It was an exceptional accolade.

A tall, dapper man, Chéret was quite a personality. He was born and bred in Paris and had everything going for him. An habitué of circles frequented by the enemies of academicism, he followed the lead of Joris-Karl Huysmans by drawing his inspiration from the eighteenth century, while using the Danish actress and dancer Charlotte Wiehe to create the prototype of a sensual and desirable Parisian woman far removed from the disembodied creatures familiar from the Salon des Artistes Français. These women became known as his '*chérettes*'. His decision to use them in advertising – a 'vulgar' art in the eyes of the leading exponents of official art – naturally drew him closer to the more militant representatives of art nouveau. From an early date he was also invited to exhibit his work at the Salon des XX in Brussels and was a regular visitor to the Sunday receptions of Albert Besnard, where he rubbed shoulders with the likes of Auguste Rodin, Jean-Louis Forain and Eugène Carrière.

'Slim and with brightly lit eyes above a twirled moustache, he had the air of a cavalry officer in spite of his necktie and wore a white linen fencing jacket' – Chéret was a famous swordsman.[2] Jane Avril recalled hearing Chéret's 'bacchantic laughter' at the noisy dinners that were held every Sunday at Le Chat Noir.[3] The press praised him to the skies, notably Frantz Jourdain in *La Revue illustrée* on 13 February 1889 and, more especially, Félicien Champsaur in *L'Événement*. Champsaur had no hesitation in hailing him as the 'Fragonard of the street, the Watteau of the crossroads, the Delacroix of the pavement and the Tiepolo of the public place'.[4]

For Joris-Karl Huysmans, writing in *Certains*, there was more talent in one of Chéret's posters than in most of the Salon paintings put together, while for Octave Uzanne, writing in his own *Nouvelle Bibliopolis*, Chéret was 'the great charmer and the life and soul of our visual circle'. But, rather than extend this already long list of contemporaries who had nothing but praise for Chéret's work, we need to examine the writings that explain the reasons for his success.

For Beraldi, Chéret 'has demonstrated an admirable instinct for creating a design appropriate to the poster,

1. He published supplements that were inserted in copies of his magazine and which for the most part comprised Chéret's posters and praised the curtains of the largest cafés-concerts, which he also covered with posters.
2. Jean Puget, *La Vie Extraordinaire de Forain*, Émile Paul, Paris, 1975.
3. Jane Avril, *Mes Mémoires*, Phébus, Paris, 2005, p.67.
4. 'The explanation for these grotesque panegyrics may be that according to an agreement between the two of them, Champsaur praised Chéret in the press in exchange for illustrations depicting his (mediocre) work!' See *La Belle Époque de Jules Chéret*, Les Arts Décoratifs/Bibliothèque Nationale de Paris, Paris, 2010, p.67.

Jules Chéret, 1896

Jules Chéret, 1889

Jules Chéret, 1896

Jules Chéret, 1891

Jules Chéret, *Pantomimes lumineuses*, 1893, showing the lithographic colour process

'THE FRAGONARD OF THE STREET, THE WATTEAU OF THE CROSSROADS, THE DELACROIX OF THE PAVEMENT, THE TIEPOLO OF THE PUBLIC PLACE.'

FÉLICIEN CHAMPSAUR, L'ÉVÉNEMENT, 1892

Jules Chéret, 1893

Jules Chéret, 1893

Jules Chéret, 1900

Jules Chéret, 1891

Jules Chéret, 1893

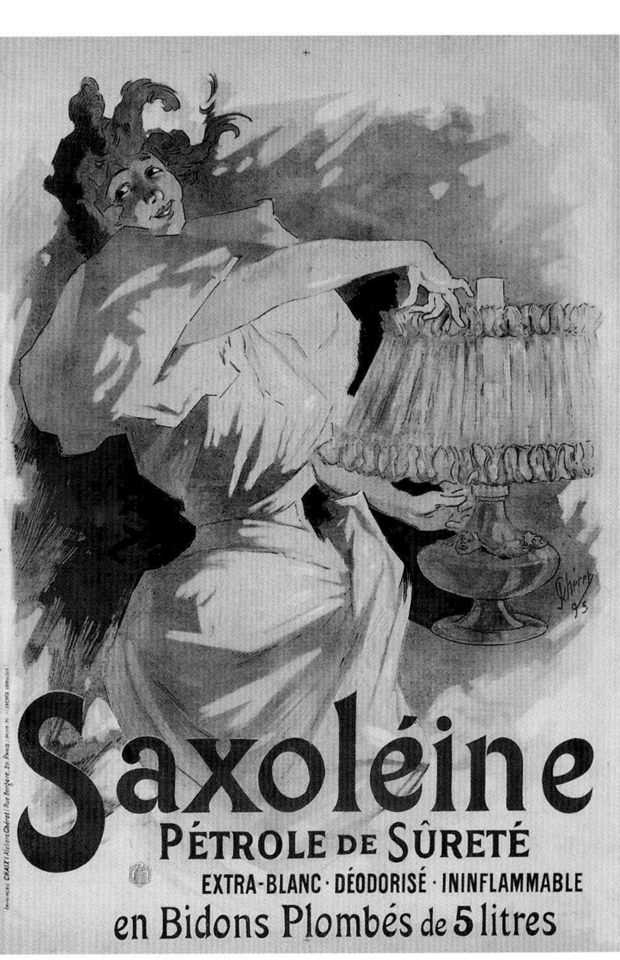

Jules Chéret, 1895

Jules Chéret, 1888

Jules Chéret

Georges Meunier, 1895

Misti, *c.* 1898

to which he has added the art of producing the maximum effect from a very small number of colours. [...] As a matter of principle, Chéret's posters are the result of three superimposed impressions. One, in black, establishes the clearly outlined and skilfully composed design before bright red – the most violent and eye-catching of colours – is applied at certain points. This second impression adds this red patch. The third creates a sense of balance between the brutal note of the red and the golden mean of a graduated background: cold tones, blues or greens, are placed at the top of the poster, warm tones, yellow or orange, are placed at the foot. [...] For Chéret's posters, this triple impression has become the normal, classic process.'[5]

Achille Segard described Chéret's working method as follows: 'The artist traces one of his paper sketches on to each of the lithographic stones. He has never used a grid. He uses the lithographic crayon to indicate the half-tones; the ink allows him to create a sense of solidity and to define essential features of the design. He uses as many stones as there are primary colours: red, yellow and blue. These three impressions are sometimes supplemented by a fourth that is designed to enrich the greys: by adding or superimposing primary colours the artist is able to produce every possible variety of colouring. When distributing his reds, he thinks of what they will become when he superimposes his yellows on them and what they will both become when his blues either black them out or enhance them. There is no technique, no amount of instruction that can help him here: it is a question of moderation and touch. One can easily sense the way in which the artist begins by distributing his most brilliant patch of colour – pure yellow or vermilion – and that it is around this area that he seeks more graduated tones, contrasts and all the nuances and subtleties that will contribute to the perfect harmony of the whole.'[6]

Ernest de Crauzat wrote no less enthusiastically about the 'hooray of reds, the repeated hallelujah of yellows and the original glory of the blues' to be found in Chéret's work.

5. Henri Beraldi, *Les Graveurs du XIXe siècle: Guide de l'amateur d'estampes modernes*, 12 vols, Librairie L. Conquet, Paris, 1885–92, esp. vol. 4, p.171.
6. Achille Segard, *Peintres d'aujourd'hui: Les décorateurs*, P. Ollendorff, Paris, 1914.

There followed the transition to the three primary colours and the use of yellow and blue to replace black in the outline of the design.

We can date this decisive development with some accuracy, for it occurred in 1888, when Chéret designed a poster for the Bal Ballier that has come down to us in two versions: in one of them, red and green are the dominant colours, whereas in the other one yellow and blue appear for the first time, marking a revolution in poster design. Segard describes this process in detail.

Writers have generally been content to reduce Chéret's talent to this technical aspect of his output, and yet nothing could be more unjust. If we examine the works being produced at this time by his contemporaries, always excepting Toulouse-Lautrec, we shall see that he was the only one to be obsessed by the idea of recreating a sense of movement, in which he went far beyond the joyous cascades of colour inspired by Tiepolo. Who else had the idea of pulling the poster in four colour scales to capture the effects in the serpentine movements of the dancer Loie Fuller? Who was more adept at capturing the swaying movements of the skaters by playing with several planes in the magnificent series of designs that he created for the Palais de Glace? And who else was able to create a quasi-cinematic vision in the twenty posters that he designed for Saxoléine between 1891 and 1900, highlighting the interplay between the woman and the lamp by approaching them from a different angle on every single occasion? This was the first campaign in the world to exploit the idea of repetition over time to establish the parameters of a brand name.

Chéret turned sixty-four in 1900, and his eyesight began to deteriorate, preventing him from devoting himself any longer to the meticulous detail of the lithograph. He turned to pastels and, above all, murals. Examples of his murals may still be seen in the Hôtel de Ville in Paris and also in Nice, where he lived out his life in the private mansion of one of his friends, Baron Vitta. It is now a museum devoted to Chéret's works. The patriarch of poster art died in 1932 at the age of ninety-six. ❧

Pierre Bonnard, 1891

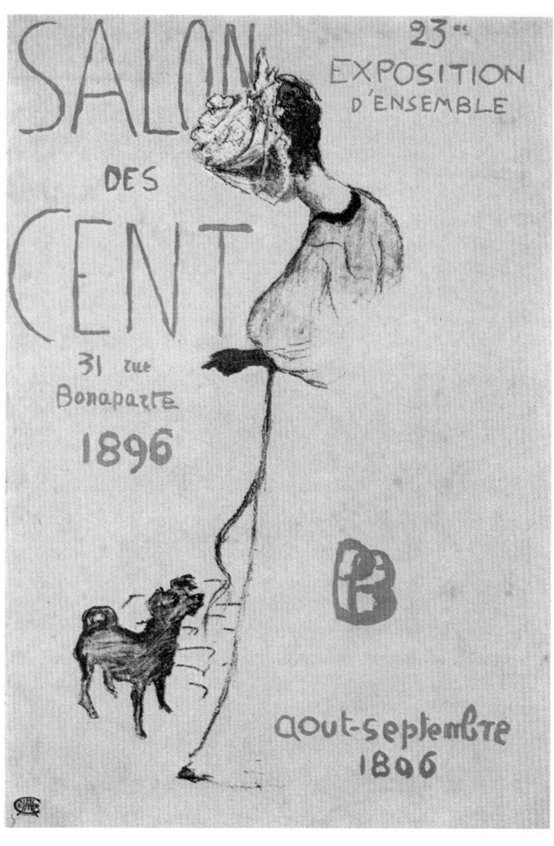

Pierre Bonnard, 1896

Édouard Vuillard, *c.* 1894

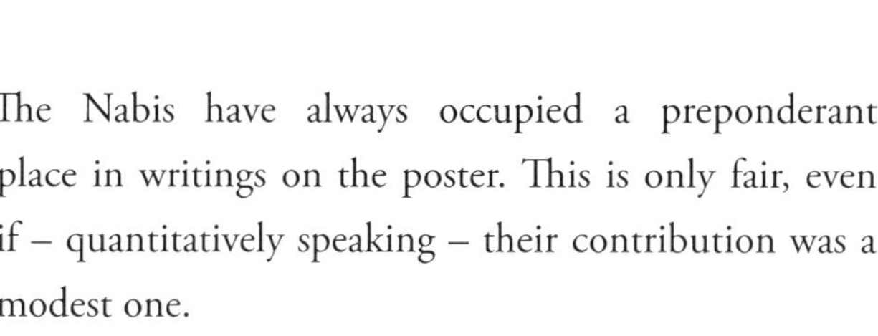

The Nabis have always occupied a preponderant place in writings on the poster. This is only fair, even if – quantitatively speaking – their contribution was a modest one.

The Nabis – the word derives from the Hebrew word for 'prophet' – were a group of students whose hard core attended the Académie Julian. All had undertaken an initiatory trip to Brittany to visit Paul Gauguin and were influenced by Japanese art and the Arts & Crafts movement. They also shared the same ideas as the advocates of art nouveau, notably their desire to remove any sense of hierarchy between the individual arts.

Although they all came to hold these views by different routes, they shared the same basic principle, as summed up by Édouard Vuillard: 'Our merit, if such it is, consists perhaps in the fact that we accepted the most varied expressions whenever they were sincere.' Their circle was large,[1] and included many who tried their hand at lithography, especially at the request of theatre managers. In 1892–3, for example, André Antoine invited his friend Henri-Gabriel Ibels to provide colour illustrations for his programmes that would not necessarily be directly related to the performances in question but which were intended to allow the artist 'to assert himself in an original way'. The manager of the short-lived Théâtre d'Art, Paul Fort, who was himself a Symbolist and a follower of Mallarmé, called on the services of Paul Sérusier, Maurice Denis, Paul Ranson and Pierre Bonnard. And Aurélien Lugné-Poe invited artists to illustrate his programmes at the Théâtre Libre: they included not only Ker-Xavier Roussel, Ranson, Bonnard, Sérusier, Vuillard and Denis but also Edvard Munch, Félicien Rops and Fernand Khnopff.

Very few of these artists were tempted to design posters. Vuillard created one for the unlikely Bécane, an aperitif for cyclists. In 1894, the politician and journalist Arthur Huc, who followed the Paris arts scene closely, invited Maurice Denis to design a poster for the Toulouse-based *La Dépêche*, a harmonious image that Jules Christophe, writing in *La Plume*, hailed for its 'calm and discreet tones' and described as 'the music of a poet'. Félix Vallotton contributed regularly to two weekly

1. See the exhibition catalogue *Nabis, 1888–1900*, ed. Claire Frèches-Thory and Ursula Perucchi-Petri, Réunion des Musées Nationaux, Paris and Prestel, Munich, 1993.

Félix Vallotton, 1898

journals, *Le Rire* and *L'Assiette au beurre*, but made only three attempts to design a poster. One, dating from 1893, was for the revue *La Pépinière* and is highly promising, not least because the subject matter, which is also explored in his engravings, suited him: using his characteristic black and white technique and exploiting his feel for movement, he produced an excellent poster. Unfortunately, his design for a handy street plan of Paris, which dates from 1894 and which was undoubtedly an attempt to make ends meet, has none of these qualities. As a design, it is merely illustrative, lacking in style. There remains the enigmatic *Art Nouveau Gallery*, which he designed for Samuel Bing, its vegetal motif no doubt being the only solution that he could find for such a commission.

Pierre Bonnard's contribution to the medium may be small but it is extremely important. Writing in 1908, Octave Mirbeau recalled that 'The first poster to burst on to the walls since Daumier's day was the work of Bonnard. So different from the joyous radiance of Chéret, *France-Champagne*, although nowadays impossible to find, inaugurated a revival of the art of lithography.' Using only three colours and bold outlines, this homage to Utamaro reveals what collector Thadée Natanson described as 'the whole ebullience of his imagination'. But the story does not end there. Toulouse-Lautrec was stopped dead in his tracks by this poster and immediately set off to find the artist.[2] Bonnard took him to the printer Edward Ancourt, a pioneer of the opera poster. The encounter marked the beginning of a long friendship with Bonnard and a lengthy working relationship with Ancourt.

2. This seems to have been a lucky chance as Bonnard, who was an indefatigable walker, reports that at the end of his life he had difficulty finding even one such poster.

There followed *La Revue blanche*, undoubtedly Bonnard's best poster. It shows Natanson's wife, Misia Sert, all wrapped up, only her devastating gaze being visible, together with a Paris street urchin selling newspapers. In the middle ground we see a man, viewed from the back and wearing a top hat, entirely monochromatic, while the background is covered with copies of the journal. According to Natanson, 'Apart from the colour of the outline, it would be monochromatic, were it not for the inventive interplay between matt and brilliant blacks, which has the effect of adding a further colour.'

The Exhibition of Painter-Engravers of 1896 is a further example of monochrome against uncoloured white paper, with two magical little touches of yellow.

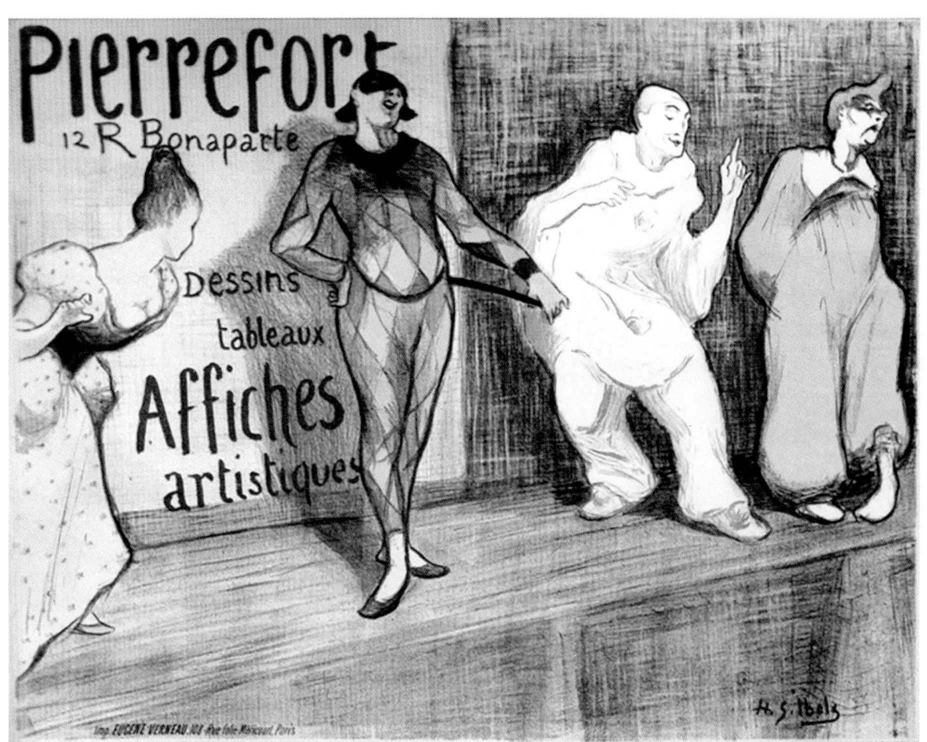

Henri-Gabriel Ibels, 1894

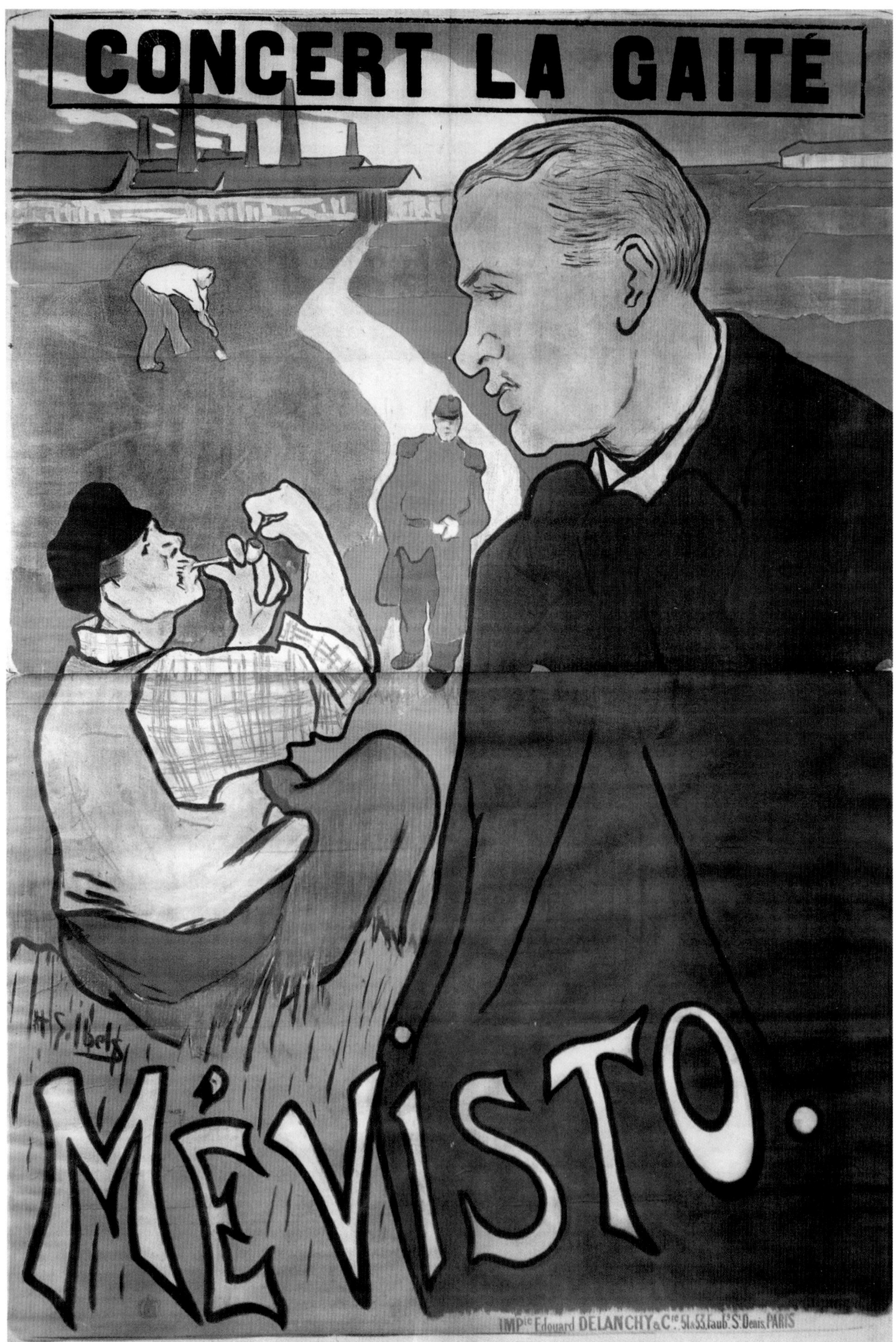

Henri-Gabriel Ibels, 1892

Ambroise Vollard's typography also plays a part here. *Le Salon des Cent* could hardly be more pared back, the elegant woman, depicted in profile, drawing attention to the little dog looking up at her. His 1897 poster for *L'Estampe et l'Affiche* is in three colours and, although more confused than its predecessor, owes its power to the personification of the young printer that has difficulty carrying an enormous box, from which sheets of paper may be seen escaping beneath the tender gaze of the elderly engraver. This effectively marks the end of Bonnard's contribution to poster art. Two lithographic posters for *Le Figaro* are ruined by their overemphatic frames and by a typeface that is without any real interest.[3]

Henri-Gabriel Ibels, whom his comrades called the 'Nabi journalist', was the only member of the group to abandon painting for works on paper. He was more interested in what we now call the media than in exhibition prints, hence the fact that he has now fallen into obscurity, his talents wholly unrecognized.

In an article devoted to Ibels in the pages of *La Plume*, Charles Saunier described him as 'one of the most perfect interpreters of the human comedy', adding that Ibels and Toulouse-Lautrec shared a gift for investing the poster with 'a higher significance, allowing it to satirize our customs and to serve as an indictment of plutocratic society'. Charles Matlack Price thought the same: 'Among less prominent, though perhaps no less talented poster designers of Lautrec's kind was H.G. Ibels, whose point of view in general and technique in particular was very similar.'[4]

Together, Lautrec and Ibels scoured circuses, fairgrounds and cafés-concerts and between them contributed eleven black and white lithographs to André Marty's *Le Café Concert* album of 1893. The panache, force and inventiveness of Lautrec leap out at the viewer, of course. Ibels was very much his opposite. Natanson wrote this touching portrait: 'There was something slightly stiff and even brusque about Ibels's whole manner. Bright-eyed and thin-lipped, he would hurry over to his friends, barely taking the time to utter a word or two or to laugh, his eyes screwed up rather than fully closed. […] He was generally on the go and rarely stood still, the sound of leather and his shoes becoming an inextricable part of his accent, which was that of the suburbs. He was touchy. At the least provocation he would turn white with fury, but on more than one occasion laughter would drive away any remnants of the threatening storm.'[5]

His works revolve around popular shows such as clowns, circus strongmen and fortune-tellers, and his prints for *L'Estampe moderne* and *La Revue blanche* as well as his posters are devoted exclusively to these themes. He also designed a number of works in smaller formats, in which capacity he hired a handful of colleagues such as Lautrec, as well as theatre programmes for Antoine and book illustrations, including *Les Demi-Cabots*, a collection of texts by Georges Esparbès and others published in Paris in 1896. Whether for the Salon des Cent, the Pierrefort Gallery or for Ibels's own exhibition at La Bodinière, his designs are notable for their juxtapositions and parades of travelling fairground entertainers: elegantly outlined, they capture the sense of movement, while the colours are never less than harmonious and delicate. According to Ernest Maindron, 'It is by dint of the most flexible of means and by a single barely indicated stroke that Monsieur Ibels achieves the extraordinary intensity of his effects. His well-positioned figures say exactly what they want to say.'[6]

Aside from his early poster of Mévisto wearing a Pierrot costume, in which he uses strikingly garish colours, Ibels adopts the same harmonious shades and the same balanced composition for his posters of artists: Irène Henry bathed in a subtle monochrome dominated by blue, Jane Debary in red and pink.

The large poster for Mévisto reveals the full range of Ibels's talent both in terms of its design and layout and its use of colour. As Saunier wrote in *La Plume* on 15 January 1893, 'In a bare-leaved suburb bounded by the tall dark chimneys of a factory can be seen a winding footpath. In the distance a farmer is breaking up clods of barren earth. Closer to hand and signalled by his limp peaked cap, a soldier wearing wide trousers half hidden by his billowing tunic is walking with a heavy gait; finally,

3. Bonnard produced only two more posters: one in 1912 for the Salon des Indépendants, the other in 1914 for Richard Strauss's *Josephslegende* performed by the Ballets Russes.
4. Charles Matlack Price, *Posters: A Critical Study of the Development of Poster Design in Continental Europe, England and America*, George W. Bricka, New York, 1913, p.67.
5. Thadée Natanson, *Peints à leur tour*, Albin Michel, Paris, 1948, p.292.
6. Ernest Maindron, *Les Affiches illustrées, 1885–1895*, G. Boudet, Paris, 1896, pp.78–9.

Maurice Denis, 1892

a layabout is smiling mockingly, a pipe hanging from the corner of his mouth. In the foreground, and seen in profile, is the actor Mévisto. […] He is studying these fellow human beings so that later that same evening, back in Paris, he can reproduce their distress and make his indolent audience shudder with their emotions.' If Ibels was an engaging painter of popular spectacles, he was also an artist whose entire output is underpinned by his sense of political engagement.

Félix Fénéon expressed his enthusiasm for Ibels's ability 'to exercise a new verve as a satirist'. He produced designs for *Le Père peinard* and *La Revue anarchiste*, which was run by his brother André, as well as for *Le Mirliton*, *L'Escarmouche*, for which he designed a poster depicting a working-class café sinister and almost deserted, with a procession of old campaigners filing past outside and visible through the window at the back, *Le Cri de Paris* and *L'Assiette au beurre*. He also produced a drawing for *Le Sifflet* in response to Jean-Louis Forain's mean-spirited *Psst…!* directed against Alfred Dreyfus. In the end, Ibels sacrificed his artistic career to his militant views.

By the end of his life Ibels had grown disillusioned. Referring to *Homage to Cézanne*, in which Maurice Denis had depicted the core of the Nabis artists, he asked why he was not among them: 'It is my fault, my very great fault! Because instead of their calm and sagacious milieu, I preferred the turbulence of political struggles alongside Briand and theatrical battles alongside Antoine and Gémier.'[7] Throughout his life he struggled with financial problems. If there is any artist from this period who deserves to be rehabilitated, then it is Henri-Gabriel Ibels.

7. Quoted by Anne-Marie Sauvage in 'Henri-Gabriel Ibels', *Nabis, 1888–1900* (note 1), 177–9, esp. 177.

René Georges Hermann-Paul was a member of the same circle. He too studied at the Académie Julian and worked on *L'Escarmouche*, on *Le Courrier français* (for which he painted a portrait of Vallotton) and on *La Libre Esthétique*, where he worked with Lautrec. He is included among the albums of prints produced by Marty and Vollard. A supporter of Dreyfus, he also worked for Zo d'Axa's *La Feuille*, for *L'Assiette au beurre* and for *Le Canard sauvage*. He produced two remarkable posters, one for the Salon des Cent, the other for a Franco-Italian fencing competition. Both are miniature jewels in the spirit of the Nabis.

It was for Mévisto that Maximilien Luce – a friend of Fénéon and the Anarchists – produced his only poster, a colourful, vibrant work. ☙

René Herman-Paul, 1896

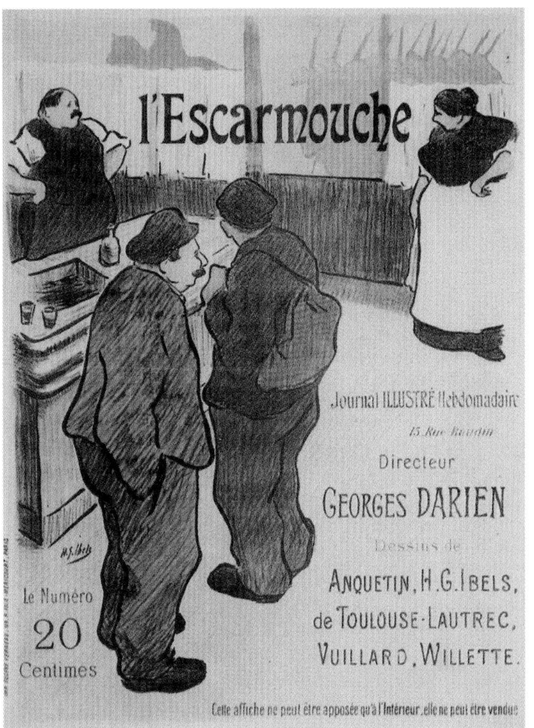

Henri-Gabriel Ibels, 1893

HENRI DE TOULOUSE-LAUTREC

Henri de Toulouse-Lautrec, 1891

Henri de Toulouse-Lautrec is one of a handful of artists whose names are familiar to a very wide audience, like Vincent van Gogh, Pablo Picasso and Salvador Dalí. His poster designs continue to be sold all over the world and have not aged in the slightest.

Lautrec was the product of inbreeding, born with a genetic bone disorder, preventing his legs from developing. Unable to pursue the activities that his aristocratic birth might otherwise have suggested, including the horse-riding enjoyed by his father, Comte Alphonse, he treated life as a spectacle and sought to depict it through drawing, for which he revealed an exceptional gift in childhood. He remained the only love of his mother,[1] who allowed him to move to Paris, where he worked first in the studio of Léon Bonnat, the elder statesman of academicism, and then in that of Fernand Cormon, who provided a breeding ground for talented young artists.

His frenzied love of life astonished all who knew him and even those whose paths he crossed only briefly. To his diminutive stature must be added a disproportionately thick lower lip, a terrible lisp and a provincial French accent so thick that it could be cut with a knife.[2] His arrogance and imagination were those of a lord of the manor unconcerned about accepted standards of behaviour and the pretensions of the bourgeoisie. He was inordinately fond of dressing up and of attending fancy-dress balls. His curiosity and his energy were both boundless. He loved every kind of spectacle and attended performances frequently, from cafés-concerts to the Comédie-Française and from the circus to the fairground, not to mention the velodrome, which he visited with his friend Tristan Bernard, and, finally, bullfighting and boxing. He frequented museums and exhibitions as well as the Jardin des Plantes, where he never wearied of watching the animals. He was also fond of his food and had two passions that appealed to his voluptuous sensuality: alcohol to fire his flashes of inspiration and women with whom he was besotted. Unable to seduce the women from his own social milieu, he sought the company of prostitutes, who dubbed him 'the dick on legs' and 'the column' and among whom he felt cocooned.

1. See the artist's letters to his mother in Henri de Toulouse-Lautrec, *Correspondance*, ed. Herbert D. Schimmel, Gallimard, Paris, 1991; Engl. trans. *The Letters of Henri Toulouse-Lautrec*, ed. Herbert D. Schimmel, Oxford University Press, New York, 1991. Spoilt as a child, he continued to demand money and expected her to keep him supplied with wine, capons, truffles and foie gras.
2. See Thadée Natanson, *Un Henri de Toulouse-Lautrec*, Cailler, Geneva, 1951, reissued by the École Nationale Supérieure des Beaux-Arts, Paris, 1992.
3. His secret was the little naps that he took throughout the day, whenever the opportunity arose. The most famous anecdote took place in London, where he was exhibiting at the Goupil Gallery and where he fell asleep on a couch. The Prince of Wales – the future King Edward VII – turned up at the exhibition but insisted on not disturbing the artist, who finally opened an eye and was informed about his visitor, whereupon he went to sleep again.
4. Natanson, *Un Henri de Toulouse-Lautrec* (note 2), p.72.

In this way he bullied his friends, dragging them around until dawn. And yet as soon as it was morning, he would often be back at the printer's.[3] Thadée Natanson recalls that 'The presses had fallen silent. The studio seemed empty. It was only when I already had my foot on one of the last steps leading down to the studio that I finally discovered Lautrec. He was not leaning over it but was lying down, full length, on a lithographic stone much bigger than himself: never satisfied but always relentless in the attentions that he continued to lavish on the stone slab right up to the very last moment, he would be adding one more retouching, before the slab left for the printer in the middle of the afternoon for the first colour to be applied to it.'[4]

According to a famous and almost certainly authentic anecdote, Lautrec came across Pierre Bonnard's poster for *France-Champagne* on a wall and lost no time in scouring the capital in an attempt to find the artist, whom he did not know but who later became one of his greatest friends. Bonnard took him to see his printer, and within six months Lautrec had designed his very first poster.

It must be admitted that Lautrec was lucky. To open the Moulin Rouge, Charles Zidler had turned to Jules Chéret, a safe choice as a designer, and whose poster was an outright success. But among his regular clients, Zidler could hardly have failed to notice the little man in the bowler hat, who enjoyed a certain reputation and was always surrounded by others. He may also have noticed the sketches that Lautrec was forever working on. Zidler was a curious individual and also an art lover. He placed his trust in the novice artist and commissioned a poster from him. And what a poster it turned out to be! Pulled in three folios, it was gigantic in size and, as such, exceptional in terms of its format. It lived up to Zidler's ambitions.

In the foreground is Valentin, the famous 'boneless' dancer and the area of white paper that draws the observer's eye to the skirt of La Goulue, then, behind it, the black mass of spectators that frames her, with, at the very edge of the image, the flat yellow surface of the lamps, while the boards of the stage provide a sense of perspective. The design is filled with life, its contours

Henri de Toulouse-Lautrec, 1893

Henri de Toulouse-Lautrec, 1892

Henri de Toulouse-Lautrec, 1893

Henri de Toulouse-Lautrec, 1895

clearly defined. Whereas Chéret, drawing on his usual bag of tricks, including a *chérette* and a riot of joyous figures, shows us what is happening outside the Moulin Rouge, Lautrec reveals its interior, evincing a talent so striking that observers were inevitably fired with enthusiasm, foremost among them Ernest Maindron: 'Here is a philosopher who speaks a new language. [...] He does not look at the bright side of things; he looks at things as they are.' As for their form, 'In spite of the simplicity of the means he employs, M. de Toulouse-Lautrec's compositions are decorative beyond anything one may imagine. In terms of color, he uses only flat tones. To achieve violent effects, he contrasts black and white with incredible deftness and know-how.'[5]

Black is certainly the key. And so we find him writing to his friend Henri Nocq in the summer of 1896: 'As for the posters, Chéret eliminated the black, it was wonderful. We put it back, it's not too bad.'[6] With the passage of time, the blacks became more intense but were also replaced by olive green, 'Lautrec green'. Otherwise Lautrec chose colours according to the subject matter and the moment of inspiration. He even used monochrome, as in *Le Pendu* (The Hanged Man), a terrifying image and at the same time a masterpiece of chiaroscuro, while the poster for the art review *L'Aube* is entirely in grey, *The Châtelaine* exclusively blue. All are symphonies in the use of a spatter technique.

Although Lautrec developed an identifiable system, exploiting the use of the diagonal, plunging views and audacious cropping techniques, he never repeated himself. Or, if he did so, it was in a spirit of playfulness: May Belfort is depicted wearing a red dress against a white background, whereas May Milton appears similarly framed against a blue background, the area left white being used to represent the dress.

Zidler invited Lautrec to design a second poster for the Jardin de Paris, which he opened in the gardens of the Champs-Élysées during the summer months. It was here that Jane Avril performed. This was the stage name of Jeanne Louise Beaudon, also known as 'La Mélinite'. A woman of spell-binding if indefinable beauty, she had nothing in common with the prostitutes and cancan dancers of the time but became the muse of the Paris intelligentsia and the friend and favourite model of Toulouse-Lautrec.[7] The frame is provided by the neck of a huge double bass extending diagonally upwards, its form

5. Ernest Maindron, *Les Affiches illustrées, 1885–1895*, G. Boudet, Paris, 1896, p.110; Engl. trans. from Gale B. Murray (ed.), *Toulouse-Lautrec: A Retrospective*, Beaux Arts Edition, New York, pp.231–2.

6. Toulouse-Lautrec, *Correspondance* (note 1), p.305; Engl. trans., p.295 (undated letter to Henri Nocq [summer 1896]).

7. Discovered by the French musicologist Théodore de Wyzewa, she went on to turn the heads of Arsène Houssaye, Catulle Mendès and Alphonse Allais, who was reduced to despair by her refusal to marry him. In the end she married the graphic artist Maurice Biais, the father of her daughter.

Henri de Toulouse-Lautrec, 1893

Henri de Toulouse-Lautrec, 1894

heavily outlined in black, while the stage boards and the theatre flats provide a sense of depth. Central to the image is Jane Avril, depicted in one of her favourite poses, her features finely chiselled. Lautrec affords proof of a striking mastery of blacks. Maindron's description has got it all wrong: 'The expression on her face is one of unutterable sadness. We sense the lassitude in it and we see that the young woman is dancing for our pleasure and not for her own.'[8] Yet this anaemic and melancholic face is precisely what constitutes her typical fin-de-siècle charm. As for the woman in question, she was altogether delighted: 'It is more than certain that it is thanks to him that I owe the fame that I have enjoyed ever since he drew that very first poster of me.'[9]

In the meantime, Lautrec had designed a poster for *Reine de joie* (Queen of Joy) for his friend, the novelist Victor Joze. It depicts a key scene in the life of a poor courtesan and shows her wheedling the ignoble Baron Rosenfeld, a banker by profession. A diagonal separates the table, which is laid, from the diners who are depicted in flat and barely outlined tones. Green is liberally used for the ignoble nobleman's hair. Understandably feeling that he had been defamed, Baron Rothschild ordered the posters to be defaced. The anti-Semites were jubilant. The Dreyfus Affair was already casting its long, dark shadows.

There followed a series of posters for Aristide Bruant that introduced Lautrec's name to a wider circle, though he initially had difficulty getting his way. Pierre Ducarre, the manager of the Ambassadeurs, complained that nobody could care less about him and that they were making fun of him, with the result that he turned instead to Charles Lévy.[10] But Bruant, who was by then a celebrated figure, insisted that Lautrec be used and that the resultant poster be displayed throughout the whole of Paris.

Bruant's massive figure takes up almost the whole of the image. Apart from his careworn face, the viewer is struck by the flat colours and, to the right, by a subtle black shadow that can be seen against a blue background. The inverse image was later to be used for Eldorado during the winter season. There followed a profile that is of no particular interest, and a poster advertising *Le Deuxième Volume de Bruant* available from *Le Mirliton*, its only merit being that it depicts Bruant as seen from the back.

These posters were followed by one for the Divan Japonais café-concert that Maindron believed was Lautrec's masterpiece and which is certainly among his

8. Maindron, *Les Affiches illustrées* (note 5), p.112; Engl. trans., p.234.
9. Jane Avril, *Mes Mémoires*, Phébus, Paris, 2005.
10. Lévy's poster was printed but was an insipid portrait devoid of any interest.

Henri de Toulouse-Lautrec, 1892

finest work. Lautrec uses an X-shaped composition that until then had been frowned on. In the foreground are Jane Avril and Édouard Dujardin, who was one of the co-founders of the *Revue wagnérienne*. A flecked diagonal spans the whole image, and from it there emerge two double basses and the conductor. The other diagonal plunges downwards and extends from the spectators to the performer, whose head has been cropped in a way that attests to the artist's creative imagination. Her black gloves reveal her to be Yvette Guilbert. The design and the magical distribution of the different colours helped to make this an iconic image.

Entirely comparable, albeit less decorative, is *Babylone d'Allemagne* (Babylon of Germany). Here, too, we have a X-shaped design, with the ascending diagonal for the horsemen intersecting with the diagonal that extends from the sentry box to the bourgeois couple on the right-hand side. The horse and the officer riding it are both white – instantly drawing the spectator's eye to them. The unequivocal gaze of the young woman as she stares at the handsome soldier adds a piquant detail to the scene.

Lautrec's later posters may be classified in various groups. Some are more like prints than posters: *La Revue blanche*, *Napoléon*, the *Elles* portfolio, *L'Artisan moderne* (The Modern Artisan), *The Simpson Chain* and *The Photographer Sescau*, which is drowned in green, are more anecdotal in character.

Mlle Églantine's Troupe was based on a photograph and is formidably effective, while *Le Salon des Cent* is a miniature masterpiece of harmony: one senses that Lautrec was in love with the young woman about whom he knew nothing at all. From 1896 Lautrec lost interest in the poster as an art form and designed them for only a small circle of friends. Natanson suggests that he was no longer receiving commissions. Be that as it may, Lautrec was certainly devastated by Yvette Guilbert's refusal to commission a poster from him: the sketch in the Musée d'Albi reveals that it would have been a masterpiece.

The Musée d'Albi contains another project for Jols that was likewise turned down. Lautrec was finding it increasingly difficult to work on the large stones that posters required but could not refuse to design one last poster for Jane Avril. We can only agree with Natanson when he writes that 'It lacks the vitality of its predecessors'. *La Gitane* (The Gypsy), finally, is a rare poster of interest only to collectors.

Toulouse-Lautrec had no disciples, even if he pointed the way ahead for his friend Maxime Dethomas and for the young Jacques Villon. There is, however, an artist who left only two posters, one for the Salon des Cent, the other for Pierrefort. They are so similar to those by Lautrec that we may be tempted to see in their artist an Émile Ajar of the graphic arts.[11] This is probably not the case, and so the mystery remains: we simply know nothing about him. ♣

11. This was the name under which Romain Gary won a second Prix Goncourt.

Jacques Villon, 1899

P. H. Lobel, 1899

P. H. Lobel

EUGÈNE GRASSET

Eugène Grasset, 1892

Eugène Grasset was born into a family of Calvinist artisans in Lausanne in 1845. He spent two years studying architecture at the Zurich Polytechnic, then left for a lengthy trip to southern Europe that eventually took him as far afield as Egypt. On his return to Switzerland, he started to acquire a reputation as an artist but had to wait until the end of the Franco-Prussian War before he could move to Paris in 1871 'with 150 francs in his pocket' but above all with a very real talent as a designer and with an impressive knowledge of all the arts, including, of course, those of classical antiquity and Japan.

Together with Eugène Viollet-le-Duc, he may justifiably be described as the true founding father of art nouveau in France. He was also a no less important figure in that he tackled practically every branch of the decorative arts.

His first mentor was the printer Charles Gillot, who made great use of gillotage, a technique which, patented by his father, was a precursor of photogravure, allowing text and image to be printed together. In 1881 he invited Grasset to provide a series of illustrations for the first modern illustrated book of any significance, *L'Histoire des quatre fils Aymon*, a masterpiece that Grasset spent two years completing and that overturned all the rules of page layout: text and image now formed a single indivisible whole.[1]

In the early 1880s Gillot invited Grasset to design furniture for his new mansion in the Rue Madame in Paris:[2] the result was a mixture of neoclassical and neo-medieval furniture reflecting the influence of Viollet-le-Duc. Relievo animals on the sideboard were a particularly bold feature.

The stentorian owner of Le Chat Noir, Rodolphe Salis, was a very different type of client. He had just moved into new premises in the Rue Victor-Massé and invited Grasset to help him design it. Grasset created a vast fireplace that was oriental and medieval in its inspiration, but his main contribution took the form of wrought ironwork for the chandeliers and two lanterns overlooking the street.

As was to be expected with an artist of a medieval bent, Grasset was also a major figure in the realm of the stained-glass window, where he worked with the master glassmaker Félix Gaudin. He also made ceramics and stoneware for Émile Müller and designed fabrics and also jewellery, the latter for the great jeweller Henri Vever. Exhibited at the 1900 Universal Exhibition in Paris, this jewellery was among Grasset's greatest triumphs.

1. The term 'masterpiece' is not always synonymous with commercial success. Three quarters of all copies produced were sold off at a reduced price.
2. This furniture is now in the Musée des Arts Décoratifs in Paris.

Eugène Grasset, first version

Eugène Grasset, second version, 1890

Eugène Grasset, *c.* 1896

Eugène Grasset, 1894

Eugène Grasset, 1897

Eugène Grasset, *c.* 1898

As Anne Murray-Robertson has observed, Grasset 'never denied the spiritual contribution that was made by the Middle Ages, but his principal objective was always to return to the sources of the decorative arts'.[3]

Together with George Auriol, he was also invited by the typefoundry G. Peignot et Fils to design a new typeface. Nor can we omit to mention, however briefly, his logo for Larousse ('Je sème à tous vents'= 'I scatter to the four winds'), an upper-case alphabet and numerous examples of commercial work such as his calendars for La Belle Jardinière and even designs for postage stamps.

But let us return to the poster.

Grasset designed his first poster in 1885, *Fêtes de Paris*, a heraldic, medieval design that he followed up two years later with his poster for *La Librairie romantique*. In a special issue of *La Plume* published to coincide with Grasset's one-man show for the Salon des Cent, Léon Maillard noted that 'It is such a perfect reproduction that it seems to be an original from long ago, albeit one that never actually existed!' The academic painter Édouard Detaille was proud to have it framed to exhibit in his salon. There followed a commission for the Théâtre de l'Odéon that marked the beginning of Grasset's lengthy association with the printer G. de Malherbe.

Grasset's first three posters for the Odéon were stock posters, with an empty space for later additions. It was a difficult exercise, but Grasset, through the skill in composition, emerged victorious. But he had yet to find his own style.

Joan of Arc marked a veritable turning point: outlines have grown thicker, the background is made up of clouds that cross the image diagonally, and the typography is beginning to evolve. The result was a success, but Sarah Bernhardt was dissatisfied with her face. Thanks to the gillotage process, it was possible to cut away part of the zinc plate and replace it with a new version with a very different hairstyle.

Between 1891 and 1894, when he triumphed at the Salon des Cent, Grasset's style achieved its full potential: a thick outline recalled the lead of stained-glass windows, while his flat tones eschewed all sense of realism. Clouds cleaved the sky, and his female figures left Chéret's sensual *chérettes* far behind them.

His posters for Marquet Ink in 1892, for the Grafton Galleries in 1893 and for the 1894 Salon des Cent all elicited considerable enthusiasm and Grasset was numbered among the Symbolists,[4] becoming associated with Maurice Maeterlinck and with the latter's

3. See Anne Murray-Robertson, *Grasset: Pionnier de l'art nouveau*, Éditions 24 Heures, Lausanne and Bibliothèque des Arts, Paris, 1981, p.69.
4. The classification is a facile one, and David Van Reybrouck is undoubtedly right to argue that Symbolism was 'one of the vaguest of all movements, but arguably for that very reason one of the most popular since Romanticism'; see David Van Reybrouck, *Le Fléau*, trans. Pierre-Marie Finkelstein, Actes Sud, Arles, 2008, p.36.

Eugène Grasset, 1899

Eugène Grasset, 1894

Eugène Grasset, 1905

Mélisande. Waxing lyrical, the critic William Ritter warmed to his theme: 'Come unto me, all you young women of Maeterlinck, O ideal sister of Grasset's most recent angelic and most modern figures.'[5] In the same special issue of *La Plume*, Henri Eon saw in these posters 'women or, rather, muses standing out in ecstatic poses on fantastical clouds – in an accentuated line recalling the figures in stained-glass windows'.

It was no doubt Anne Murray-Robertson who coined the best definition of Grasset's style when she called it 'neo-Botticellian'.[6] The fascination exerted by Grasset's female figures could induce a state of near ecstasy. For William Ritter, the woman depicted in the Grafton Galleries poster was the very embodiment of 'etiolation and decadent anaemia', while *The Acid Thrower* seemed 'lost and cadaverous through fear'. She had 'this strange and distracted air of someone who would always be expecting some great misfortune to strike a beautiful garden in the sunshine'.[7] This remark applies with particular force to Grasset's series of decorative panels. In short, Grasset's female figures titillated the Symbolist imagination, the more so because his model was almost certainly imaginary. We know nothing at all about Grasset's emotional life except that he was a fiercely solitary individual, so much so that we are bound to ask ourselves if this Symbolist woman was not herself a symbol.

Extending the debate in the pages of *La Plume*, Léon Maillard provides us with a fine description of Grasset's style: 'Nothing scandalous, nothing brutal, but a fusion, an accord, an intimacy between the subject and the means of reproduction.' Or take Henry Bordeaux, who writes that Grasset's posters 'are mysterious poems in terms of their precision, making a strange contrast with those of Chéret'.[8] All of these remarks are valid, and they all apply equally to Grasset's commercial posters such as Masson Chocolate, which depicts a mother and her child at home, and Mexican Chocolate, with its extraordinary image of a gaucho and his horse. For his poster for À la Place Clichy, a tourist wearing a pith helmet is seen choosing one of the shop's rugs. And for Georges Richard, a woman deep in thought is seen holding an enormous four-leafed clover, which was the firm's trademark.

All the larger American stores had a representative in Paris, who recommended that they make contact with the younger generation of artists. For the puritanical middle classes living on the East Coast, the Calvinist medievalism of a designer like Grasset, with its impression of what Edmond Rocher called 'cold grace', was a perfect match. Chéret and Mucha would have shocked such clients with their sensuality, whereas Lautrec was simply unthinkable.

After an initial – and very early – commission for Frank Leslie's *Illustrated Newspaper* in 1882, Grasset designed two covers for *Harper's Magazine* in 1889, depicting well-behaved young women carrying baskets of fruit and flowers. In 1892 an archangel playing a hunting horn heralded his success in America,[9] where he won a Gold Medal at the Boston Exhibition.

In 1893 *The Century Magazine* invited Grasset to design a poster to promote *A New Life of Napoleon*. Depicting the emperor on a white stallion, it is a magnificent example of a style that superficially may seem purely illustrative, but his pupil Paul-Émile Berthon encourages us to look more closely at these images: 'When he draws a horse, he lengthens or shortens its limbs depending on his needs and he arranges the mane in coils or curves, but he always respects the shape of the hooves, the bone structure and the details of the head.' The 'Wooly Horse' was unbelievably successful,[10] prompting the publisher to produce a three-panel version measuring 100 x 220cm/39.37 x 86.61in that covered the walls of New York.

Grasset had been a retiring figure appreciated by only a small circle of art lovers, but he was finally revealed to a much wider public by Léon Deschamps, who organized a one-man show of Grasset's work at the second Salon des Cent in 1894. Grasset did not have a penny and had kept practically none of his work, so that Deschamps had to go knocking on the doors of printers and collectors in order to assemble a collection of the artist's

5. *Eugène Grasset*, special number of *La Plume*, 6/122 (15 May 1894), 93. Grasset had links with the Rose+Croix movement and with the Idealists, sending his work to their salons.
6. Murray-Robertson, *Grasset* (note 3), p.114.
7. *La Plume* (note 5).
8. Bordeaux was a prolific author who subsequently fell into oblivion.
9. Bizarrely, a third illustration for *Harper's* is preserved in the library of the Musée des Arts Décoratifs. It represents a nativity scene in a setting far removed from Galilee. It is also interesting to note that these illustrations were printed in Paris.
10. *Harper's* commissioned a further poster five years later in 1895, this time for Napoleon in Egypt.

Paul Berthon, 1898

Maurice Pillard-Verneuil, 1900

Eugène Grasset, *Grafton Gallery*, 1893

Eugène Grasset, *Méditation*, 1897

Paul Berthon, 1895

work. It was a triumph.[11] 'We shall always remember our illustrious friend being terrified and not daring to show his face but summoning us to a nearby café at six in the evening to have news of the event.'[12] It was also a revelation for many young artists, including Louis Rhead, who on his return to New York wrote that 'I was very happy to have been able to profit from the influence of M. Grasset, whose singular talent I admire unreservedly.'

None of this affected Grasset, who from 1890 devoted much of his energy to teaching at the École Guérin, then at the Académie de la Grande Chaumière, remaining there practically until his death in 1917. In 1896 he published *La Plante et ses applications ornementales*, on which he sought the assistance of two of his pupils, Maurice Pillard-Verneuil and Mathurin Méheut, following this up in 1905 with his *Méthode de composition ornementale*, a monumental study that allowed him to hand down the principles of art nouveau to a new generation of artists. In around 1905 his poster for Suzy Deguez revealed a sensuality and a technique to which Mucha was no stranger.

Among Grasset's disciples, it is Berthon who left the largest body of work. In particular he designed a poster for Cléo de Mérode that in turn inspired the one commissioned from him for the Salon des Cent in 1897. His Symbolist women and his use not only of floral motifs but also of medieval musical instruments were clearly influenced by Grasset, but Berthon found his own personality in a palette extending from yellow to red and passing through ochre and green. Although he also responded to prestigious commissions such as the de luxe edition of *Les Maîtres de l'affiche*, Berthon devoted much of his time to a series of decorative panels that depicted women, of course, but also crowned heads of state and landscapes. He died prematurely in 1909.

Among Grasset's other disciples, pride of place goes to Maurice Pillard-Verneuil, who produced a number of the plates for *La Plante et ses applications ornementales* and, working on his own this time, for *L'Animal dans la décoration*. Together with the Breton painter and ceramicist Mathurin Méheut,[13] he published *L'Étude de la mer* in 1913–14. Augusto Giacometti, who was to be one of the masters of the Swiss poster, should also be mentioned here, as should Arsène Herbinier, who designed a handful of posters, including one for the Salon des Cent. ❧

11. Deschamps had thought that he would lose money on the exhibition but in the pages of *La Plume* he could boast that it had proved a money-spinner. Every item was sold.
12. Quoted by Murray-Robertson, *Grasset* (note 3), p.186.
13. Among his posters are those for Dr Pierre's Toothpaste and, above all, the disinfectant Laurénol no. 2.

Alphonse Mucha, 1902

A shooting star in the Paris sky, Alphonse Mucha left such an impression on the local art scene over the course of a mere five years that many commentators have described what was to become art nouveau as 'the Mucha style'.

He has often been contrasted with Eugène Grasset, but this assessment seems oversimplistic. Mucha was from a different generation and respected Grasset as a mentor. The two men were clearly very different: one was a Swiss Calvinist and a loner by nature, while the other an extrovert Slav who frequented Paris's bohemian quarter.

The same is true of their female figures: the stiff coldness and semi-nudity of Grasset's figures contrasts with the curvaceous sensuality and warm tones of Mucha's figures with their flowing hair and magnificent jewels. Even so, it needs to be remembered that they shared the same ideas and pursued careers that were ultimately very similar.

Both artists rejected the term 'art nouveau'. For Mucha, art was 'eternal'. Both were interested in the social aspect of the renewal of the decorative arts, hence Mucha's willingness to produce decorative panels.

In the world of books, Mucha's *Ilsée* is acknowledged as being no less important than Grasset's *L'Histoire des quatre fils Aymon*. And whereas Grasset privately designed furniture for Charles Gillot, Mucha, invited by Georges Fouquet to design the shop front and the interior of his new jeweller's, brought art nouveau to the streets of Paris. He also designed jewellery for the firm, while Grasset did the same for the jeweller Henri Vever. Their work was exhibited at the 1900 Universal Exhibition in Paris. Both men were interested in the different branches of the decorative arts: fabrics, ceramics and wrought-iron work.

On a more trivial level – although it has to be remembered that Mucha was active for a mere five years, Grasset for fifty – Mucha published his *Documents décoratifs* in 1902 and his *Figures décoratives* in 1904–5 and taught at the Académie Colarossi in the same street as the Académie de la Grande Chaumière, where Grasset was a member of the teaching staff.

Both men, finally, enjoyed a signal official honour when they were invited to design postage stamps for their respective countries.

Mucha was born in Ivančice in the depths of Moravia in 1860 and spent some time in Vienna, where he was introduced to Count Karl Khuen, for whom he designed a series of murals and who paid for him to study in Munich. Here he was struck by the floral figures of Hans Makart, a painter popular with the local middle classes. By 1887 he was in Paris, where his solid foundations as an artist allowed him to find work. His talents as a designer did not pass unnoticed, and he produced numerous illustrations, including a set for *Scenes and Episodes from the History of Germany* produced in collaboration with Georges Rochegrosse and published by Armand Colin.

A sequel was made to appear much prettier in an attempt to turn it into something closer to a Christmas story, from which it was not in fact far removed. Just before Christmas 1894 Sarah Bernhardt, who was to return to the role of Gismonda in Victorien Sardou's play at the Théâtre de la Renaissance the following January, was keen to have a new poster to advertise the event. The publishing house of Lemercier entrusted Mucha with the task.[1] Although he was terrified by the challenge, Bernhardt herself was delighted with the result. He became famous overnight, and she signed a five-year contract with him. By the following year Champenois had become the actress's printer for a six-year period. Between then and his departure for the United States Mucha no longer needed to go hunting for work. Although Champenois paid him a comfortable salary, Mucha soon realized that he had fallen into a trap, which he complained about with increasing bitterness over the course of the years that followed, since he was required to meet his publisher's numerous demands without enjoying any of the profits.[2] For collectors and his numerous clients, this was a blessing. The elongated format of the poster allowed him to depict the whole figure and certainly appealed to Sarah Bernhardt.[3] The warm tones, the

1. Mucha first drew Sarah Bernhardt in 1890 and may even have met her by then. In any event, the commission in 1894 was not a complete surprise.
2. For more on this episode, see our chapter on the decorative panel.
3. This was not the case with Grasset's poster.

Alphonse Mucha, 1895

Alphonse Mucha, 1896

Alphonse Mucha, 1899

Alphonse Mucha, 1898

Alphonse Mucha, 1897

Alphonse Mucha, 1894

Alphonse Mucha, 1896

Alphonse Mucha, 1896

sumptuous ornamentation and Mucha's attention to the details of her costumes all delighted the actress.

This system remained essentially the same for the six posters that followed. Framed by a semicircle, the actress's name appears at the top, together with the name of the play. She invariably appears full-length, dressed in the costume that she wears in the main scene in the play in question and that is reproduced in detail, including the jewellery that Mucha himself occasionally designed for her. Lack of time presumably meant that the background to the *Gismonda* poster is non-existent, but in every other case the composition is both detailed and harmonious. Gold, silver and bronze are the preferred colours.

Mucha found his style almost at once and at the same time developed the design elements that were to become his hallmarks: the outlines, which vary in thickness depending on the elements that he wanted to highlight; the pastel colours that do not prevent him from achieving a subtle relief, notably in the case of the face, but also for the clothes, with their exaggerated folds and pleats; and the circle or orb on which the actress rests or sometimes sits. Mucha makes much play with the actress's reddish-brown hair, even devising extravagant curls. The vegetable motifs likewise contribute to the same exuberance.

With the exception of his homage to Sarah Bernhardt, who is depicted from the front, Mucha's female faces and busts are generally seen in profile, their hair elaborately detailed: *Zodiac*, *Salon des Cent*, *Job* and *Byzantine Heads* are all examples of this approach. In his decorative panels the figure is depicted in every conceivable position.

By combining all of these elements, which he assembled as he saw fit, Mucha was able to meet a need that continued to increase.

Mucha's most accomplished posters are in the double-colombier format, two of the best examples being *Job*, in which the female figure is depicted as a brunette seated on an orb and superimposed on the brand name, which was that of a type of cigarette paper; and *Perfecta Cycles*, a purely graphic work, notably in terms of the treatment of the face, while the figure's hair is a riot of scrolls and arabesques.

Mucha was one of the first designers to make regular use of photographs in his work, eventually developing a system when he started to produce monumental paintings.

He soon abandoned his small studio in the Rue Campagne-Première and established new premises a few yards away in a vast studio in the Rue du Val-de-Grâce, where he could work at his ease. Here he employed a number of assistants and even installed a small lithographic press during his work on *Ilsée*. His one-man show at the Salon des Cent was a triumph, and he became a ubiquitous figure in the small world of poster-mania, designing the cover for *La Plume*, a number of covers for *Cocorico* and the covers used when sending out instalments of *L'Estampe moderne*.

In 1897 he caused a sensation at Galerie de la Bodinière and above all at the Salon des Cent.

The previous year he had received a visit from Léon Deschamps, the founding editor of the literary and artistic review *La Plume* and a man famous for discovering new and talented artists, and offered him a poster. It was a magnificent example of his work, but Mucha, feeling unsure of himself, explained that he had not yet completed the details, prompting Deschamps to reply: 'Finish this work as it is and you will have produced a masterpiece of the decorative illustrated poster.' And so it proved. As Deschamps went on, 'The six or seven thousand people who currently own a copy of this poster, which has been unprecedentedly successful, are all here to corroborate our judgment.'

There is something paradoxical about the case of Alphonse Mucha. The public adored him, and he sold more panels and posters than all his rivals put together.[4] And yet the praise was always slightly stinting, even in the pages of *La Plume*. For Paul Redonnel, Mucha was 'one of those who have willingly returned to their epoch', while Henri Degron asked: 'His profession? It is by a miracle that he has one! His inspiration? It is always

4. With the obvious exception of Chéret, who designed ten times more posters than Mucha.

Alphonse Mucha, 1899, 1896 and 1902

Alphonse Mucha, 1896

honest and pellucid and suggests that he is a poet. What more?' As if he was justifying himself! Critical voices failed to speak out in support. Arsène Alexandre referred only to the 'profound charm of the coils shaken by the wind'.[5]

There were several reasons for this. First, Mucha burst upon a scene whose leading actors were Chéret and Grasset, with the result that the critics looked askance at the arrival of a newcomer who was overturning existing hierarchies and destroying traditional certainties. This, moreover, was a time when the Dreyfus Affair was at its height, and Mucha had nothing to reassure his contemporaries.[6] As a protégé of Sarah Bernhardt, he had Dreyfus's supporters on his side, but the motley colours of his Slav shirts were found shocking by more than one observer. He was treated as a Hungarian, which cannot have pleased him. And it was claimed that Sarah Bernhardt had found him in a gypsy encampment. But all of this matters little, for posterity has accorded him the place in history that he deserves as the embodiment of a style and of a whole period.

As was the fashion at this time, his new studio resembled nothing so much as an old curiosity shop in which Japanese artefacts were ranged alongside furniture of every style and provenance. Also in evidence were the Byzantine wall-hangings of which Mucha was inordinately fond. His studio was always packed with visitors, preventing him from working, even though he was at his desk from nine in the morning until often late at night.

His son, Jiří, has left an account of some of the ploys that he used in an attempt to prise himself free.[7] He would dine at four in the afternoon, for example, in order to be left in peace at a time when others traditionally dined. And when he was invited out, he would accept four or five invitations for the same evening, spending only a short time at each. The more his fame increased, the less time he had for himself, even though he still found the time to travel.

5. See 'Alphonse Mucha et son Œuvre' published as an offprint of *La Plume* in 1897.
6. Writing in *L'Estampe et l'Affiche*, Ernest de Crauzat expresses a degree of hostility that speaks volumes.
7. Jiří Mucha, *Alphonse Mucha: His Life and Art*, Heinemann, London, 1966, p.189.
8. See Alfred Weidinger, 'Alphonse Mucha and the Pavilion for the Ottoman Provinces of Bosnia-Herzegovina at the Exposition Universelle in Paris in 1900', *Alphonse Mucha*, ed. Agnès Husslein-Arco and others, Prestel, New York, 2009, pp.49–55.
9. Jiří Mucha, *Alphonse Mucha* (note 7), p.231.

With the turn of the century, a number of factors brought about a change in his life. For the 1900 Paris Universal Exhibition he designed a Pavilion of Man that never saw the light of day. Conversely, he was asked to help design the Bosnia-Herzegovina Pavilion, an invitation he accepted with tremendous enthusiasm.[8]

Recalling the events of 1900, Mucha explained that 'for the past five years my works had largely met the needs of day-to-day life, but the energy I had put into them had not been in proportion to their mission. From wallpaper to cutlery, from furniture and jewellery to decorative panneaux – everything had been given away to others, while the needs of my own nation had remained unanswered. That was why, on the threshold of the new century, I was desperately trying to discover how I could make even a modest contribution to my own people.'[9]

But 1900 was also the year when Mucha regained his freedom as his contracts with Champenois and Sarah Bernhardt both came to an end.

He decided to turn over a new leaf and devote himself to painting, while at the same time starting to brood on a vast project that he took on following his return to Prague in 1910 and that occupied him between then and his death in 1939. This was his great historicist narrative in twenty large canvases, *The Slav Epic*.

A final factor undoubtedly played a part in Mucha's decision to leave the French capital, for a young compatriot, Maruška Chytilová, had fallen madly in love with him and had moved to Paris in order to study there. Mucha broke off his relationship with his mistress, Berthe de Lalande, and married Maruška in 1906. Then, armed with numerous recommendations, he left for the United States. Here he quickly tired of painting society portraits – they are in any case of no more than middling quality – but found an enthusiastic audience among the Slav community, most notably in Chicago, where a wealthy industrialist, Charles R. Crane, provided him with an income for life, allowing him to return to Prague and complete *The Slav Epic*. ❧

GEORGES DE FEURE

Georges de Feure, 1897

Georges de Feure was another of the great exponents of art nouveau, but for a long time his reputation suffered as a result of the mystery surrounding his life and the morbid nature of his subjects. But, as his biographer, Ian Millman, has written: 'I very quickly discovered that de Feure was a talented and multifaceted artist. Not only was he a Symbolist painter but also an illustrator and a poster artist. Even more significantly, he played a major role decorating Bing's Art Nouveau Pavilion at the 1900 Universal Exhibition. In short, he was an outstanding example of those "universal artists" who thrived at the end of the nineteenth century and who included Grasset, Mucha and Van de Velde.'[1]

We shall limit ourselves to his career as a poster artist, although it is worth mentioning that his life was notable for its highs and lows. He collaborated not only with Samuel Bing but also with the Maison Moderne of Julius Meier-Graefe and the Maison Krieger. He also wrote ballet scenarios for Ravel and Debussy. By 1910 he was even building aeroplanes. Fifteen years later he designed one of the pavilions at the International Exhibition of Modern Industrial and Decorative Arts. Other commissions included interior designs for the home of Madeleine Vionnet and a boudoir for the International Exhibition of Art and Technology in 1937. Meanwhile, he continued to paint, evolving from an unsettling Symbolist to a singular landscape painter.

De Feure settled in Paris in 1889 and began designing posters in 1892. Although it is impossible to deny that their style was highly individual, it is also difficult to claim that in themselves they were sufficient to establish his reputation. They are a riot of garish colours, of awkward figures and invasive lettering. With the exception of his poster for *Fonty*, their design leaves much to be desired. In short, these posters were potboilers intended to advertise such ephemeral stars of the cafés-concerts as Naya, Isita and Fonty herself. But they must have brought his name to wider attention since he was also responsible for the poster of Loie Fuller as Salome in her own adaptation of the legend, a poster which, picking up an idea of Chéret's, was reproduced in six colours. The result is utterly terrifying. De Feure was no doubt aware of the fact that his many other lithographs depicting the femme fatale – images redolent of a morbid Symbolism and depicting pallid creatures in prognathous profile amidst floral decoration of almost psychedelic colours – were reserved, unsurprisingly, for an audience like that of the Salon des Rose+Croix.[3]

For a series of posters that de Feure designed for the circle of poster lovers associated with Edmond Sagot

1. See the monumental study by Ian Millman, *Georges de Feure: Maître du symbolisme et de l'Art nouveau*, ACR Éditions, Courbevoie, 1992. This monograph exists only in French.
2. Ibid., p.6.
3. According to the art critic F. Vieilliard, 'The only interesting and original submissions are those of Monsieur de Feure with his strange watercolours in which the most disparate but skilfully juxtaposed tones are grouped together in bizarre harmonies'; quoted in Millman, *Georges de Feure* (note 1), pp.38–40.

Georges de Feure, 1898

Georges de Feure, 1894

and including *Le Salon des Cent* and *Le Journal des ventes*, he rethought his typical female figure and created an elegant modern young woman, not necessarily an angel, but no longer a demon. Tightly framed, the woman is reproduced head and shoulders.

Le Salon des Cent takes up the framing device also used by Grasset, but instead of the pure young girl caressing a flower, we have a hard-faced woman wearing a hat, a fox fur round her neck and caught in the act of snapping the stem of a rose that she is about to affix to her corsage.

Paris-Almanach is calmer. It depicts an elegant woman luxuriously dressed in a variety of browns and visiting a museum. The background consists of a crowd of art lovers looking at anything but the paintings. She is convinced that she will be able to engage their attention.

For *Le Journal des ventes*, the woman is seen in profile. The lettering is maladroit but this cannot be the result of chance. *The Original Lithographs* is undoubtedly the most elegant and intimate of de Feure's posters. Although the woman is white-faced – the artist uses a blank area of the paper to create this effect – she is focused on her reading.

For *Pierrefort*, de Feure seems again to have been possessed by his demons, for it depicts a black widow as a femme fatale whose gaze we would best avoid. To complete this series of posters, de Feure responded to a commission from a shop in Carcassonne by the name of Astre et Soux. In *À Jeanne d'Arc*, Saint Joan stares back at us with the eyes of a vamp. With its pronounced hips and breasts, her armour is the result of the workings of a delirious imagination.

A final series of posters in the dying moments of the century was more conventional, intended, as it was, to advertise the thermal baths at Liège and the newspaper *La Dépêche*. For the latter de Feure chose to depict an elegant woman, full-length, while placing the accent firmly on the printed fabrics that she is wearing. For *Jane Derval* in 1905, the clothing is even more cumbersome, a sumptuous dress worn by a puffy-cheeked and graceless woman.

A strange and invariably daring artist, de Feure was paying tribute in this way to the art of the mural. ♣

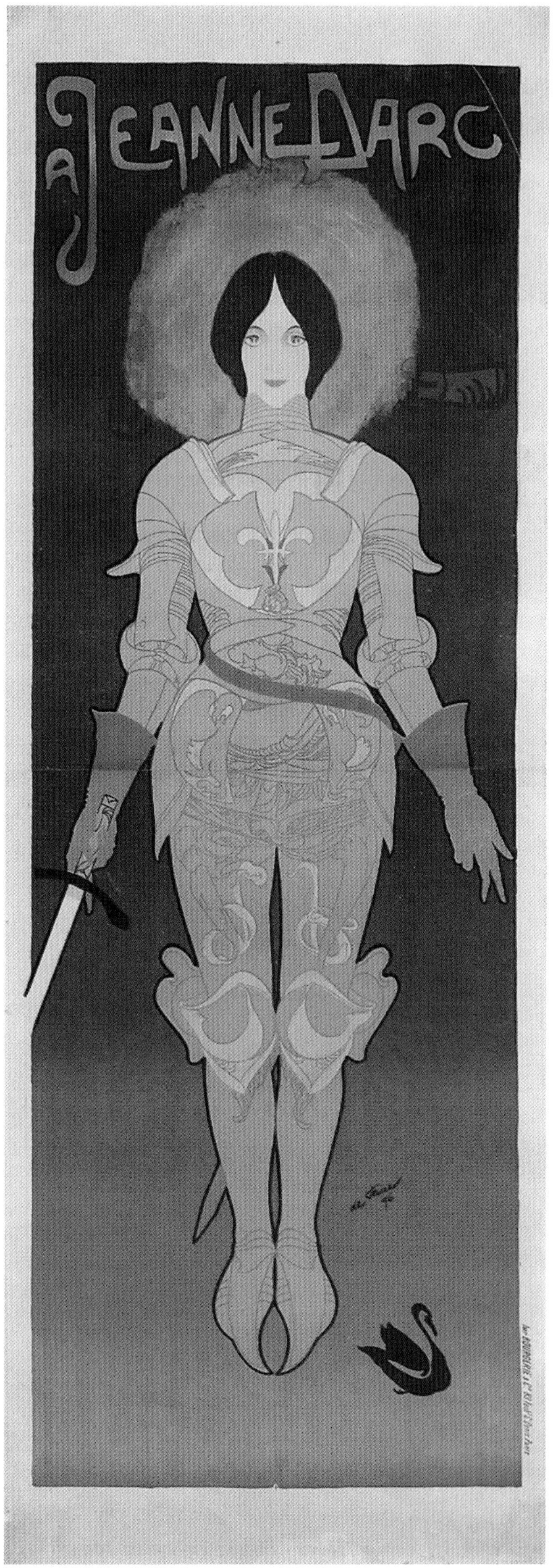

Georges de Feure, 1896

Manuel Orazi, 1900

Manuel Orazi, 1900

Manuel Orazi was the last great representative of the floral style of art nouveau that flourished in Paris. Unfortunately, there is as yet no major study of his life and works, with the result that we know very little about him. He was born in Rome in 1860 and arrived in Paris in the late 1880s. Like all the artists of his generation, he combined within his works a whole series of disparate influences, including Byzantine, classical, Symbolist and the occult.

He was particularly adept at handling the whiplash curve. His earliest work was for the theatre: his poster for Théodore Dubois's *Aben Hamet* at the Théâtre-Italien in 1884 reveals a skilful interplay of text and music. That same year he collaborated with Auguste Gorguet on a poster for Victorien Sardou's *Theodora* at the Théâtre de la Porte-Saint-Martin that assumes the form of a Byzantine mosaic. His poster for Massenet's *Thaïs* at the Paris Opéra in 1894 depicts a fragmentary papyrus. He was drawn to the world of horseracing, and his prowess at designing ornaments and jewels was second only to that of Mucha, notably in the latter's poster for Job cigarette papers. His delicate pastel-shaded *Dream of Christmas* was designed for the dancer Liane de Pougy at the Olympia Theatre in 1899, while his poster for the Maison Moderne was a veritable inventory of art nouveau motifs centred around a seated woman seen in profile.[1] For the Wine-Growers' Association, he designed a classical scene framed by grapes and vine leaves. For the 1900 Paris Universal Exhibition he produced two posters that were much admired at the time: *The Palace of Dance* depicts a ballerina pouring coloured bubbles from a ewer, while *Loie Fuller*, produced in various shades of colour, is made up of abstract motifs to which Orazi has added his strikingly elaborate monogram.[2] He went on to design a magnificent *Magic Calendar* in the form of an ancient grimoire that could also be a hoax, after which he devoted himself mainly to illustrating esoteric works. His masterpiece postdates the First

1. He also designed *objets d'art* and furniture for the store.

2. Ernest Maindron also refers to a poster for the Peugeot Velocipede 'which could pass as one of the models of the genre' and also for a poster for a gas heater known as the *héliogène*. But no known copies exist. The afterlife of posters is dependent, therefore, on the goodwill of dealers and collectors.

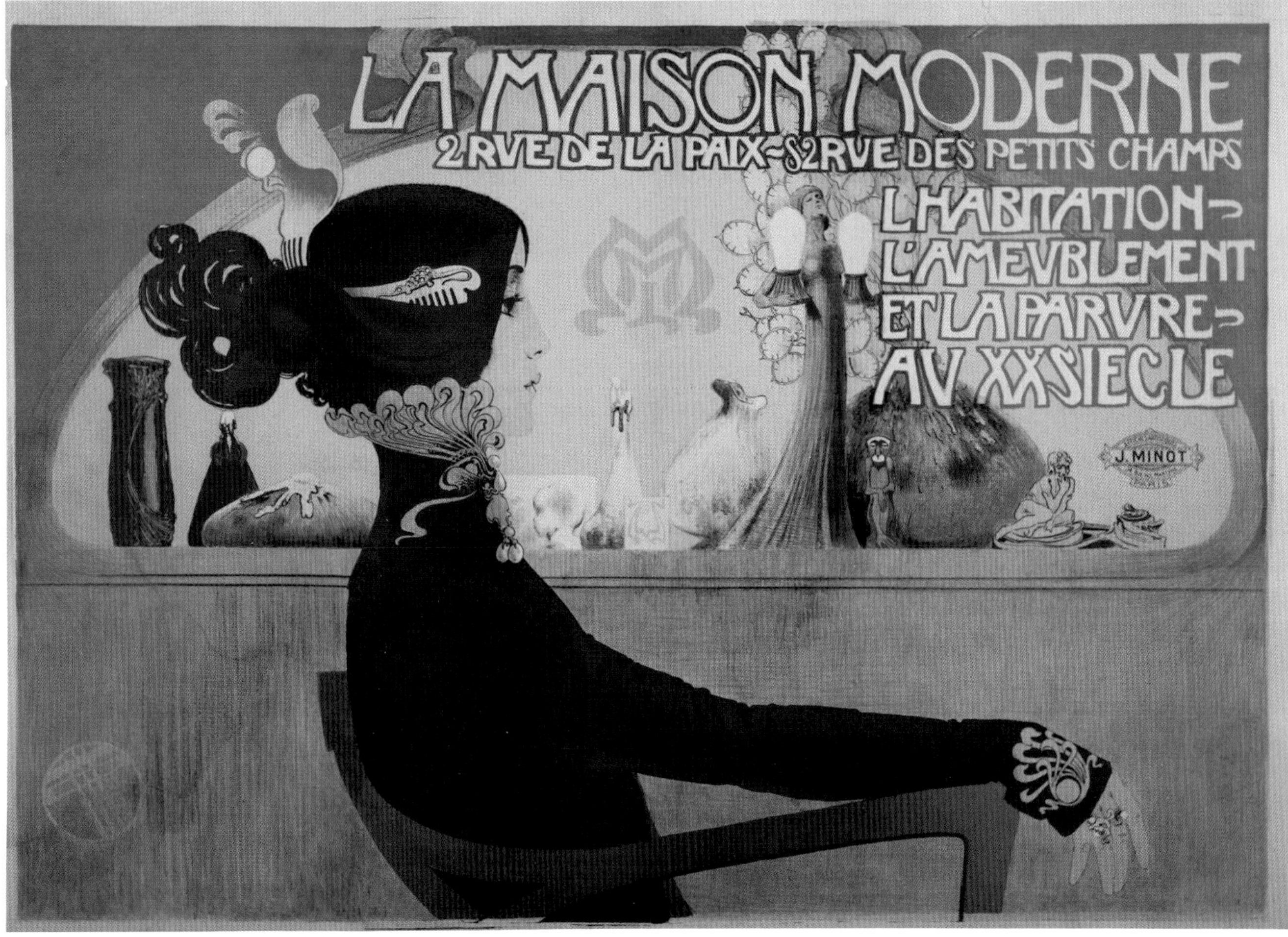

Manuel Orazi, 1902

Louis Théophile Hingre, 1898

Marc Auguste Bastard, 1896

Arsène Herbinier

Jane Atché, 1896

Henri Thiriet, 1898

World War, when he designed the sets and costumes for Jacques Feyder's 1921 film *L'Atlantide*.

Another name that deserves to be singled out from the cohort of artists who followed in the footsteps of fashion is that of Henri Thiriet. Although we know nothing about him as a person, the posters that he designed are remarkable for their quality, with their rich palette of flat tones, clear outlines and elegant design. His compositions for the *Exposition de Blanc à la Place Clichy* and for Berthelot – a brand of absinthe – are worthy of being placed alongside the very best, and the same is true of his winged angel for Omega Cycles. His poster for Griffiths Cycles reveals an exuberance confirmed by his incredible poster for Dayton Cycles.

Outside Paris, the only French city worth mentioning is Toulouse, thanks to the Cassan printing works and the journal *La Dépêche* attracting artists to the area. Local artists, too, were inspired to design posters, notably Jane Atché for Job and Arthur Foäche for *La Dépêche*.

Of the artists who followed their lead, many exaggerated the hair motif or produced such an invasive riot of floral designs that the results were often little more than a caricature of the art nouveau style and in some cases simply absurd. Among the artists least guilty of these excesses were Louis Théophile Hingre, Arsène Herbinier and Vincent Lorant-Heilbronn.

Maurice Réalier-Dumas belongs to this same group of artists, additionally sharing their same essential approach to outline and flat tones, creating a curious, yet elegantly minimalist version of their work. His posters are almost all of them vertical in format and depict an elegant woman. Their long dresses in the classical, contemporary or Empire style were used to advertise gas lighting, Jules Mumm champagne and *Paris-Mode*. A peasant costume served to promote Blandy madeira, depicted beneath a brilliant Roussillon sun. His masterpiece was his vast mural for St Catherine's Church in Villeneuve-sur-Lot. ❧

Armand Point, 1898

G. Lian, *c.* 1900

Bernard Artigue, *c.* 1905

Louis Théophile Hingre, 1897

Théophile-Alexandre Steinlen, 1896

By the end of the 1880s the climb to the top of the Butte Montmartre was a rite of passage that no lover of the city's night life, no crowned head and no artist was able or willing to forgo. The Chat Noir and the Moulin Rouge found imitators in every country.

A smooth talker with an exuberant imagination, the owner of Le Chat Noir, Rodolphe Salis, posed the following question on one of his election posters: 'What is Montmartre? Nothing. What should it be? Everything.' It was one of his favourite jokes. And yet he almost succeeded in achieving his aim in all of the areas that interested him. In June 1885 he moved from the cramped confines of the Boulevard de Rochechouart to a private mansion in the Rue Victor-Massé, which he refurbished as a medieval inn filled with all manner of bric-à-brac contributed by Paris's bohemian artists, including two new lanterns by Eugène Grasset and even work by Edgar Degas. The reopening was followed by five days of carnivalesque binges that spilled out into the rest of the quarter. Literary and political figures came to Le Chat Noir from all over the world. Behind its lewd and farcical aspects, we tend to forget Salis's exhortation that hung over the entrance: 'Passant, sois moderne.'

In 1889, seasoned impresario Charles Zidler opened the Moulin Rouge in the Place Blanche, where it still stands. It was an overnight success thanks to its star attraction, nowadays known all over the world as the cancan, a dance ultimately derived from the quadrille or *galop* but here invested with an element of the risqué and the louche.

Thanks to these two beacons of the bohemian lifestyle and to the Universal Exhibitions of 1889 and 1900, Montmartre flourished. Dozens of cabarets, cafés-concerts, dance halls, clubs and taverns opened.[1] Abandoning the Left Bank that had been their former preserve, artists settled here in large numbers, finding a perfect alcoholic environment in which to pursue their bohemian lives, find inspiration and, ultimately, work.

The quarter's spirit and the embodiment of its aspirations from his admission to the Circle of Hydropaths in 1878 to his death in 1920, when he was elected president of the Republic of Montmartre, was Adolphe Willette.[2] He helped to launch Le Chat Noir in 1881, when he designed its first sign and painted a series of murals.[3] For the inaugural ball of The Incoherents at the Élysée-Montmartre in 1885, he dressed as a Pierrot and thereafter was known as Pierrot-Willette. A prolific designer, he worked for *Le Courrier français* but was also active as an interior designer, whose murals and stained-glass windows were admired throughout Montmartre. In his memoirs, he recalls being paid 3,000 francs for four oil paintings for Le Clou, which was no mean sum in 1885. In 1888 his one-man show was advertised by a poster by Chéret.

The first generation of poster lovers placed Willette on a par with Chéret and Grasset, expressing regret that he devoted so little time to poster art. For Ernest Maindron, he was 'not only a perfect designer but also a lithographer of the greatest ability', which is true. His lines were animated and bold, and above all he felt comfortable using black and white, most notably for the Salon des Cent, for *La Revue déshabillée* and for the International Exhibition of Commercial and Industrial Products. His rare colour plates prove that his visual style was by no means fixed: *L'Élysée-Montmartre* is over-busy, its use of colour inept, its lettering poorly integrated. His two posters for Van Houten Cocoa have nothing in common with each other: one, delicately coloured, is an ineffectual pseudo-Hispanic scene, while the other attests to a surprising attempt to reflect contemporary taste, with a Dutch woman seen from the front, thickly outlined, against a uniform background made up of the branches of cocoa trees. His advertisement for Fer Bravais – an iron supplement to prevent anaemia – is a delicately coloured print and is not really a poster at all except by virtue of its added text, while his poster for the Nice Carnival on the Côte d'Azur is a perfect example of the principle that a poster is not an illustration, especially when it is as weighed down with motifs as this one is.

There remains Willette's election poster for 1889, when he stood as an anti-Semitic candidate.[4] A monochrome allegory, it expands on all the clichés surrounding the subject of anti-Semitism and did much to harm his posthumous reputation.

1. Willette, Steinlen, Grün, Roedel, Truchet, Neumont and their colleagues all contributed to the interior design of these establishments with countless murals and stained-glass windows.
2. Ferdinand Bac sees him as a kind of maybug flying around Montmartre: see Ferdinand Bac, *Adolphe Willette, 1857–1926*, Lienart, Paris, 2014.
3. Miraculously saved for posterity, both the sign and the mural *Parce domine* are now in the Musée Carnavalet in Paris.
4. This was also the age of anticlericalism.

Caran d'Ache, 1895

Willette, 1898

Willette was a complex and paradoxical individual and, as such, a mirror of the era in which he lived, which was that of the Dreyfus Affair that divided France in two. It can, of course, be claimed that Montmartre was a cultural exception inasmuch as it brought together anarchist revellers and artists in a spirit of drunken camaraderie.

Among those with whom Willette consorted in Montmartre were men who had supported the Commune of 1871, including the remarkable Colonel Maxime Lisbonne.[5] Willette was also close to the militant socialist Théophile-Alexandre Steinlen (Steinlen was a witness at his wedding in 1909) and produced designs for anarchist journals such as *Le Canard sauvage* and, later, *L'Assiette au beurre*. For years he waged a campaign against René Bérenger, a senator known as 'Père la Pudeur' on account of views that would have embarrassed even a Mrs Grundy. He also defended the Dreyfusard caricaturist Gustave Joussot in a case where Joussot was accused of plagiarism and spent his whole life fighting for authors' rights, which were finally recognized in 1912. Three years earlier he had become the president of the first Society of Authors' Rights in France. It was also his ideas that lay behind the creation of the Society of Humourist Painters, which for many years held an annual salon starting in 1904. Its first president was Charles Léandre.

Willette and Léandre were among the first artists to install themselves in Montmartre. Léandre was a subtle pastellist and an excellent lithographer, who preferred black and white to colour. He was known above all as a caricaturist who specialized in cover designs for *Le Rire*.

The issue of 16 April 1898 was targeted at the Rothschilds and is an example of the anti-Semitism that was rife at this period. But he also provided the cover for *Le Populaire* announcing the death of the Marxist Jules Guesde in 1922. His few posters were designed to promote stage shows: the cabaret *La Lune Rousse*, *Les Cantomimes de Xavier Privas* and Yvette Guilbert's tour *Montmartre en Ballade*. But he also designed a poster for the Salon des Peintres Humoristes.

Of French ancestry, Emmanuel Poiré was born in Moscow in 1858, moving to France in 1877 and taking the name of Caran d'Ache, meaning 'pencil' in Russian. After a period spent in Germany, where he developed a love of 'Junker uniforms and parades',[6] he triumphed with

5. A former colonel at the time of the Paris Commune, Maxime Lisbonne was sentenced to death, a sentence commuted to exile to New Caledonia. In 1885, following his return to France, he opened the Taverne du Bagne, which was modelled on the canteen used by the convicts in Nouméa. Prison slang was used to describe even the glasses of beer. It was perhaps not surprising that the tavern closed after three months, although it made episodic attempts to reoffend.

6. Michael Herbert, *La Chanson à Montmartre*, La Table Ronde, Paris, 1967, p.67.

Théophile-Alexandre Steinlen, 1897

his Napoleonic *Epic* at the Chat Noir's shadow theatre but left only a single really good poster, *The Russian Exhibition at the Champ-de-Mars*. Maindron sought to encourage him: 'The day when M. Caran d'Ache tackles the large-format illustrated poster, he will achieve something remarkable.' He preferred to devote his time and energies to the satirical journal *Psst…!*, working with Jean-Louis Forain whose only poster worth mentioning was designed for the second Salon du Cycle.

Back at the Chat Noir, four other designers deserve a mention: Ferdinand Bac, who designed three posters for Yvette Guilbert; Abel Faivre, who worked for the magazines *Le Chat noir* and *Le Rire*; Lucien Faure, who is remembered for his posters advertising a review at the Moulin Rouge titled *Les Caucaseries de la Butte*, a body-building device developed by Eugen Sandow ('Eugen the Magnificent') and Strock Cycles; and Fernand Fau, who designed two posters, one for the cabaret Le Tréteau de Tabarin at 58 Rue Pigalle, the other for the Salon des Cent.

With Steinlen, we come to the last real giant of the period. In terms of both quality and quantity – he designed some seventy posters – he was never a marginal figure as a poster artist but was above all what Francis Jourdain has termed a 'great image-maker'.[7]

Steinlen arrived in Paris in 1881 after a period spent in Mulhouse, where he designed textiles. In Paris he became friendly with Aristide Bruant, the author of songs celebrating Paris street life and a man in whom he must have found a kindred spirit.[8] Bruant took Steinlen to the Chat Noir, where he met Willette, and it was for the Chat Noir that he produced his earliest designs in 1883. He followed Bruant to *Le Mirliton* and provided illustrations for its magazine as well as for the two volumes of Bruant's *Dans la Rue*. Even so, he did not sever his links with Salis, for whom he designed the emblematic poster *Tour of the Chat Noir* in 1896. Five years earlier he had began what was to prove a lengthy and successful collaboration with the magazine *Gil Blas*, for which he produced more than seven hundred illustrations. He also worked on ninety-two numbers of *Le Chat noir*. It has been calculated that between 1883 and 1911 he worked on fifty-six magazines in Paris.[9] These included not only *Le Rire*, one edition on which he worked with Lautrec, but also four magazines of a more politically active kind: *Le Chambard socialiste*,

7. See Francis Jourdain, *Un Grand Imagier: Alexandre Steinlen*, Éditions Cercle d'Art, Paris, 1954, p.16.
8. Bruant was not yet the populist anti-Semite whose only goal was to make his fortune.
9. These figures are taken from Phillip Dennis Cate and Susan Gill, *Théophile-Alexandre Steinlen*, Gibbs M. Smith, Salt Lake City, 1982, p.36.

Théophile-Alexandre Steinlen, 1894

Théophile-Alexandre Steinlen, 1893

Théophile-Alexandre Steinlen, 1899

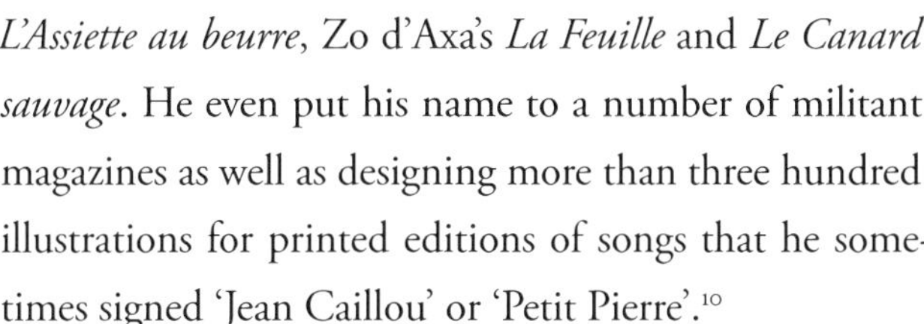

L'Assiette au beurre, Zo d'Axa's *La Feuille* and *Le Canard sauvage*. He even put his name to a number of militant magazines as well as designing more than three hundred illustrations for printed editions of songs that he sometimes signed 'Jean Caillou' or 'Petit Pierre'.[10]

In a world of wit and humour, Steinlen gave the impression of a man of gravity, especially when compared with Willette and Forain. Irony, sarcasm and indifference were all alien to him.

According to Francis Jourdain, 'Steinlen believed that every artist claiming a populist aesthetic should have other dreams than those of seeing his paintings on display in a museum. [...] More than anyone else at this time, he was able to adapt his chosen profession to the conditions of the fight he was waging.'[11] It was only logical, therefore, that Steinlen would not be represented in the classic collections of lithographs published by Marty and Vollard. It should also be noted that his paintings – including those in very large formats – were all of the highest quality.[12] His career took the opposite course to that of his colleagues, illustrations and lithographs leading him to paint canvases, including those that were demonstrably inspired by his posters for Comiot Motorcycles and Vingeanne Sterilized Milk.

Steinlen worked hard, breaking off only for the long walks that provided him with his inspiration. Like Lautrec, he was always making sketches, but unlike Lautrec, it was in the street that he found what interested him. 'A loafer like so many others?' asks Francis Jourdain. 'No. He was a loafer like no other. [...] He looked and he saw. [...] His figures are not *symbolic* but *representative*.'[13] He gazed affectionately at the young dressmakers

10. Both names involve a play on words involving the term 'lithographic stone'.
11. Jourdain, *Un Grand Imagier* (note 8), pp.17–18.
12. See the collection in the Petit Palais in Geneva.
13. Jourdain, *Un Grand Imagier* (note 8), pp.13 and 27.

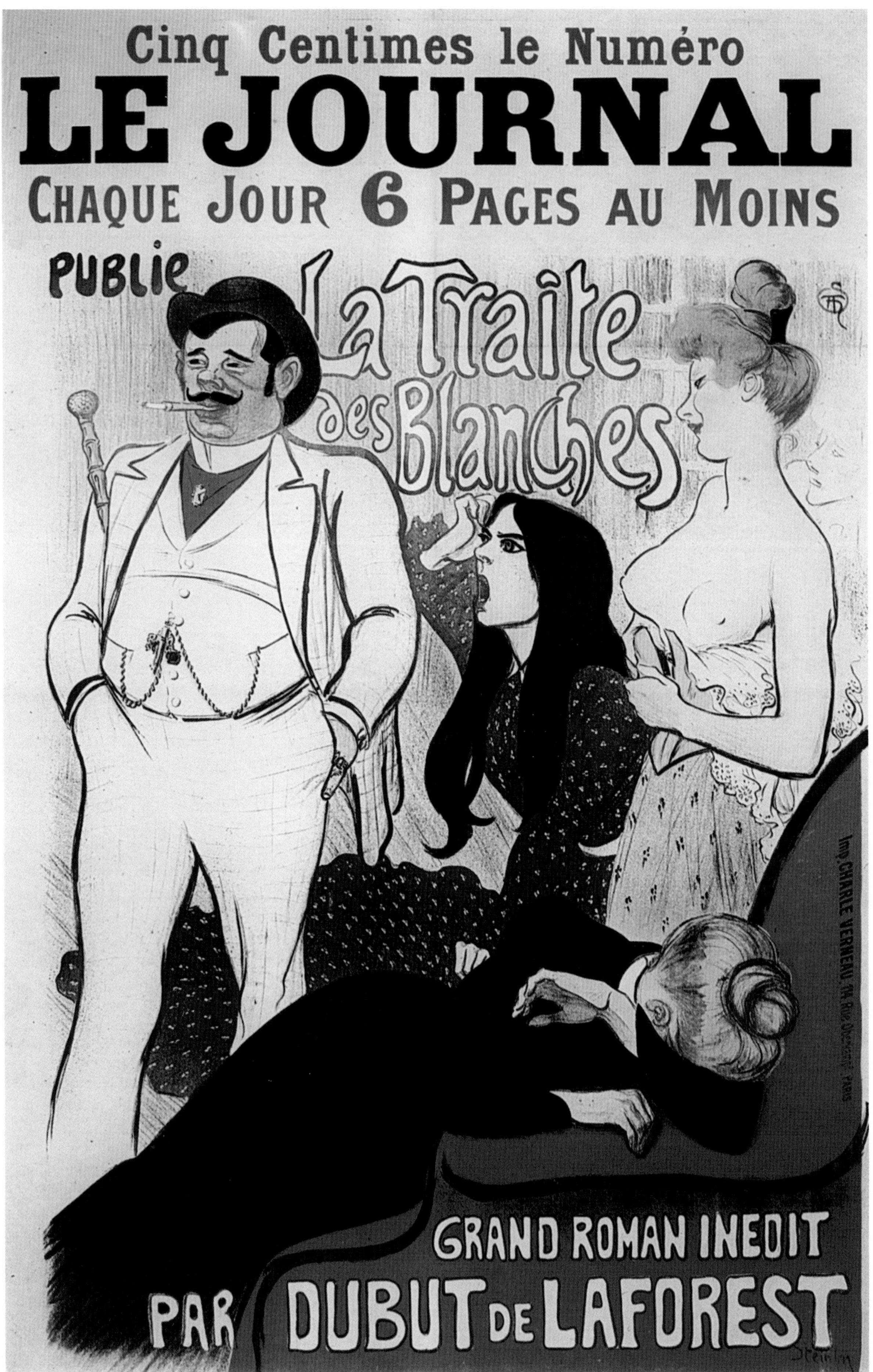

Théophile-Alexandre Steinlen, 1899

and at the dances held on 14 July. He saw the tragedy in the whores and the pimps who prowled around the city gates and he captured the hopelessness of the destitute and the homeless. He was horrified by mining accidents, by social repression and by war. And he was fired by anger to take up the cause of the proletariat in its struggle to break free from its chains. To the black of his illustrations he added the red of spilt blood. His friends were Zola, Anatole France, Georges Courteline and Jules Renard, who called him 'the incorruptible'. He illustrated many of their books.

With the exception of his early posters, which are simple chromolithographs or images lacking in any identifiable style, his posters fall into two categories: *intimiste* and warm-coloured for advertising purposes, dark and exhortative in the case of the others.

Adolphe Brisson recalled 'a man who spoke softly and at length, a distant expression in his eyes' and who preferred a life of quiet domesticity with his wife, his daughter and his numerous cats to the noisy nightlife of Montmartre. On his wife's death, he continued to lead the same kind of life with a statuesque black woman.

Théophile-Alexandre Steinlen, 1894

Steinlen did not really have a calling as a poster artist. His friend George Auriol noted that 'like everyone else, he fell under the spell' of Chéret, adding that 'in his eyes the lithograph was a vulgar profession, one that had been chosen by chance by a man of genius but otherwise good only for advertising furniture polish and farm machinery'.[14]

14. Réjane Bargiel and Christophe Zagrodzki, *Steinlen Affichiste: Catalogue raisonné*, Éditions du Grand-Pont, Lausanne,1986, p.12.

Since he had to make no major concessions, the poster was undoubtedly a source of considerable income for him. And he soon saw it as the tool of militant propaganda that it is. Following a confused design for Léon Gastinel's pseudo-Japanese ballet *Le Rêve* (1890), he found his style with his poster for *Mothu et Doria* (1893). As Auriol has noted, 'He merely transposed to the stone the principal lines of the project that he had conceived and which he freely reworked, without any recopying. He has undoubtedly seen Lautrec's work, including his use of outline and of spatter technique. As for the rest, he remains in firm control of the design and

Théophile-Alexandre Steinlen, 1899

Théophile-Alexandre Steinlen, 1896

the distribution of the colours. From the very outset he achieves a stylistic maturity.'

In the case of his poster for Yvette Guilbert at the Ambassadeurs, the influence is more obvious. Here the upper half of the image is divided vertically, with – in the background – a theatre flat and an auditorium whose light fittings recall those of the Moulin Rouge. Yvette Guilbert is depicted full length, very lightly outlined, with her famous black gloves. Steinlen was probably realizing what the singer had dreamt that Lautrec would have produced, a design that she had rejected with a grimace of disapproval.

This brings us to an *intimiste* series of designs that were to lay the foundations for Steinlen's later reputation. For his exhibition at the Galerie de la Bodinière – a rite of passage for all artists seeking recognition at this time – he depicted two cats. In his poster for Vingeanne Sterilized Milk three cats are seen staring greedily at a bowl of milk in the hands of the artist's daughter, Colette. The poster is a triumph: never before had a poster breathed such a simple spirit of domestic bliss. As Francis Jourdain has written, it was 'simple, generous and effective'. Ten thousand copies in varying sizes were printed by Verneau, and the British rights were also bought by Nestlé, which ordered a further ten thousand copies.

Next came the French Chocolate and Tea Company, a poster which in this writer's opinion is Steinlen's masterpiece, a harmonious composition with warm-toned colours and imbued with the tenderness linking mother, daughter and cat. The same tenderness is also found in his 1905 poster for the baby food Racahout des Arabes, although here he was working from memory, Colette having now grown up. His rendering is also closer to that of a print, which works less well in this context.

Comiot Motorcycles of 1899 belongs to the same family of images. Against a rudimentarily rustic

Théophile-Alexandre Steinlen, 1907

Paul Balluriau, *c.* 1899

background an elegant young woman is making her leisurely way through a gaggle of startled geese. Steinlen also made an oil painting of this scene, but it is considerably less successful.

Last but not least is Steinlen's 1905 poster for the Chéron Veterinary Clinic, an elaborate composition centred around a young animal-lover that allowed him to express his extraordinary talent for drawing animals.

For his printer Charles Verneau he designed an enormous poster measuring 238 x 304cm/93.6 x 120in and made up of six separate sheets. Street life was clearly a subject that never ceased to inspire Steinlen, and the present result is on a commensurately high level, depicting, as it does, popular Parisian types ranging from female workers and bare-headed washerwomen to flat-capped workers and a top-hatted bourgeois. A second image, *The Boulevard*, never saw the light of day.

Ernest de Crauzat was enthusiastic about what he saw: 'Far more effective and far more likely to promote the idea of art than Puvis de Chavannes,[15] this is art, this is truth, an art that we cannot applaud too much.'[16]

Steinlen also designed two posters of heraldic power. One was for Le Chat Noir. Seated on a red plinth, the eponymous feline is made up of a large area of black that is subtly outlined, its head surrounded by a kind of halo spelling out Salis's motto 'Mont-Joye – Montmartre'. The cat stares back at us, a hieratic presence. The poster exists in a number of variants, each with a different wording. A similar design was used when the night club was sold at auction in 1898. The other poster worth mentioning here is the one that Steinlen designed for *Cocorico*, a magazine devoted to the graphic arts. He showed great skill in incorporating the abnormally lengthy text into the lower half of the image, encroaching on the body of the cockerel but leaving the creature's upper half free in order for it to utter its famous cry of 'Cocorico', the French equivalent of 'cock-a-doodle-do'.[17]

Passing swiftly over a series of images of lesser importance, including publicity posters for the Pyrenean resort of Vernet-les-Bains, for Alphonse Duvernoy's opera *Hellé* and a delightful series for Western Railways, we arrive at a group of militant posters, starting with magazines such as *La Feuille* and a small poster for Zo d'Axa's 1895 autobiography *De Mazas à Jérusalem*. For *Le Journal*, he produced a vast allegorical fresco that makes great use of light and shade to advertise Zola's novel *Paris*, which appeared in instalments in the paper's pages in 1897–8. Next came a poster for the novel *The White Slave Trade* by Jean-Louis Dubut de Laforest that was a violent indictment of pimping. For this, Steinlen designed a brothel scene that features an impassibly brutish pimp contemptuously parading three of his victims in front of him, the black area of the woman crying in the foreground echoing the hair of the one who is shouting, while the third woman looks on with a dazed expression in her eyes. The poster caused a scandal and led to a court case when the censor demanded that the third woman's breasts be covered, which was duly done. Without overstating his case, Steinlen summed up to perfection the ignominy of the scene.[18] Also for *Le Journal*, he designed a poster advertising *The Mysteries of the Pointed Tower*, a sensationalist novel by Marie-François Goron. The poster is equally sensationalist.

For the socialist magazine *Le Petit Sou* he designed a poster depicting the figure of Marianne – the typical embodiment of the French Republic – encouraging a crowd of workers to revolt. 'If the poor did not make so much noise,' commented Charles-Louis Philippe, 'the rich would not even notice that they existed.' The poster that Steinlen designed for the anarchist journal *Les Temps nouveaux* that was published by one of his friends, Jean Grave, is less interesting in terms of its graphic design.

Finally, Steinlen designed a poster for a state adaptation of Zola's novel *L'Assommoir* (The Low Dive), a large-format example of his work that allowed him to express himself more fully. It depicts the scene in which Coupeau meets Gervaise. Drunks can be seen at the bar in the background. The pair's emotion is palpable. The whole drama is summed up in a single image. Steinlen was even able to insert a smaller poster within the larger one, allowing him to avoid contaminating the main image with the information that it contains.

15. Steinlen is alluding to the large billboards that the Union pour L'Action Morale commissioned from Puvis de Chavannes. Clearly uninspired, the artist designed a third-rate poster depicting *St Genevieve as a Child at Prayer*.
16. See Bargiel and Zagrodzki, *Steinlen Affichiste* (note 15), p.44.
17. The cockerel was reproduced on boards and covers, many of them designed by Mucha.
18. He brought the same intensity to his illustrations for Maupassant's short story *La Maison Tellier*.

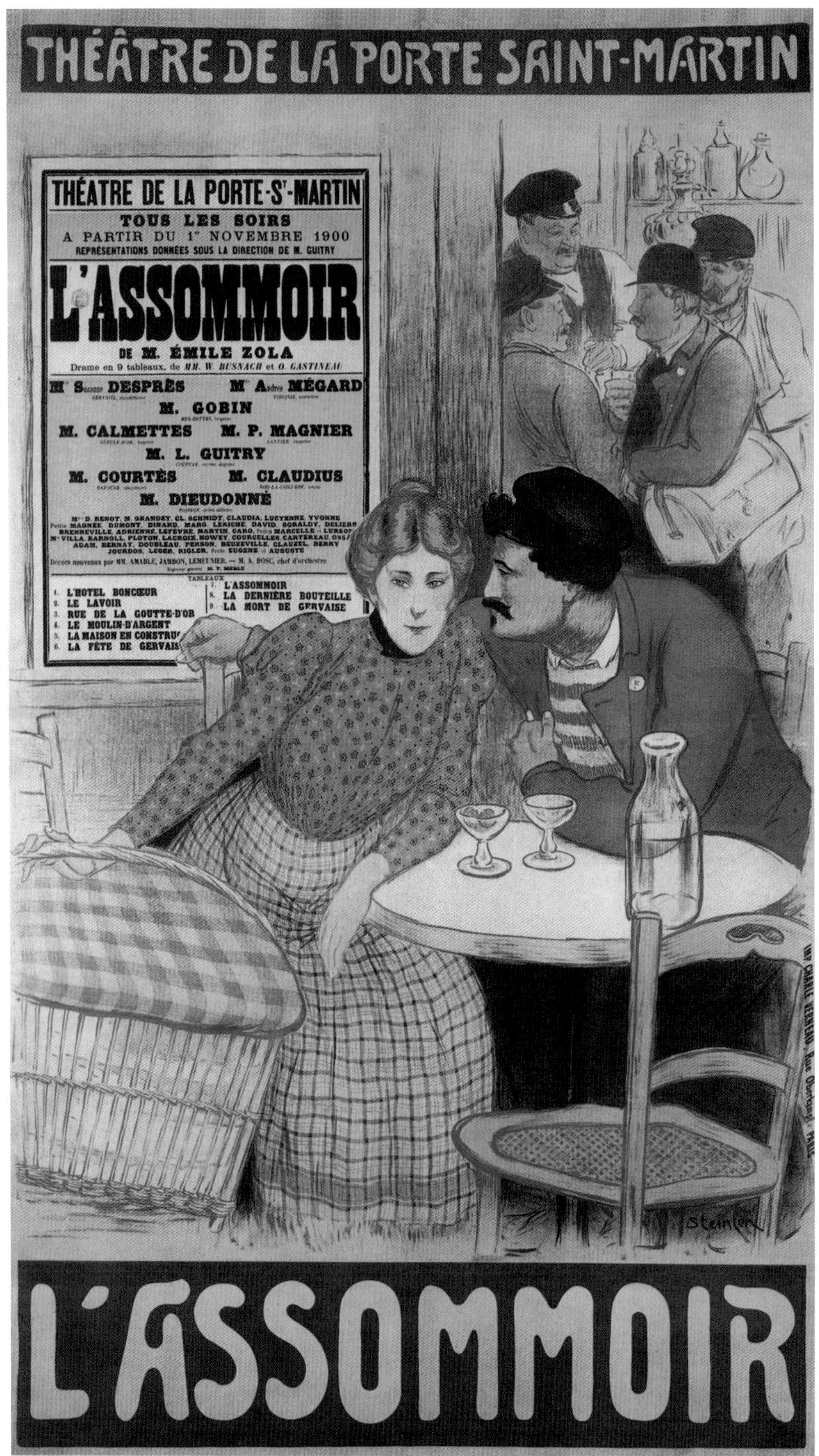

Théophile-Alexandre Steinlen, 1900

Auguste Roedel, 1895

Maurice Biais, 1901

Just before the war Steinlen championed the French Tenants' Association 'against the privileges of property owners'. The desperate look on the face of the father who, close to tears, is being thrown out on to the street, together with his whole family, is almost impossible for the observer to bear.

Steinlen also designed posters to advertise his own exhibitions, and to promote his own illustrations, including those to Émile Morel's book on miners in northern France. Then came the war. It was entirely consistent with the whole of his earlier approach that he should set himself apart from other poster artists, preferring to depict civilian and military suffering rather than focus on patriotic bombast and enemy insults.

Quite apart from a talent that allows us to rank him among the finest designers of his generation, Steinlen also occupies a special place in the history of the Belle Époque poster by virtue of the depth and the reflective and visionary nature of his work: Adolphe Brisson spoke of his 'secret ardour as an apostle'.

His one true disciple was Paul Balluriau, some of whose posters are almost indistinguishable from those of Steinlen himself, notably those he designed for *Le Journal*. His illustrations for *Gil Blas* and *L'Assiette au beurre* likewise reveal his mentor's imprint.

Auguste Roedel was one of the first artists to settle in Montmartre, a quarter that he soon came to embody like no other. Joining forces with Willette, he sat on the organizing committee that ran the local carnival, the Vachalcade. He was also the founding director of the monthly *La Vache enragée*. For a special edition in 1897, he designed an improbable cover depicting a

Jules-Alexandre Grün, 1904

Weiluc (Lucien-Henri Weil), 1900

Jules-Alexandre Grün, 1906

woman wearing a Louis-Philippe dress and dealing the coup de grâce to a bull in the manner of a matador. He was responsible for a number of excellent posters, the best of them being one for Monopole Linen depicting a washerwoman, obviously inspired by Steinlen but stiffer in execution, who sees three little men rising out her ironing board, all of them made from the same hard collars as the ones she is currently ironing. For the Moulin de la Galette and the Moulin Rouge he designed a series of stock posters, all of them clearly – and beneficially – inspired by Steinlen. Known as 'the king of the cavalcade', Roedel was destroyed by absinthe, dying in 1900.

Maurice Biais was another of the eccentric figures whom Montmartre attracted. He was born in Corbeil in 1872, the son of a notary, who cut off his son's livelihood when he moved to Paris. There he made a promising start, creating an excellent poster for the Maison Moderne for whom he also designed furniture. He additionally produced two posters for the Folies-Bergère and one for Quinquina Vouvray, a tonic wine made by Ernest Bourin in Tours. Against a uniform background, Biais plays with the black masses of the clothes and of the white uncoloured paper to depict a hugely overweight waiter and his top-hatted, cigarette-smoking, roistering client. We find the same allusion to Lautrec's poster for *Le Divan japonais*, in which the bare-headed woman seen from the back is Jane Avril, with whom Biais was madly in love.

Courted by the most brilliant men, Jane Avril became engaged to Biais – an example of the unfathomable mystery of love. They may have had a son together. He devoted a poster to her, but it is a singularly maladroit

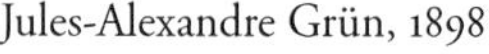
Jules-Alexandre Grün, 1898

Jules-Alexandre Grün, 1898

affair, after which he turned to gambling and drink.[19] But the affair was rekindled and in 1911 the two of them were married, after which they settled in the suburbs. When war broke out, Biais was called up. Gassed in the trenches, he returned home, disappearing increasingly often, not to sanatoriums, as he claimed, but to gambling dens. He even stole Jane Avril's jewels before death came as a blessed release. As a final unpleasant surprise, a trunk was found to contain the women's dresses that he wore as a transvestite.

Louis-Abel Truchet was another artist who in 1918 died of injuries sustained in the war. He could hardly have been more different from Biais in terms of his stature as an artist. He studied at the Académie Julian before settling in Montmartre and creating a wonderful stained glass window for the École des Beaux-Arts in Paris that has unfortunately not survived. An outstanding neo-Impressionist painter, he had a unique ability to describe the Paris of the dances and cafés-concerts as well as the boulevards and the Tuileries, treating the same subjects in his decorative lithographs as in his other work. His posters are extremely rare, but all of them are of the first order: for Morel Tyres he drew children who recall the world of the Nabis, whereas his posters for the Touche Concerts, for the department store À la Place Clichy, for Aiglon Cycles and for the Monte-Carlo Fair, all feature designs reminiscent of Ibels and Steinlen.

The young Jules-Alexandre Grün did not arrive in Montmartre until early 1890. He had already exhibited at the Salon of 1886, when he was only eighteen, the youngest exhibitor in the Salon's history. To his imperial Christian names, he added premature baldness. He was

19. For more on the affair between Biais and Jane Avril, see François Caradec, *Jane Avril au Moulin Rouge avec Toulouse-Lautrec*, Fayard, Paris, 2001.

Jules-Alexandre Grün, 1902

Jules-Alexandre Grün, 1898

soon admitted to the intimate circle of Willette, Steinlen, Roedel and Truchet, all of whom were his senior by ten or so years. His old friend Fursy – the stage name of the actor Henri Dreyfus – described him as 'this merry live wire without whom there was no decent ball at the École des Beaux-Arts and who repaired every day to the Auberge du Clou, where his friends would habitually gather'.[20] He quickly became indispensable since he paid for the drinks himself. For the second Vachalcade in 1897 he even designed a number of smaller posters inviting 'the kind ladies of Montmartre' to draw his chariot. He soon became the preferred poster artist of many of the cabarets and cafés-concerts.

In 1893 and 1894 he designed two posters for Le Concert des Décadents that reveal the direct influence of the fashionable shadow plays of Le Chat Noir, depicting black silhouettes against a white background. Two other posters from this period, for the Divan Japonais and, above all, for Le Carillon, point to an evolution in the artist's use of a black field that is not outlined in any way. During the summer of 1895, in the cabaret's garden, Fursy created the Carillon Tribunal. Grün adopted the black background, to which he added red, extending the colour beyond the judges' traditional robes. His *Vachalcade 1897* and his later *Benefit Ball for the Moulin Rouge* were both banal by comparison.

Grün's portrait of a group of singers at the Trianon – *Les Chansonniers de Montmartre* – confirms his talents as a cartoonist.

Grün finally settled on his style in 1898 with his poster for L'Âne Rouge: against a black background from which there emerges a village constable recognizable by

20. Quoted by Alain Weill and Israel Perry, *Jules Alexandre Grün: The Posters / Les Affiches*, Queen Art Publishers, New York, 2005, p.8.

Jules-Alexandre Grün, 1898

During the heyday of the poster, there was no lack of sites where such objects could be displayed, and it was with an endearing insouciance that nightclub owners and cabaret entertainers took their chance. With such colourful figures, moreover, quarrels and tiffs were commonplace: after being discovered at Le Carillon, Fursy opened Le Tréteau de Tabarin, before falling out with his partner and opening La Boîte à Fursy. In turn, he merged with Le Tréteau, reviving its fortunes and leasing La Scala. The intolerable Rodolphe Salis (caricatured in the top right-hand corner of the poster above, where he is seen on a donkey weighed down with sacks full of banknotes) ended up falling out with everyone, starting with his brother Gabriel, who had rejoined him and who opened L'Âne Rouge in 1899 and who tired of both the tightfistedness and the character of his brother. The name L'Âne Rouge was suggested by Willette, who was the first to abandon Le Chat Rouge and who took his cue from Rodolphe's red hair. Bruant likewise made good his escape and opened Le Mirliton. ❧

Jules-Alexandre Grün, 1905

his buttons, a ravishing bare-chested beauty places one of her arms round the famous red donkey that was the symbol of the nightclub.[21]

Grün went on to design *Where Are They Coming From?* and *Where Are They Taking Her?* for Le Tréteau de Tabarin and Le Violon respectively. By now he had developed an identifiable style, beginning with his typical female figures. Just as commentators refer to Chéret's young women as '*chérettes*', so I would propose the term '*grünettes*' for Grün's.[22] But whereas the *chérette* is a charming Parisian, the *grünette* is clearly a tart who reflects the age's canon in terms of her beauty: a full bosom with a plunging neckline, her corset tied so tightly as to produce a wasp waist and a well-rounded posterior. (False bottoms were on sale at this period for those women who felt that nature had left them insufficiently endowed.) His cast of characters also included old and ruddy-faced revellers and local policemen, although the *grünette* was often found posing alone, her various positions designed to show off her bosom or rear.

The lightness of Grün's style has meant that his work has never been taken entirely seriously, which is unfortunate. The dominant use of black, with a shirt front or the reflection of a top hat enough to indicate a party-goer or a line of buttons and a belt sufficient to suggest an officer of the law, is entirely original, allowing Grün to use the white background for the text.

Red is by far his favourite colour for dresses and hats, though it may sometimes be replaced by a brilliant yellow or green. We have to wait until 1906 to see blue appear in a poster produced to mark the reopening of the Paris Casino. Grün was never the man to show a lack of imagination, and the posters that he designed to advertise revues at La Cigale, La Scala and L'Européen provided him with especially evocative themes. Neither *Ya du linge* nor *T'y viens-t-y* nor *C'est d'un raid* nor *Veux-tu grimper?* was too complicated for him to illustrate.

He left only a single account of his working method, and in it he confirms the lightness of touch that he brought to all of his commissions: 'I am very fond of posters,' he told his interviewer, Paul Duverney, in 1899: 'and this kind of work has always tempted me, even from my debut, as an artist. But, all the same, I do not make special efforts to do them; I take orders when they come, but do not seek them. One exhausts one's-self [sic] by doing posters only, and at length one is obliged to repeat one's self.'[23] This was undoubtedly a dig at Chéret.

Grün's sex bombs delighted collectors, and he was the only designer to have his copyright printed on much of his work: 'This poster may not be given or sold.'[24]

By the turn of the century Grün had decided that it was time to settle down. He married Marie-Juliette Toutain, the daughter of the paymaster-general for navy pensioners, and moved into a private mansion in the Boulevard Berthier, one of many such houses built at the end of the nineteenth century that also included an artist's studio. But his break with Montmartre was a gradual one, for he still accepted commissions.

Grün now turned to painting, gaining recognition in 1911 with his vast canvas *A Friday at the Salon des Artistes*, but he did not turn his back on the poster as an art form, gravitating rather in the direction of commercial advertising. He signed a contract with Herold, an agent who used Verneau, Chaix, Bourgerie and Daubendis as his printers. Of these, the last named 'printed all of his posters on rotary presses using aluminium plates'.[25]

Grün was interested in bicycles ('the little queen') and eventually cars, too: Marot-Gardon, L'Autotouriste and Gallus Studded Tyres. For Herold he also designed posters for Gabron Automobiles and Lorraine-Dietrich, but there were few products for which he did not produce posters, including the Silbermann Fireplace, the general knowledge magazine *Je sais tout*, the Larousse encyclopaedic dictionary, Angostura Bitters, Bannier Preserves and Byrrh. His typical female subject had settled down and was no longer omnipresent, while both his palette and his cast of characters had increased in size and number.

By the turn of the century Grün was working for Western Railways (London and Brittany) and Northern Railways (the beach at Mesnil-Val), but the most notable series of posters from this period were the five that he

21. This poster illustrates the fickleness of the contemporary censor, who in 1901 had refused a licence for *Enfin seuls* (Finally Alone!). It was evidently less shocking for a topless woman to stroke a donkey than for her to be depicted in the arms of a man.

22. Weill and Perry, *Jules Alexandre Grün* (note 21).

23. Paul Duverney, 'A Chat with Grün'. *The Poster*, 2/9 (March 1899), 99–102, esp. 99–100.

24. This measure merely served to stimulate the market, for there are now copies in every collection.

25. In ten years the huge flat machines that had been Camis's pride and joy were obsolete.

Jules-Alexandre Grün, *c.* 1905

Jules-Alexandre Grün, *c.* 1905

Jules-Alexandre Grün, 1905-1910

Jules-Alexandre Grün, 1905

designed between 1905 and 1910 to advertise Monaco. Here his style may be said to have burgeoned, and his palette, which until then had been grounded in black, the colour of night, discovered colour at the same time that he himself discovered the Riviera. His posters for the Monaco Motorboat Exhibition are real gems.

Prior to this, Grün had designed the largest poster to be printed during this period, measuring 400 x 480cm/157.50 x 189in, it was made up of a dozen panels and printed by Chaix in 1902 for High-Life Tailor. In it he managed to find room for all of his favourite figures – and all of them appeared, of course, against a black background. Following the war, Grün devoted himself almost exclusively to painting until Parkinson's disease brought his career to an end.

Lucien Métivet studied with Lautrec in Fernand Cormon's studio. The two men became friends and were often to be seen together at the bars and nightclubs of Montmartre. Métivet abandoned painting for theatre design but above all became one of the most prolific illustrators of his day, working for *Le Rire* and *L'Assiette au beurre*, among others. In 1905 he won the competition organized by *The Century Magazine* to illustrate the life of Napoleon – Lautrec's entry was famously rejected. But he also designed three excellent posters for the music-hall singer Eugénie Buffet, which are among his very best works.

Another of Cormon's students was Louis Anquetin, who designed only two posters. One of them – sinister and barely comprehensible – was a black and white poster to advertise the launch of *Le Rire*, while the other was a more cheerful affair for the singer Marguerite Dufay.

The final artist to be mentioned in this chapter on Montmartre is Fernand-Louis Gottlob, who was a member of the Société du Cornet,[26] which provided him with a passage of safe-conduct. A painter and prolific illustrator who, like Métivet, worked for *Le Rire* and *L'Assiette au beurre*, he designed posters for two major events, the Salon des Cent and the second Salon de la Lithographie. Both are painterly, rather than graphic, works. ❧

26. This society, to which a number of historians seem to have attached great importance, was founded by Bertrand Millanvoye, the owner of Le Carillon, together with Georges Courteline and Paul Delmet. It existed to gamble for drinks using dice, hence the use of the term 'cornet', meaning 'dice box' in the French title.

Lucien Métivet, 1893

Poulbot, *c.* 1900

Albert Guillaume and Francisco Tamagno, 1897

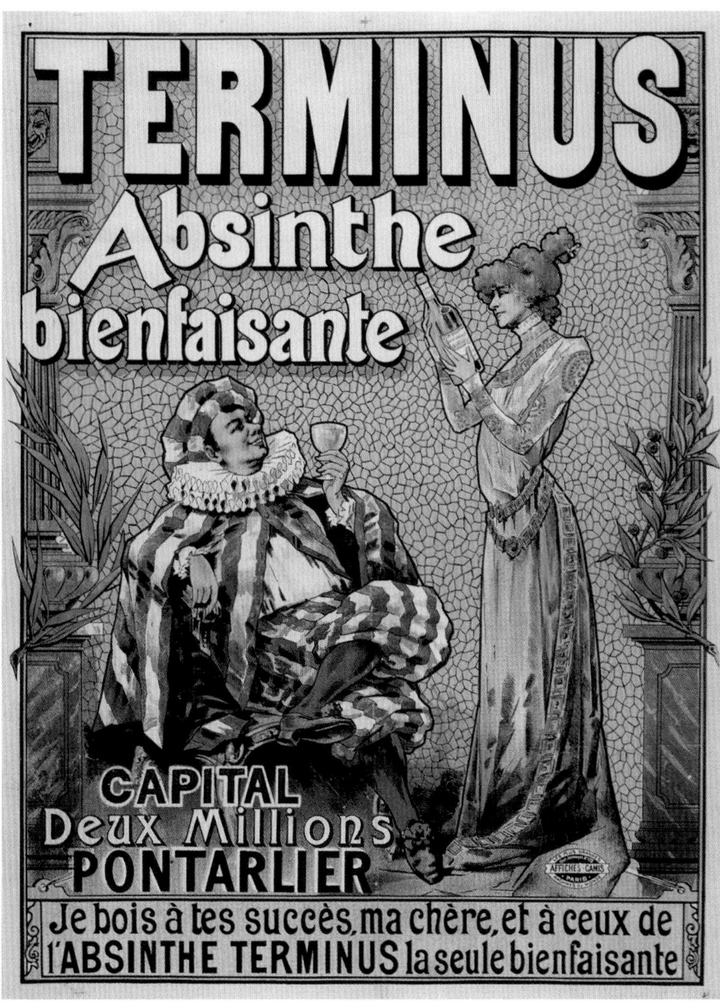

Francisco Tamagno, 1892

Albert Guillaume, *c.* 1900

With the exception of Jules Chéret, the grand masters of the poster designed relatively few posters, even though they made a major contribution to the golden age of the medium and ensured that posters became collectors' items. As a result, industry and commerce became all the more demanding, and the larger printing firms, which had equipped themselves with presses capable of producing huge print-runs of large-format posters, signed contracts with artists who became professional designers, while often continuing as painters and engravers. This chapter offers a survey of the key figures in this development.

Victor Camis brought together a team that included Francisco Nicolas Tamagno, Firmin Bouisset, Henri Gray and Albert Guillaume, making his the most prestigious team in the field. (Camis had also brought Gustave Jossot's name to a wider public, which had required a certain courage.)

According to a contemporary encomium, 'The Société Camis was founded only a few years ago in Paris and deals almost exclusively with art posters. It has managed to apply the presses that use the Marinoni system to the production of large-format posters, surpassing even the Americans in terms of its boldness. One of its creations, *The Little Girl of Menier Chocolate*, is a good example of the ingenuity of the artists that Monsieur Camis, an artist in his own right, has succeeded in luring to his firm.'[1]

After completing his studies in Turin and Rome, Nicolas Tamagno moved to Paris and immediately began working for Camis, for whom he designed one hundred or so posters. Édouard Cointreau employed him on a regular basis to design posters advertising his make of brandy and featuring the figure of Pierrot. His most famous posters are for Peugeot, Liebig, Cusenier,

1. Daniel Bordet, *Les cent plus belles affiches de l'Imprimerie*, Dabecom, Paris, 2004, p.63.

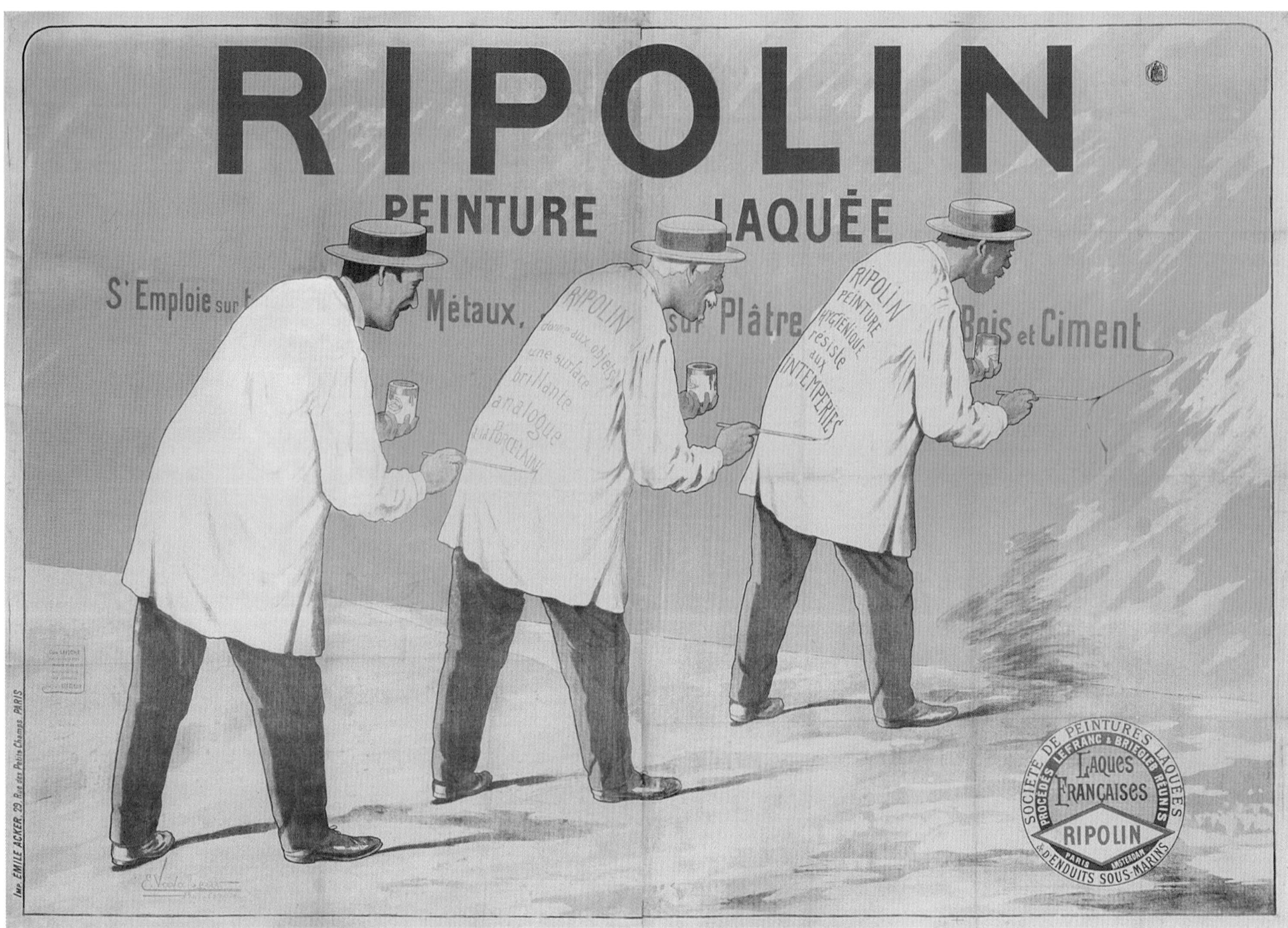

Eugène Vavasseur, 1898

Pernod and Terminus (a brand of absinthe). A skilled draughtsman, he was able to adapt his style to suit the taste of his clients. When his contract with Camis expired in 1905, he moved to Gallia, then in 1908 to Pecaud, before returning to Italy in 1913.

Albert Guillaume was the son of one of the leading architects of his day and husband of Suzanne Bloch-Levallois, whose father designed the commune of Levallois-Perret in Paris's north-western suburbs. His ambitions often transcended those of the traditional fine arts. In 1900, for example, he joined forces with his brother to open the Théâtre des Bonshommes Guillaume at that year's Paris Universal Exhibition, using marionettes to pillory the mores of the age. Though the enterprise failed, Guillaume was by no means lacking in a certain facile talent, his comic and bawdy canvases enjoying a huge success. The same was true of his numerous posters with their cast of comic characters: a circus strongman for Armour Meat Extract and a fat army officer for Dupit Grog. But he also tapped a more elegant vein for his posters for La Scala and the Palais de Glace, both of which reveal a skilful use of half-tones.

Firmin Bouisset worked for Alexandre Cabanel and Jean-Joseph Benjamin-Constant before enrolling at the École des Beaux-Arts. An excellent portraitist, he exhibited at the Salon, while for his posters he found a real money-spinner with a little schoolgirl for Menier Chocolate. His two children, Yvonne and Jacques, were then pressed into service for the most varied advertisers, including Maggi, Job and Poulain Chocolate.

Firmin Bouisset, 1893

O'Galop, 1913

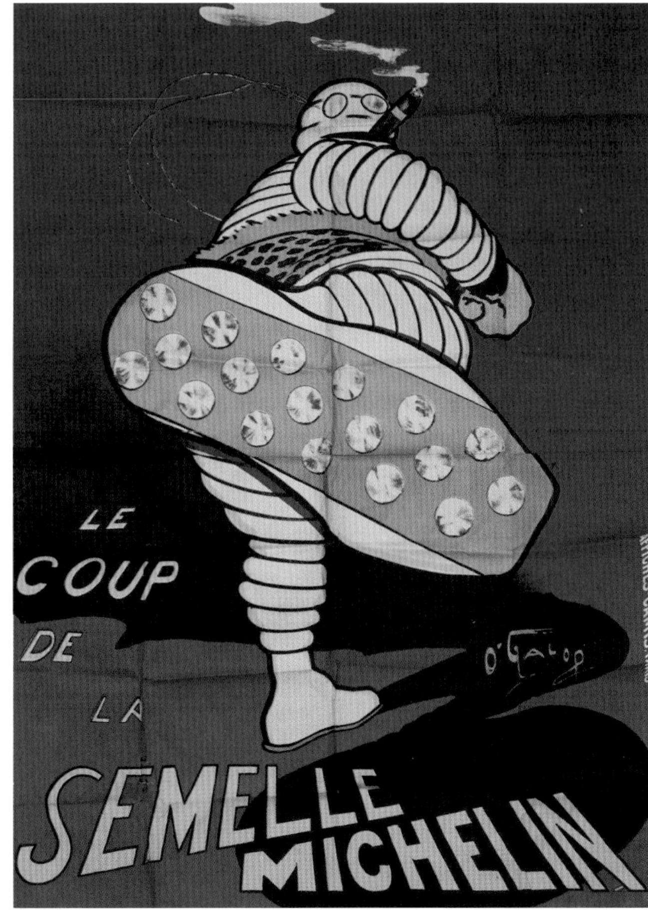

Henri Boulanger, known as Gray, 1898

Pal, 1898

Eugène Ogé, 1900

For the 1899 Salon des Cent, Bouisset designed a poster depicting a little girl surrounded by extravagant floral motifs in a style indistinguishable from Mucha's. The critic of *L'Estampe et l'Affiche* was incensed: 'Why has Firmin Bouisset, the creator of so many charming compositions of children, abandoned the world of graceful simplicity and thrown himself into one of confusion and over-ornateness? Mucha's influence is all too apparent in even the finest artists, including those endowed with a real personality.' In fact Mucha and Bouisset were good friends. Perhaps this was some kind of an in-joke.[2]

2. See Claudine Dhotel-Velliet, *Jane Atché*, Le Pont du Nord, Lille, 2009, p.59.

Henri Gray was the professional name of Henri Boulanger, whose speciality was the bicycle poster, in which he tried his hand at practically everything, including an unlikely series of scantily-clad women in space for Phébus and Brillant Cycles and for Stella Petroleum.

Pal was born in Bucharest as Jean de Paleologu and is believed to have been a descendant of the last ruling dynasty of the Byzantine Empire. He was also the undisputed star of Paul Dupont's printing works, for which he designed a vast number of posters. His typical female figure is instantly recognizable: a buxom blonde sex symbol in a more or less complete state of undress or else disguised as a knight or a cowgirl. In whatever guise she appeared, she certainly laughed at the censor. Pal worked in those areas of industry where the demand was greatest: bicycles (Clément, Cleveland, Columbia,

Eugène Ogé, 1904

Humber and Rudge, to name the most important), aperitifs (Cusenier and Abricotine), soap, gas burners and acetylene and shows such as the Folies-Bergère and the Casino de Paris. He also turned his hand to tourism whenever the opportunity arose. Pal was also in demand in London, where he signed his work 'Price'.

Eugène Ogé was the chief attraction at Charles Verneau's printing works, where he began his career designing posters. But although he was named as 'principal collaborator', he was allowed to sign his work only after 1894.[3] As his reputation grew, so he started to work for other firms, finally breaking with Verneau in 1902, when he designed *Here is the Enemy* for the anticlerical journal *La Lanterne*.

3. Patient work has allowed these to be identified: see Anne-Claude Lelieur, *Eugène Ogé: Affichiste, 1861–1936*, Agence Culturelle de Paris, Paris, 1998.

⌃1903. **Heads of state are meeting in an attempt to resolve international tensions**, resulting in total derision. A closer look reveals that the French president, Émile Loubet, and Tsar Nicholas II are discussing the best way of having a boy. Meanwhile, Wilhelm II is serving drinks to the Japanese emperor, Mutsuhito, while Pope Pius X and King Victor Emmanuel III of Italy sign a reconciliation agreement. Edward VII and Jacques Lebaudy – the owner of a sugar empire and the self-proclaimed emperor of the Sahara – share memories of the African colonies. Behind them Leopold II of Belgium is depicted gazing fondly at a portrait of his mistress, Cléo de Mérode. Uncle Sam, finally, is seen handing a drink to an African American child that is perched on his knees.

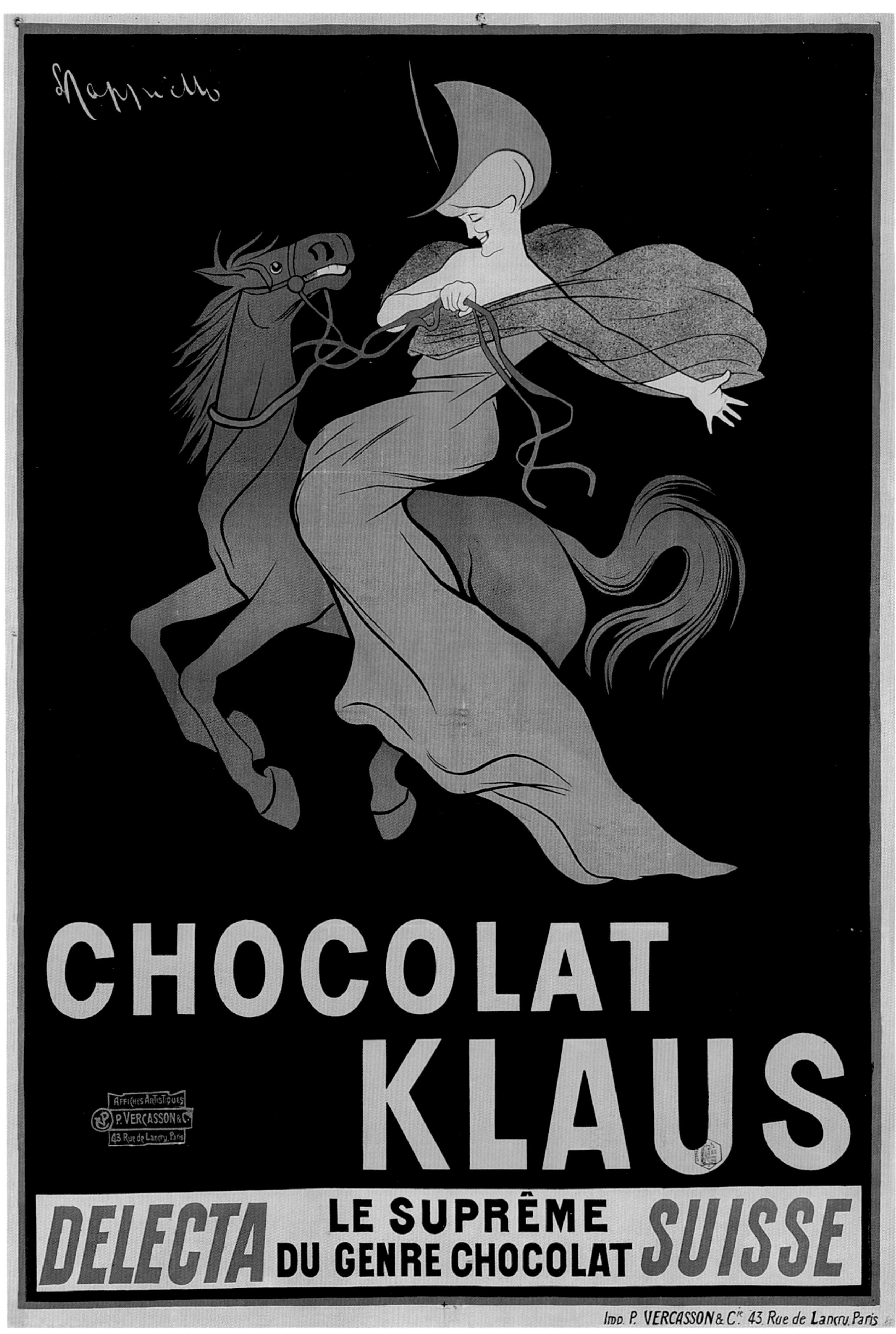

Leonetto Cappiello, 1903

Ogé's early work is clearly inspired by Chéret, notably in his posters for the Concert of the Twentieth Century, for the annual fair at St-Germain, the Fête des Loges, and for Pontarlier Absinthe, while the art nouveau style was the manifest influence behind his posters for the International Book Fair and Waterman's 'Ideal' Fountain-Pen. By the turn of the century he finally found his metier in the world of caricature with Dubonnet Tonic Wine and Géraudel Pastilles, which guaranteed his lasting success. In his attempts to create a popular kind of imagery, he turned to exaggerated lines, fearing neither the ugly nor the vulgar, and his method proved to be undeniably effective.

He favoured terrible children, as in Ibled Chocolate, Poulain Chocolate and Cygne Biscuits, bloated drinkers in his posters for Lion and Éclair Beer and fat servants in his poster for Léon Gonnet's 'ideal' dye. He exploited another vein that caught the public imagination when he included political figures and crowned heads of state in his work: among those who are readily identifiable are Queen Victoria and Paul Kruger advertising Dr Trabant's Pastilles[4] and the Prince of Wales drumming up trade for men's outfitters Bugnot & Cie. The method was most successful when Ogé combined the figures in his larger posters, including those advertising La Coquille Soap and Menthe-Pastille, a liqueur designed to aid digestion. From this mass of posters, the occasional nugget emerges, most notably his poster for Brunswick Billiards, which is a veritable jewel of poster art.

Over the years, a tendency may be seen to emerge, as advertisers sought to identify themselves with a specific character. Suffice it to mention Eugène Vavasseur's poster of the Ripolin Brothers painting each other and the Bibendum character devised by d'O Galop – the pseudonym of Marius Rossillon – to promote Michelin Tyres.

The arrival of Leonetto Cappiello also brought new blood to an ageing medium. Cappiello failed to find a new solution to the problem between 1900 and 1903 but continued to depict his typical female figure against a uniform background in his posters for Furet Corsets and Ducros Absinthe, while his series of posters for various brands of champagne followed in the tradition of Chéret. His breakthrough came in 1903 with his poster for Klaus Chocolate, which even though very few copies were produced – his publisher Vercasson claimed that there were only twenty-five – proved astonishingly successful with its depiction of a female rider dressed in green and seated on a red horse. Nothing like it had been seen before. And it worked. From now on Klein's customers demanded the 'chocolate with the red horse'.

From our own point of view, Cappiello had an advantage in that, unlike his predecessors who rarely expressed themselves on their work, leaving critics to speak on their behalf, Cappiello has left a detailed account of his working method and, indeed, of his whole development.

He began by looking for a defining blob or area that would contrast with its surroundings. One such splash of colour is the skirt of La Goulue in Toulouse-Lautrec's *Moulin Rouge*.

Next came the arabesque, a vague enough term, but one that Cappiello defined as 'this primitive lightning flash, this momentary feeling of excitement that overwhelms the imagination, this lightning flash of life'. He then 'sought the arabesque, fashioning and refashioning it until it encapsulated the subject and, once established, remained unchanging'.[5] It measured no more than 4–5 cm/1½–2in. It could also be defined, no doubt, as an idea that materialized in graphic form – the 'graphic expression of the idea', as Jean Carlu was later to put it.

Finally, there came the third element: surprise. It was this that ensured the success of the poster for Klaus Chocolate, which for Cappiello was the first of its kind.

In the face of all logic and realism, Cappiello surprised and delighted the world with his Cinzano red zebra, his green devil for Maurin Quina and his fire-spewing Pierrot for thermogene wool.

Within a few years Cappiello had become the leader of a new generation of poster artists who sought to establish rules governing the subject of advertising and the ways in which it can and should communicate with its audiences.

4. During the Boer War, the French public tended to be on the side of the Boers. A more politicized version exists, *Take Dum-Dum Pills*, with bullets replacing the pills. The poster was immediately censored in the interests of the Entente Cordiale.
5. Michel Laclotte and others (eds.), *Cappiello: 1875–1924. Caricatures, Affiches, Peintures et Projects Décoratifs*, Éditions de la Réunion des Musées Nationaux, Paris, 1981.

Gustave Jossot, 1898

Gustave Jossot, 1903

If the caricature has a presiding genius – and this is not a term I use lightly – then his name was Gustave Jossot.

A remarkable and yet ultimately unclassifiable anarchist, Joussot was the only member of his generation to invest the caricature with the status of modern art: 'In my view a gob that twisted or contorted by suffering, anger, laughter or fear is a thousand times more beautiful – in spite of its ugliness – than the insipid and inexpressive head of the Venus de Milo. Ah, expression and movement are an art unto themselves!'[1]

It is impossible to be clearer than this. Nor is it possible to draw a clearer line between Jossot's artistry and the aesthetic of the two dominant movements of the time, Symbolism and post-Expressionism.

1. Michel Dixmier and Henri Viltard, *Jossot: Caricatures. Da la révolte à la fuite en Orient (1866–1951)*, Paris Bibliothèques, Paris, 2010 (catalogue for an exhibition at the Bibliothèque Forney in 2011), p.24 (undated letter from Gustave Jossot to Noël Clément-Janin, [Nov–Dec 1897]).

Jossot is unique because he was not posturing. Rather, he continued to produce great art through the medium of the caricature.

The son of upper middle-class parents from the French provinces who provided him with a back-up plan, he arrived in Paris after various vicissitudes and produced designs of shocking banality before things fell into place in 1893, when he exhibited a number of watercolours on a gold background at the Salon des Indépendants. Léon Maillard, the editor in chief of *La Plume* was astounded: 'When I saw these strange and symbolic caricatures by Jossot, I nearly leapt out of my skin, as one does at an unexpected shock. I was neither apprehensive nor surprised, but was simply not prepared. […] And in them

Gustave Jossot, 1897

there was no reminiscence, nothing oriental, no trace of Japan, Jossot just makes reference to medieval gargoyles, which he does with considerable skill.'

Jossot was adopted by the Salon des Cent and invited to design a poster for its fifth exhibition: an academician who had to pay for his admission. In parallel he published *Artistes et bourgeois*, enjoying a sly dig at the whole of this small world. He poured scorn on the whiplash curve, creating grotesque pieces of furniture. And it worked. Pierre Puvis de Chavannes invited him to open a section on caricatures at the 1895 Salon des Artistes Français. That same year he was also asked to exhibit at the Libre Esthétique in Brussels, where a fellow exhibitor was Aubrey Beardsley – an interesting encounter between two artists who, each in his own way, was in the process of unsettling and shocking his bourgeois contemporaries. With *Mince de trognes* (Thin of Face), he went even further in terms of what one writer has called his 'Expressionist distortion'.[2] The album was to be called *Sales gueules* (Ugly Mugs) and Jossot had already designed the poster for it.

L'Assiette au beure welcomed the new work with open arms: Jossot would be a veritable pillar of the paper.[3] He never followed mere fashion. One after another he targeted all of the institutions which as a good anarchist he execrated. His thick outlines and flat colours gave rise to characters from which terrifying faces emerged. He placed them onstage with a feel for movement and a violence that added to the monstrous nature of the subject matter.

Jossot favoured short, ringing titles: *Circulez!* (Keep Moving) for the police, *Fixe!* (Attention!) for the army, *Cra* (Caw) for the clergy, *Les Tapinophages* (a nonce word derived from the Greek for 'humble' and 'devouring') for judges and *Dressage* for teachers.

Jossot even succeeded in breaking into the poster market, while continuing to lay claim to his identity as a caricaturist and refusing to countenance the least concession in terms of his individual style. His first poster dates from 1894, an advertisement for Auger Gingerbread of Dijon. The result is strange, although the scene is a classic one. In 1897 he was engaged by Victor Camis after Camis had printed his poster for Le Manillon, an advertisement for oxygenated absinthe. The poster is a masterpiece in three colours playing with the black background and the uncoloured white paper to construct the image. He also designed a poster for Camis's company, a long-haired art student drawing on a lithographic stone. The lettering is chaotic, the colours garish.

Next came the trilogy of works that made him famous. His poster for Saupiquet Sardines shows five celebrities eating said sardines. It is a curious exercise in which he succeeds in distorting the figures in question to the point where they are barely recognizable, yet the style is still Jossot's own. The poster, printed in a large format, leapt out from the wall. But this was true of all of his posters. They 'caught the eye', as poster artists used to say. How could a classic poster, with all its implied concessions, hope to compete with one by Jossot?

From this point of view, Jossot's poster for Amieux – a rival of Saupiquet – is altogether exemplary: emerging from the night, a hirsute rag-and-bone man, wearing blue overalls and carrying his pannier on his back, checks that a tin of sardines is marked 'Amieux Forever'. Perhaps there is a hint of irony at the idea that the poor fellow, possibly famished, is examining an empty tin. The image is arresting. As for the beam of light from the man's lantern in which Jossot has written the caption, this is a fantastic graphic trouvaille. The poster made an impact, just as Jossot had predicted: 'The poster must roar and compel the passer-by to look at it. My loud colours have drummed up a huge amount of publicity for Saupiquet and Amieux. In four or five years the female servants who go to the grocer's for a tin of sardines will no longer remember my vast hoardings, still less my signature, but they *will* remember the name of the product that my posters etched into the heads. […] At the risk of offending collectors, I have to say that my posters are not intended exclusively for them. Before them, there is the wholesale merchant and the industrialist for whom the poster was made.'[4]

Édouard Cointreau took a close interest in the advertising to which he devoted half of his profits during

2. This perfect definition is provided by Dixmier and Viltard, *Jossot: Caricatures* (note 1), passim.
3. Élisabeth and Michel Dixmier, *L'Assiette au beurre*, François Maspero, Paris, 1974. Jossot contributed eighteen complete numbers and several separate designs.
4. Dixmier and Viltard, *Jossot: Caricatures* (note 1), p.36 (letter from Gustave Jossot to Noël Clément-Janin, Dec. 1897).

Adrien Barrère, 1902

the second half of the 1890s.[5] He worked with Camis, whose enormous presses he admired, and had already chosen one of Camis's trainees, Nicolas Tamagno, to design a poster for his triple sec Cointreau, depicting a Pierrot wearing a pince-nez. For another of Cointreau's brands, Guignolet, by contrast, Cointreau took Camis's advice and could only congratulate himself for doing so: Jossot's poster is an extraordinary minimalist image in only two colours that is almost hypnotic in its impact.

Also worth mentioning here is Jossot's sardonically ironical poster for the men's outfitters, Lejeune, a strange illustration captioned 'Always Young' and depicting a dandy all in green resting a condescending hand on the balding pate of the poor tailor who, dressed in red, is clearly terrified at having to take his client's inner-leg measurement.

The last of Jossot's posters to mention is *À bas les calottes* (Down with the Clergy), a work of unprecedented violence that he designed for the launch of the journal *L'Action* in 1903, when he was in his element.

With the death of his father, Jossot found himself in receipt of a private income that allowed him to retire from a world in which he had continued to evolve but which he had never ceased to denounce. For a time he lived at Coulommiers and Rueil, then paid several visits to Tunisia, where he was attracted by Muslim mysticism and where he settled in 1911. Two years later he converted to Islam and became Abdul Karim Jossot ('the slave of the generous').

Jossot failed to find the peace he was looking for, but his works were another story. True to himself, he wrote with disarming irony: 'What have I done in North Africa? This is a question I've been asking myself for thirty-five years. Clearly it was stupid of me to have left Paris. I wanted people to forget me and I think that I have succeeded beyond my wildest dreams.'

5. Alain Weill and Les Bâtisseurs de Mémoire, *La Saga de la marque mondiale Cointreau / The Saga of the World-Wide Brand Cointreau 1849–1999*, Éditions du Chêne, Paris, 1999 (bilingual edition).

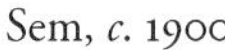
Sem, *c.* 1900

Daniel de Losques, 1908

Beside him, everything else indeed seems well-behaved and serenely classical.

Jean-Louis Forain was a great cartoonist during the final decades of the nineteenth century and also an excellent post-Impressionist painter. He was succeeded by two other artists who arrived in Paris almost simultaneously: Sem and Leonetto Cappiello.

Sem was born Georges Goursat and was thirty-seven when he came to Paris. He had perfected his style in the provinces, replacing Forain's pen and crayon hatchings with designs reduced to their essential outlines, using flat tones and pellucid compositions. He also created a new genre that no longer used humorous or sardonic captions, turning himself instead into a chronicler of fashionable society, most notably in *Les Courses* (The Races), *Les Promenades de L'Avenue du Bois* (Walks in the Avenue du Bois) and *Maxim's*. Between 1900 and 1914 he published no fewer than fourteen such albums. He designed posters all his life. They are large-scale cartoons on a uniform background: *Mayol*, *Dranem*, *Max Dearly* and – his best – *Colette*, which is in two colours apart from the white of the paper. There were also posters for revues such as those at La Scala and the Casino de Paris as well as for liqueurs like Benedictine depicting an impeccably dressed maître d'. Here, too, the black, the yellow background and the white of the paper are all in perfect harmony. Above all, there is Sem's masterpiece, *Footitt*, the grinning portrait of a clown in a garish red, yellow and green that is striking in its modernism.

Cappiello settled in Paris in 1898 and immediately joined the staff of *Le Rire* on the strength of a cartoon of his compatriot, the composer Giacomo Puccini. He designed his first poster – *Nos Actrices* (Our Actresses) – the following year for the humorous magazine *Frou Frou*, depicting a woman dancing against a yellow background.

Leonetto Cappiello, 1899

Her little sister advertised the Folies-Bergère. Between them, these two posters opened the doors of commercial advertising to Cappiello.

For all that Sem and Cappiello tapped the same rich vein, Cappiello was also adept at using stars whom he sketched for commercial posters: Jeanne Granier and Albert Brasseur for *Grands Chais du Médoc* and Réjane and Jeanne Granier for *Les Magasins des Cordeliers*.

After studying law and medicine, Adrien Barrère ended by turning to cartoons. He also designed two decorative panels based on them: *Les Professeurs de la Faculté de Médecine* (The Teachers at the Faculty of Medicine) and *Les Professeurs de la Faculté de Droit* (The Teachers at the Faculty of Law), both of which sold like hot cakes. Rarely for this period, Barrère devoted himself almost exclusively to designing posters from the very beginning of his career. An excellent cartoonist, he used thick outlines and bright flat colours, producing a veritable gallery of portraits of the stars of the cafés-concerts. He had a particular gift for depicting his characters in a theatrical setting and for his ability to play with perspective, notably in his posters for *Dranem* and *Polin*. He also worked for the theatre and for the famous Baret Tours and when a review became fashionable, he would design delightful friezes depicting all the venue's artists, notably for the Folies-Bergère. He also took an interest in the cinema, designing two hundred posters for Pathé, always with the same ease and assurance.

Daniel de Losques was a promising artist who had great success with his posters for Mistinguett and Spinelli, only for him to be killed in the war in 1915.

Adrien Barrère, *c.* 1900

Adrien Barrère, *c.* 1900

Armand Rassenfosse, 1899, detail

BELGIUM

Georges Privat-Livemont, 1896

Georges Privat-Livemont, 1897

Crespin and Duyck are generally regarded as the pioneers of the Belgian poster, which they steered in the direction of the French style of the period. A painter and decorator by training, Crespin spent the greater part of his career working with his friend the architect Paul Hankar, for whom he designed a splendid poster that plays with the tools of the architect's trade, including the T-square and the plumb line. His other posters attest to a strictly symmetrical art nouveau style. Belgium was enjoying an economic boom and was an important player in international affairs: its industrialists and tradesmen were dynamic and ambitious, and many of them appealed to advertising in order to build up their empires – Delacre Biscuits, Jacqmotte Coffee and the Delhaize chain of shops were only three among many.

Georges Privat-Livemont dominated the advertising scene and was the alter ego of Alphonse Mucha in every respect apart from being his disciple – his earliest poster dates from 1890, five years before Mucha's. To the reds and ochres that made up Mucha's warm palette, he added greens and blues that created a colder impression. He used a double line of black and white to outline his images, and yet his touch remained light. He often preferred to depict his subjects in profile. Finally, his approach to his female subjects was more Symbolist than Mucha's. He worked in every cultural domain, including a poster for the fifth annual exhibition of the Cercle Artistique de Schaerbeek, as well as for products as varied as Robette Absinthe, the Bec Auer (a light fitting incorporating an incandescent burner) and Bitter Oriental, three of his undisputed masterpieces. And he also worked for the press in the guise of *La Réforme*. In 1902 and 1903 he additionally designed the poster for the Salon of the Automobile Club of France.

Henri Meunier made his name with a radically different style that drew on Japanese and minimalist elements and incorporated flat tones. Time seems to stand still in his posters for Dietrich postcards and for the Ÿsaÿe Quartet. For the Rajah Café he chose an approach closer to art nouveau, with a background comprised of a single flat tint but designed with extraordinary elegance.

Henri Meunier, 1898

Henri Meunier, 1896

Henri Meunier, 1899

Henri Cassiers, 1898

Émile Berchmans, 1900

Armand Rassenfosse, 1910

Auguste Donnay, 1897

Armand Rassenfosse, 1899

Émile Berchmans, 1896

For Pepinster Chocolatiers he used a contrast between the dominant yellow and the blue of the pot and cup and of the cloud of aroma that holds the viewer's attention. His poster for Starlight Soap is delicately outlined and has a pictorial poetry all of its own.

Victor Mignot was another artist who developed a very individual style. Each of his posters conveys a riotous sense of movement, with the main figure in the foreground, while the other figures that are arranged behind it, together with the typography, causing the viewer's eyes to spin, while still attracting our attention and never losing their legibility. Here one thinks above all of Berton Champagne, Léon Mans Cycles and *The Record*.

Léon Dardenne was also a prolific poster artist, even if his style was more conventional. Georges Gaudy specialized in bicycle posters. Henri Cassiers was closely associated with American Line and with the illustrations for Émile Verhaeren's *Toute la Flandre*.

'And now we need to speak of the triumphant triumvirate of Liège,' Alexandre Demeure de Beaumont struck a note of enthusiasm in describing what he called 'the three musketeers who are actually four':[4] Émile Berchmans, Auguste Donnay, Armand Rassenfosse and the Imprimerie Bénard. He was right to include Bénard, since the printer's influence is clear from the work of each of the three artists, notably in their use of half-tones.

Rassenfosse was a disciple of the great lithographer Félicien Rops, who exerted a formative influence on his career.[5] One of the first artists to devote himself to the poster in Belgium, he has been described by Yolande Oostens-Wittamer as 'an engraver to the very depths of his soul and yet one who remained sensitive to half-tones highlighted by insistent or spontaneous strokes'.[6] His favourite subject was a woman adapted to suit the product that was being advertised – not that this precluded the use of flat tones or even a bold outline, as in his poster for the *Tournoi de lutte de Liège* (Tournament of Liège).

Berchmans designed over seventy posters and was the most political of this group of artists. His women extend from a poetical evocation, as in *The Fine Art and General Insurance Company Limited*, to family scenes as in *Starlight Soap*, but they also include boldly outlined portraits as in his poster for Bock de Koekelberg and a more monumental style reserved for official occasions.

Donnay, finally, was less prolific and more skilful in his use of the art of suggestion: hands running over printed sheets for Imprimerie Liégeoise or hands that are tightly clenched while snatching a box from the flames of a fire, as in his poster for The Fine Art and General Insurance Company Limited. Between these two extremes, he played with outlines and with colour.

Henry van de Velde, who in 1899 left for Weimar to found a school of decorative art that was one of the precursors of the Bauhaus, had the previous year designed a poster for Tropon foods. By creating a stylized image of the three sparrows that were emblematic of Tropon's brand name and by preserving the curves of art nouveau, he was responsible for masterminding what was to prove a key campaign in the history of advertising. ♣

4. Alexandre Demeure de Beaumont, *L'Affiche belge: Essai critique. Biographie des artistes*, Château de Daussinanges près Clairac, Chez l'auteur, 1897, p.77.
5. They invented a process known as 'Ropsenfosse'.
6. Yolande Oostens-Wittamer, *L'Affiche belge, 1892–1914*, Bibliothèque Royale Albert 1er, Brussels, 1975.

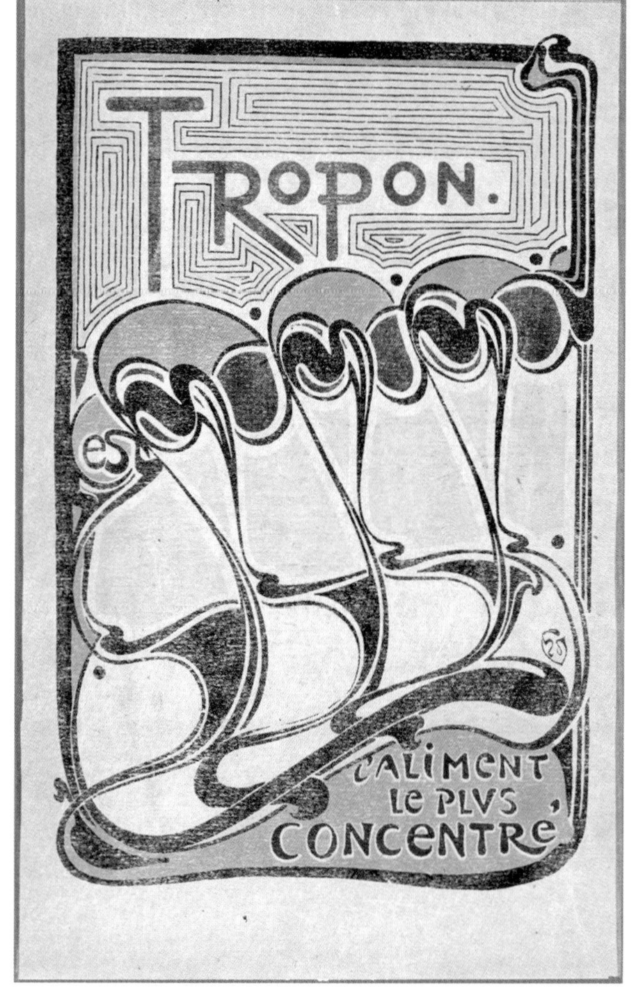

Henry van de Velde, 1898

Jan Toorop, 1895, detail

THE NETHERLANDS

Jan Toorop, 1895

Theodorus Nieuwenhuis, 1893

Johan Thorn Prikker, 1896

With their narrow streets and canals, the towns and cities of the Netherlands were ill suited to encouraging the growth of the large-format poster, and the country's inhabitants had to wait until 1893 to witness the appearance of the first posters worthy of that name. This was the year in which the avant-garde architect Hendrik Petrus Berlage designed a poster for the tramway, its strict symmetry destined to become a characteristic of the Dutch poster in general. Perfectly outlined, the decorative elements are innocent of even a hint of the whiplash curve.

That same year Theo Nieuwenhuis designed a strange poster for a make of cooking oil, Delftsche Slaolie, a bizarre composition of bottles bathed in yellow and adopting the same principle of symmetry as that found in Berlage's poster. The result might almost be a Rorschach test.

In 1895, for the same advertiser, Jan Toorop designed the first Dutch poster to become known and acknowledged abroad. Toorop was born on the island of Java, becoming a member of the Libre Esthétique in Brussels in 1888 and soon gaining recognition as a major artist. His hybrid style comprising whiplash curves and Indonesian marionettes was visually stunning. With the passage of time, it was a style that grew more austere, while also embracing the most striking colours, notably in his 1900 poster for the Tourist Association in the coastal town of Katwijk aan Zee.

Another strange poster was designed in 1896 by Johan Thorn Prikker, a terrifying representation of the crucified Christ for the journal *L'Art appliqué* that seems to reflect a very strange concept of advertising.

That same year, 1896, also witnessed the appearance of a great commercial poster designer, Johann Georg van Caspel, whose perfect mastery of colour, often in the form of flat tones, was combined with a subtle use of outline to produce a series of masterpieces that includes posters for Karstel Cocoa, *De Hollandsche Revue*, Wilhelm Ivens's photographic studio in Nijmegen and Hinde-Rywielen Cycles. His characters are even depicted smiling.[1] Another artist working in the same vein was Georg Rueter.

Jacques Zon, to whom Delftsche Slaolie entrusted its advertising in 1898, was another leading exponent of the floral art nouveau style, his typical female figures manifestly inspired by Mucha and Georges Privat-Livemont.

1. Caspel rightly found a place in the pantheon of Roger Marx's *Les Maîtres de l'affiche* with plate 240, the last in the volume for 1900.

Two other minor artists left a handful of successful designs: Carel Adolph Lion Cachet with his silhouette for Boele Cigars and Theodorus Molkenboer with his wood engraving of the Amsterdam bookbinder Elias P. van Bommel, who is depicted in profile.

Albert Hahn was an excellent poster designer notable for his political commitment (*Fatum* and *Stemt Rood*). As was the case with many other countries, the Netherlands' brief flirtation with the commercial art poster barely survived the turn of the century, although Chris Lebeau, Adriaan Roland Holst and Antoon Molkenboer helped to extend the lifespan of the art nouveau theatre poster through their rigorous symmetry and limited use of colour, a development continued by Jacob Jongert after the war. Bart van der Leck's 1914 poster for the Batavier Line from Rotterdam to London opened the way for a new vision that was to become that of De Stijl. ♣

Johann Georg Van Caspel, 1899

Roland Holst, 1919

Albert Hahn, 1912

Jacques Zon, *c.* 1898

Theodorus H. Molkenboer, 1897

Beggarstaff Brothers, 1894, detail

GREAT BRITAIN

Dudley Hardy, 1894

The art poster took its time to reach Great Britain, but when it did, the exhibition by the dealer and collector Edward Bella at the Royal Aquarium in 1894 was a revelation for Londoners. Bill-sticking had been chaotic until then, but now things moved very quickly. The Advertising Stations Rating Bill of 1889 had laid down the rules for outside advertising and regulated the purchase of reserved sites, leading to a considerable reduction in the number of companies. But one positive consequence was the standardization of formats. The basic size was the double crown,[1] the size used for theatre advertising. The market was dominated by the company David Allen & Sons, which had been founded in Belfast in 1857, soon establishing offices in London and Manchester and, briefly, in New York and Melbourne, controlling the whole network of printers, where it had artists under contract, and also supplying its major clients, the theatres. It controlled 75 per cent of the market.

David Allen & Sons also had its own team of bill-stickers with a large number of hoardings at its disposal and it printed what were called 'stock posters', on which touring companies could insert their names, together with the place and date of their provincial tours. Their main rival was Weiner, which controlled the Viennese market but which was also a presence in Paris and London with a catalogue of more than 500 stock posters.

Even so, the situation in London was very different from the one in Paris. In his seminal *Book of the Poster*,[2] W.S. Rogers offers a number of reasons for this disparity, foremost of which, in his view, were the climatic conditions and pollution – London's famous fog – that persuaded poster artists to use strong and vivid tones – 75 per cent of British posters were printed in colours in which reds and yellows predominated. The second reason, Rogers believed, was that British poster artists rarely drew their designs direct on the stone, preferring to leave that task to lithographic draughtsmen.[3] And printers did not lavish the same degree of care on commercial work as they did on a work of art.[4]

Finally – and with the exception of Aubrey Beardsley and the Beggarstaffs, who were superior artists, if marginal ones – Rogers considered that the best English poster artists did not have the genius of their Gallic counterparts. The subtleties of tone, the rendering and the colours of French *affichistes* were incomparable, but they had the stature of true artists, and they paid themselves accordingly, which was clearly not to the liking of British advertisers. If we add a Victorian puritanism, then we shall understand why Great Britain was not the country of choice for the artistic poster. As a result the British ignored two exceptionally talented artists who merely served to demonstrate the truth of the adage that a prophet is not without honour, save in his own country.

Beardsley's meteoric career ended with his death on the Riviera at the age of twenty-five. Although a marginal figure, he none the less revolutionized the English theatre poster. His 1894 poster for the Avenue Theatre was a bombshell, shattering English conformism and sparking a veritable scandal. Writing in 1908, Julius Meier-Graefe[5] described Beardsley as one of the 'Superboys' and recalled discovering the artist's work in London: 'Of a hundred important artists born within so many years, a certain number are indispensable [...] because they affect their age and because they are symbolical of ourselves [...] and to have seen every one of [Beardsley's] fragments is a more urgent necessity than to know a single picture by Burne-Jones or Watts'.[6] Beardsley achieved instant notoriety with his illustrations to Oscar Wilde's *Salome* (1894) and with his work on *The Yellow Book* and, later, on *The Savoy*.

As early as 1895, Marion Harry Spielmann had offered a perceptive account of Beardsley's position in an article on 'Posters and Poster-Designing in England', hailing him as 'a draughtsman of weird and singular power, who, after importing into his art elements so suggestively opposite as his distorted echoes of Chinese or Annamite execution and Rossettian feeling, seen with a squinting eye, imagined with a Mephistophelian brain, and executed with a vampire hand, showed a deep natural instinct for the beauty of line, for the balance of chiaroscuro, and for decorative effect.'[7]

1. The double crown measured 50.8 x 76.2cm/20 x 30in.
2. W.S. Rogers, *A Book of the Poster*, London, Greening & Co., 1901.
3. This practice also existed in France, but the big names also worked closely with the printers and kept a far closer eye on the workers.
4. But posters cost far less – nothing ever comes free.
5. The great German critic who founded *Pan* in Berlin and the Maison Moderne in Paris and who was an avid traveller.
6. See Julius Meier-Graefe and others, *Modern Art: Being a Contribution to a New System of Aesthetics*, 2 vols, G.P. Putnam's Sons, New York, 1908, vol. 2, p.253.
7. M.H. Spielmann, 'Posters and Poster-Designing in England', in Arsène Alexandre and others, *The Modern Poster*, Scribner, New York, 1895, pp.33–67, esp. p.57; Spielmann's piece had already appeared under the same title in *Scribner's Magazine*, 18/1 (July 1895), 34–47, esp. 44.

Aubrey Beardsley, 1894

Also in 1895 Charles Hiatt recalled the effect produced by Beardsley's work: 'Nothing so compelling, so irresistible had ever been posted on the hoardings of the metropolis before. Some gazed at it with awe, as if it were the final achievement of modern art; others jeered at it as a palpable piece of buffoonery: everybody, however, from the labourer hurrying in the dim light of the morning to his work, to the prosperous stockbroker on his way to the "House," was forced to stop and look at it. Hence, it fulfilled its primary purpose to admiration; it was a most excellent advertisement.'[8] With only three colours and flat tones, Beardsley created a masterpiece. His few other posters were constructed along similar lines, while in terms of his design he had a considerable influence on the American artist William H. Bradley as well as on the Viennese Secessionists.

James Pryde and William Nicholson were brothers-in-law who traded under the name of the Beggarstaff Brothers. Their principal inspiration was Henri de Toulouse-Lautrec. Interviewed by *The Idler* in January 1896, they replied: 'One man we admire, and that is Lautrec. He is one of the few artists who understand what a poster is and should be.' They also studied Japanese fabrics and engravings. Their approach – the 'lost outline' – was nothing if not original, as Nicholson explained with typical British understatement: 'We cut 'em out of paper. Outlines, y'know. Terrific size. Then we walked round and had a look at it, t'see whether we'd alter the colours. So much easier with coloured papers than paints.' But the Beggarstaffs denied that they were no more than a pair of merry andrews. As Pryde explained: 'People are rather prone to imagine that, because a thing looks easy when finished, it must have been easy to do, but I can assure you that, although our posters have been criticised by purchasers in an off-handed manner, as "simple as a child's drawing", it has taken all the artistic knowledge which Nicholson and I have been able to gain to produce the results which you see.'[9]

At the poster exhibition organized by Edward Bella at the Royal Aquarium in 1894, they presented four

8. Charles Hiatt, *Picture Posters*, G. Bell, London, 1895, p.220.

9. The first part of the quotation comes from a brief memoir of William Nicholson published in *Postscript to Image* in 1949 and reproduced by Colin Campbell, *The Beggarstaff Posters*, Barrie & Jenkins, London, 1990, p.112; the remainder of the quotation is from 'Arcades Ambo: The Beggarstaff Brothers at Home', originally published in *The Idler* in January 1896, reprinted in *The Journal of the Decorative Arts Society*, 2 (1976), 44–50; and in Campbell, *The Beggarstaff Posters*, pp.113–15.

Aubrey Beardsley, 1894

Beggarstaff Brothers, 1895

Beggarstaff Brothers, 1894

projects that had no brand names attached to them but which they offered to advertisers. As Charles Hiatt noted: 'The Beggarstaff's showed four posters which advertised Nobody's Blue, Nobody's Candles, Nobody's Niggers, and Nobody's Pianos. If each "Nobody" is not rapidly converted into "Somebody," the various manufacturers and proprietors of the articles mentioned above much be very stupid people.'[10] Evidently they *were* very stupid since not one of their posters was sold.

The Beggarstaff Brothers' brief career lasted from 1894 to 1899 and was a series of disillusionments. After a diffident *Hamlet* for a touring production starring Gordon Craig, their poster for a stage production of *Don Quixote* at the Lyceum remained at the planning stage.[11] It was only when they finally appealed to an agent in 1896 that they were able to design a poster for Rowntree's Elect Cocoa that was widely distributed. There followed a poster for *Cinderella* at Drury Lane but *A Trip to Chinatown* was ruined by terrible typography, while their Beefeater poster found few takers and was finally printed by *Harper's Magazine* in an edition intended only for collectors.

10. Hiatt, *Picture Posters* (note 9), p.232.
11. Margaret Timmers, *The Power of the Poster*, V&A Publications, London, 1999, p.43.

But as deplorable as their professional success may have been, the Beggarstaff Brothers exerted a tremendous influence on foreign artists. Six of their posters – practically their entire production – were reproduced in Roger Marx's *Les Maîtres de l'affiche*. As a result it was in continental Europe that the Beggarstaffs received the recognition they deserved, for all that it came too late. The lost outline exerted a major influence on the whole of Europe. Ludwig Hohlwein used it regularly, as did the Polish-born artist Franz Laskoff. The Vienna Secession was clearly aware of developments in Britain, and when it organized its exhibitions in Vienna, it extended invitations to architects from the Glasgow School, including Herbert McNair and Charles Rennie Mackintosh, whose posters were no less revolutionary.

By contrast, the Arts & Crafts movement exerted little influence. A follower of William Morris, Walter Crane designed a handful of historicist posters but his

Beggarstaff Brothers, 1895

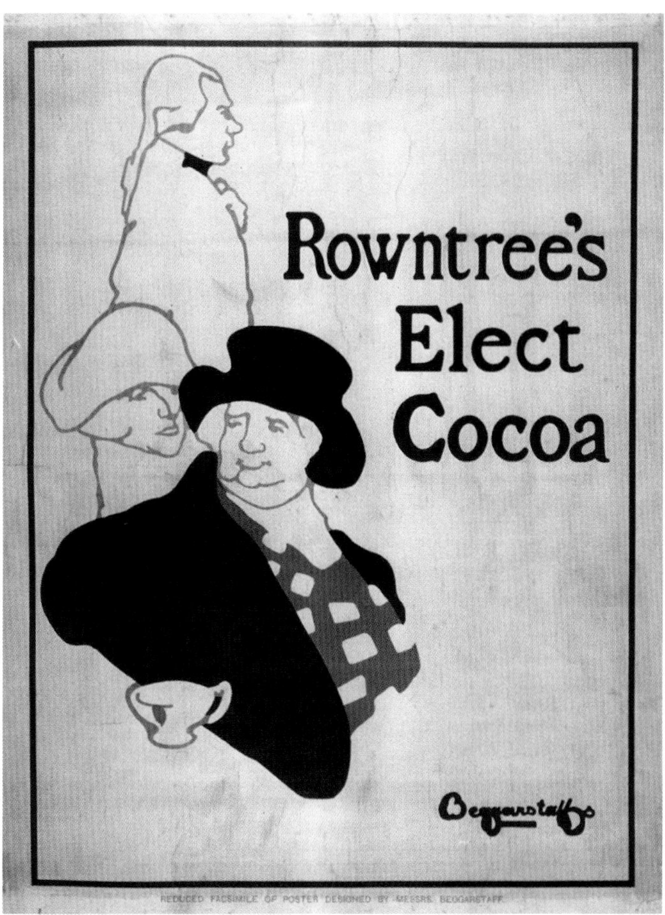

Beggarstaff Brothers, 1896

A. S. Forrest, 1898

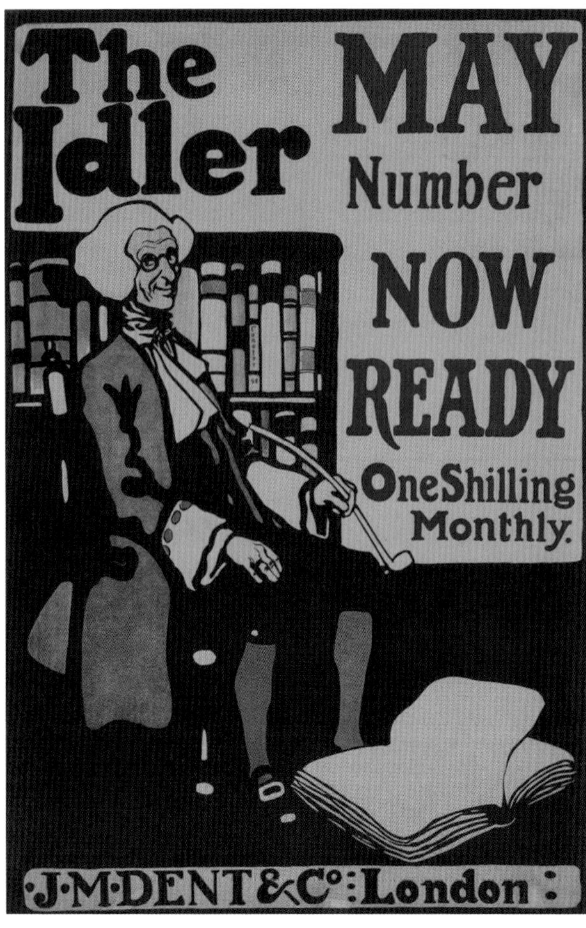

Edward Gordon Craig, 1898

Mosnar Yendis, 1897

Leonard Raven-Hill, 1894

Dudley Hardy, 1894

underlying thinking was clear: 'I fear [...] that there is something essentially vulgar about the idea of the poster unless it is limited to simple announcements of directions, or becomes a species of heraldry or sign-painting.'[12] Behind Crane's comment lies the Arts & Crafts' characteristic refusal to engage with the world of commerce and industry.

Theatres adopted the double-crown format and relied on good printers, remaining loyal to the best artists, giving rise to the true English poster. Two artists in particular played a key role in this development: Dudley Hardy and John Hassall. Two figures more remote from the inner circle of the art nouveau movement would be hard to imagine. 'They had similar temperaments,' wrote Bevis Hillier. 'Heavily moustached, boozy and ribald, they had the air of officers recently risen from the ranks. [...] On pier-ends they had their pictures taken together on the popular "tin-types", sticking their beaming faces through pictures of ballet-dancers and nannies. They rode about in pony gigs, sporting straw hats like those worn by Edwardian murderers and pork butchers in modern stage productions. They drank themselves silly in Paris cafés, sang in lusty baritones and roistered along the boulevards.'[13]

Hardy and Hassall were characters straight out of Jerome K. Jerome, who was in fact one of their friends and instrumental in helping Hardy to achieve success by asking him to design a poster for his magazine *To-Day*. Hardy's first poster – *A Gaiety Girl* – dates from 1893 and clearly reflects the influence of Jules Chéret, while reducing to a minimum the artistic effects employed: minimal colours, a splash of red for the dress, touches of black, and no background. Only the face reveals any degree of detail, suggesting that it is lit from below by the stage footlights. The poster is simple and effective – and it proved successful. But Hardy's real triumph came with his *Yellow Girl*, constructed along similar lines and depicting a radiant young woman dressed in yellow.

Hardy's biographer, Alfred Edwin Johnson, writes as follows about the poster: 'The effect was startling, and no advertisement ever achieved its purpose more simply or more completely. The Yellow Girl refused to be ignored. There was something almost immodest in the way she danced, with mincing steps, along the decorous streets of London.'[14]

These were Hardy's best posters, although he enjoyed a long career, producing designs for the theatre – he was under contract to the Savoy and to the printers Waterlow

12. Walter Crane quoted in Spielmann, 'Posters and Poster-Designing in England' (note 8), p.65.
13. Hillier, *Posters* (note 9), pp.82–3.
14. Alfred Edwin Johnson, *The Book of Dudley Hardy*, A & C. Black, London, 1909 quoted by Hillier, *Posters* (note 9), p.98.

Dudley Hardy, 1894-1895

John Hassall, 1898

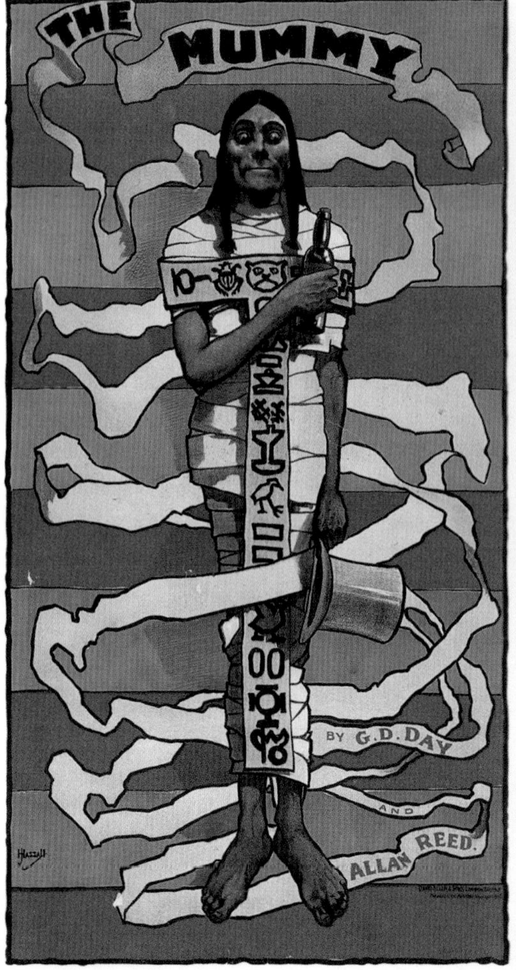

John Hassall, 1898

John Hassall, 1897

John Hassall, *c.* 1893

& Sons – as well as for major clients like Liebig. He was at his happiest depicting a single figure, proving less adept at group compositions. Ultimately he was the link between the French art poster and a new and totally British approach using a practically non-existent background, a mere handful of details, bright colours, a marked outline and integrated typography. His posters had everything that was needed to create an impression and, crucially, did not require the assistance of skilled lithographers. The uncontested master of the genre was Hardy's friend John Hassall, whom he initially influenced.

Bevis Hillier, as always accurate in his assessment, admits that Hassall may not have been a great artist but that he was undeniably a man of genius.

After leading a life of adventure, including a spell spent as a farmer in Manitoba in western Canada, and studies in Antwerp and Paris, Hassall experimented with painting but the results were mediocre. He tried his hand at magazines before answering a small ad from David Allen & Sons. Turning up for the interview with nothing to show, he was asked to produce a sketch that became the poster for the play *The French Maid*. Sensing his talent, they offered him a seven-year contract, marking the start of a prolific career that is believed to have produced as many as 600 posters. Far more skilful and inventive than Hardy, he used uniform backgrounds, clearly outlined designs and flat tones. His theatre posters extend from a single rabbit sitting on its haunches against a yellow background for *The Wild Rabbit* to a well-characterised couple for *Poppy and Her Trainer: The Sporting Girl*, the couple in question being drawn in profile against a uniform background of grass, with only a sliver of sky visible in the distance. It is here that the horses can be seen racing, providing a touch of genius. His poster for *Little Bo-Peep* is a little gem of harmony, while his stock poster for a touring production of *Cinderella* depicting the heroine descending a flight of stairs is simply stunning. He was supremely adept at reproducing the movements of a crowd, notably in *How London Lives* and *Beeston Tyres*. In short, Hassall never ceased to reinvent himself. When tackling advertising, he abandoned his flat images and instead constructed readily intelligible and effective posters whose starting point was an eye-catching and amusing idea, then using the interplay of light and shade to produce a sense of perspective. His most famous poster is for the coastal

John Hassall, 1896

resort of Skegness. Designed in 1909, it represents a jolly fisherman skipping along the beach and enjoying the bracing the sea air. Hassall influenced almost everyone who came after him and had two disciples: Cecil Aldin, who drew gentleman farmers and fox hunters and who, like Hassall, designed an advertisement for Colman's Mustard, and Will Owen. But he also left his mark on the work on Will True and George Scotson Clark.

A handful of book illustrators also designed the odd poster, including A.S. Forrest for *The Idler*, Edward Gordon Craig for *The Dome* and Lewis Baumer for *Pall Mall* magazine and *Punch*, while Leonard Raven-Hill and Phil May produced amusing cartoons. Alec Ritchie designed a number of highly original posters from which he removed every unnecessary decorative element and positioned his figures like cut-outs. Hal Hurst and Frank Chesworth opted for a floral art nouveau style.

For his automobile and bicycle posters W.S. Rogers created feminine figures who have a Gallic grace to them, whereas their flat tones and outlines are English in style. No less English is Mosnar Yendis – a reverse spelling of the artist's real name, Sidney Ransom – and the same is true of his sense of humour as illustrated by his designs for *The Poster* and for the Szalay Home Trainer.

By the early years of the twentieth century the French model was already moribund, leaving Britain to set an example to the rest of the world.

The critics and collectors who dominated the world of poster art during the 1890s were French and hence chauvinistic or at the very least Francophile where foreign artists were concerned. For them, the only good posters were art posters signed by the artist who in that way gave himself the credentials of a truly creative individual.

As a result they were happy to co-opt to their pantheon figures such as Beardsley and the Beggarstaffs, all of whom were held in high regard. But with their distorted view of the subject, *affichomanes* judge a poster by reference to its decorative effect, evidently convincing themselves – if they ask the question at all – that it is the value added by a signature that sells the poster in question. This explains why Marx's *Les Maîtres de l'affiche* reproduces six posters by the Beggarstaff Brothers – a huge number – and five by Dudley Hardy, whose affinities with Chéret were bound to render him sympathetic. And yet there are none by John Hassall, which is certainly not an accident. He was regarded as not sufficient of an artist, while his stylistic approach, entirely different from all that was being practised on the Continent at this time, was undoubtedly disturbing. The golden age of the French poster was well and truly over.

That great collector Lluís Plandiura bought many of Hassall's posters and, significantly, invited him to design the poster for the great exhibition that he organized in Barcelona in 1901. It was an invitation that marked the definitive end of French hegemony in the field of the poster. Ludwig Hohlwein had said very clearly that it was during a visit to London that he encountered a genuine influence – in the introduction to the study that he devoted to Hohlwein, Hermann Karl Frenzel spoke of the style of the 'sober' British who had supplanted the French in public esteem.

In Germany and the whole of central Europe, as well as in the Nordic countries where the poster developed rather later, it was the English model that triumphed. Idolized by collectors, the art poster now gave way to the modern poster that was placed in the service of advertisers. ❧

John Hassall, 1901

John Hassall, *c.* 1898

John Hassall, *c.* 1899

Dudley Hardy

William Henry Bradley, 1895, detail

UNITED STATES OF AMERICA

William Henry Bradley, 1895

Joseph J. Gould Jr, 1896

Edward Penfield, 1896

William L. Carqueville, 1895

Before 1900 there was no connection between the American poster and its European counterpart. As W.S Rogers noted in 1901, 'It is the country of big things'.[1] It was also the country of Phineas Barnum. Writing in *The Poster* in 1898, the English impresario Charles Cochran recalled that 'Seven years ago, when I first visited America, I was struck with the horrors that looked down upon one from the hoardings. The huge theatrical posters, although beautifully printed, were entirely lacking in taste as regards design and colour.'[2] Other authors agreed on this point. The principal American printers – Currier, Forbes and Strobridge – were all abreast of the latest technology and used the most up-to-date lithographic presses, but their workforce, mostly made up of Germans, was familiar only with popular imagery and with the chromolithograph that was best suited to appealing to a largely illiterate audience. Their major clients were popular shows and miracle cures.

When change came, it came, logically enough, from literary circles in the form of the numerous journals that were appearing in increasing numbers on America's East Coast. Their publishers were fully conversant with all that was happening in Europe and took their cue from that. Theodore Child, *Harper's Magazine*'s Paris correspondent, approached Eugène Grasset – Chéret and Mucha were considered too risqué for puritanical America. From then on Grasset worked regularly for *Harper's Magazine* as well as with one of its rivals, *The Century Magazine*. His 'Wooly Horse' – so called on account of its luxurious mane – had appeared in his Napoleon poster in 1894 and had found an enthusiastic following.[3]

But the true breakthrough came in 1893, when *Harper's Magazine* invited Edward Penfield to design its monthly cover and make a poster out of it, a policy that it pursued for the next six years. Penfield has often – but wrongly – been described as a disciple of Théophile-Alexandre Steinlen. Although both men shared a love of cats, Penfield drew his inspiration, in Charles Matlack Price's view, from Egyptian sarcophagi that he had seen at the Metropolitan Museum of Art in New York, resulting in 'a treatment bold and flat of mass, with cleverly contrasted colors and heavy black outlines'.[4]

1. W.S. Rogers, *A Book of the Poster*, Greening & Co., London, 1901, p.85.
2. Charles B. Cochran, 'Theatrical Posters in America', *The Poster*, 1 (1898), 62–3, esp. 62; see also Charles Matlack Price, *Posters: A Critical Study of the Development of Poster Design in Continental Europe, England and America*, George W. Bricka, New York, 1913, pp.149–227
3. Napoleon was certainly a popular figure. As already observed, *Century Magazine* held a competition in 1895 that was won by Lucien Métivet.
4. Price, *Posters* (note 2), p.231.

Edward Penfield, 1896

Edward Penfield, 1897

Edward Penfield, 1896

Edward Henry Potthast, 1895

Frank Hazenplug, 1895

Louis John Rhead, 1895

Maxfield Parrish, 1897

Ethel Reed, 1895

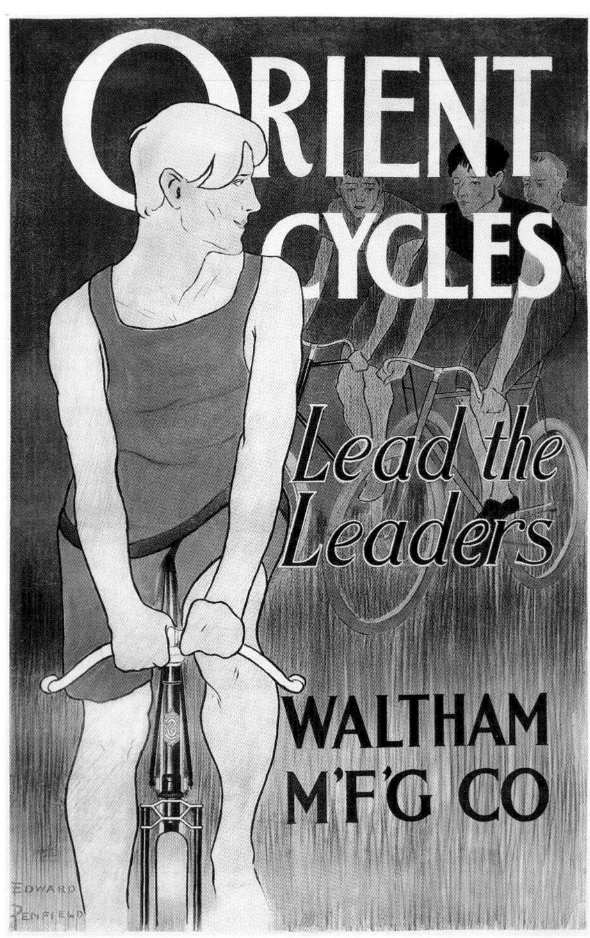

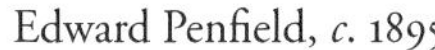

Edward Penfield, *c.* 1895

William Henry Bradley, *c.* 1896

Louis John Rhead, 1895

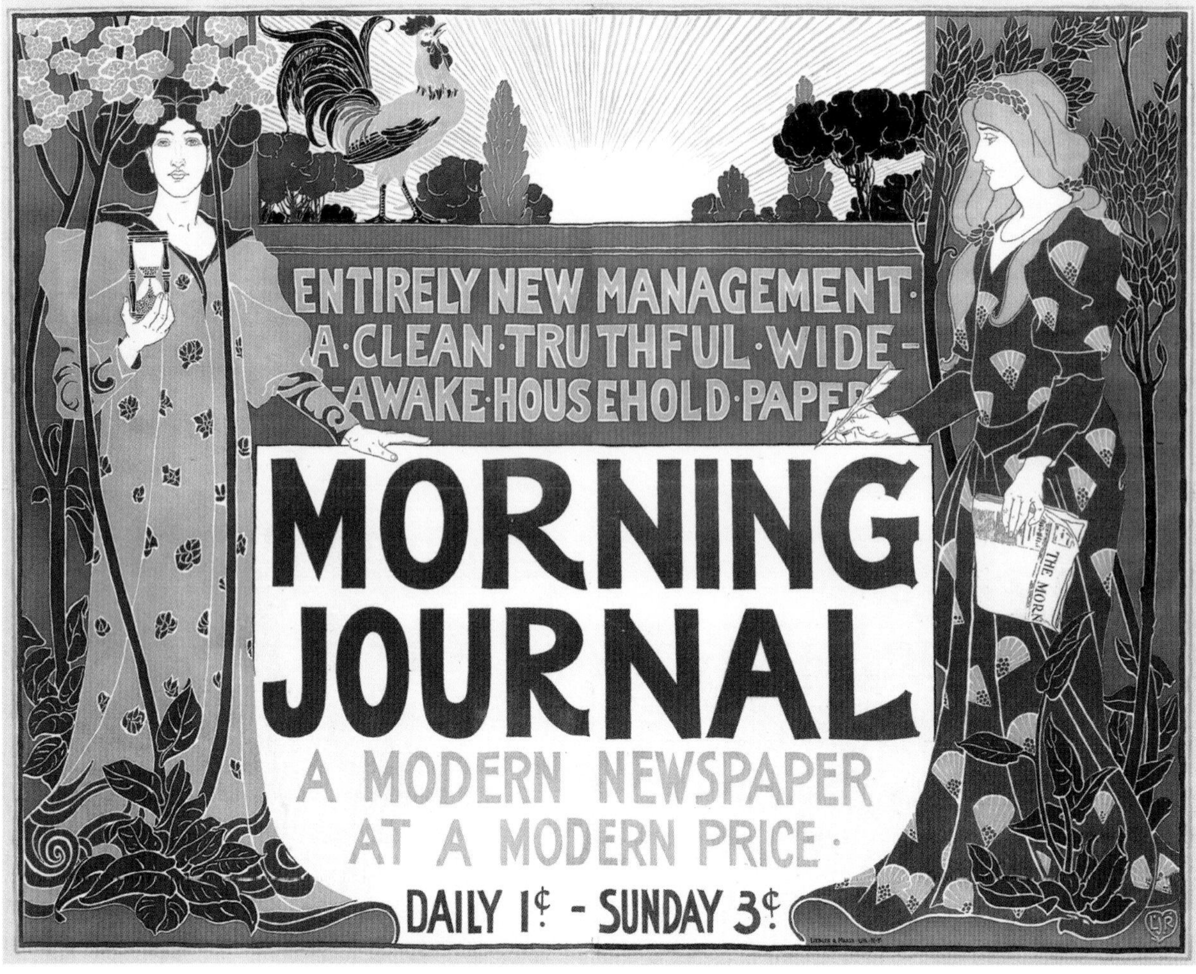

Blanche McManus, 1897

Ethel Reed, 1895

In his Introduction to *Posters in Miniature*, Penfield had written that 'We are a bit tired of the very serious nowadays, and a little frivolity is refreshing'.[5] And yet his images lead us to question the accuracy of this statement, for the figures who people these scene of bourgeois life are rarely seen to be smiling, and if they read, it is merely to dispel their boredom. Joseph J. Gould and William Carqueville were Penfield's respectable disciples. Both men worked for *Lippincott's Magazine*.

The second great American poster artist was William H. Bradley, who was clearly familiar with Beardsley's work.[6] He was a master of the whiplash curve and of cleverly constructed decorative arabesques. His training as a printer enabled him to produce many of his books himself.[7] For *The Chap-Book*, *The Inland Printer* and his own ephemeral *Bradley His Book*, he could switch with remarkable deftness from a somewhat rigid art nouveau style to the sort of exuberance attested by his Twins for *The Chap-Book*, a tribute to Beardsley but lacking the latter's morbidity. His poster *When Hearts are Trumps* is an icon of art nouveau. Frank Hazenplug was one of the artists he influenced.

The third grand master of American poster design was born in Britain: Louis John Rhead arrived in New York in 1883. He designed his first poster in 1890, creating more than a hundred in total and becoming the only Anglo-Saxon graphic artist to be accorded a one-man show at the Salon des Cent in Paris in 1897. While never concealing his debt to Grasset, he shared with his French colleague a vision close to that of William Morris's Arts & Crafts movement and combined a rich palette of warm colours with sophisticated outlines. He was the only designer to be able to insist on large-scale formats for posters advertising *The Sun* and *The Morning Journal*.

Rhead also designed commercial posters advertising Quaker Oats and Lundborg's Perfumes, for example. Only Penfield and Bradley were as successful in persuading advertisers to commission their work, albeit in the much more limited field of bicycles.

For his part, Maxfield Parrish had a very personal style drawing on Pre-Raphaelite symbolism and often featuring naked women in the great outdoors. His posters for *Scribner's* and *The Century Magazine* are striking images that also include photographic elements.

The United States also saw a number of women who managed to break into the profession. For two years Ethel Reed was extraordinarily successful in Boston, designing twenty-four posters, several that are among the very finest, notably mischievous little girls in a floral setting and a woman of great beauty that is undoubtedly a self-portrait. A fascinating and fantastical figure, she left for Europe at the end of 1896 and ended her life in obscurity.

Blanche McManus returned to the United States in 1893 after completing her studies in Paris. She, too, worked for publishers – she is known to have designed at least eight posters – and she, too, returned to Europe, travelling to France in 1900.

Florence Lundborg was the only female poster artist active on America's West Coast, designing a series of posters for the magazine *The Lark* that reveal the influence of the Arts & Crafts movement. She later engraved them on wood, investing them with an unusual quality. After that, she turned to painting.

By 1900 the movement had more or less come to an end, disappearing with the same abruptness as it had appeared and in that respect mirroring developments elsewhere in the world.[8] The bold designs of artists working in a distinctively individual style were no longer felt to be appropriate, and magazines grew tired of publishing posters that gave pleasure merely to collectors, while doing nothing to boost their sales.

The Leyendecker Brothers, Joseph Christian and Frank Xavier, with their spruce young men advertising Arrow Collars and Shirts; Charles Dana Gibson and his Gibson Girl; and Howard Chandler Christy contented themselves with providing blandly beautiful illustrations. The case of James Montgomery Flagg is a good example of this stylistic recidivism. In 1917 he designed both a masterpiece of graphic artifice for his propaganda poster *Wake Up, America!* and a recruitment poster featuring Uncle Sam for *I Want You*, the illustrative realism of which he was to retain for the rest of his career. ☙

5. Percival Pollard, *Posters in Miniature*. With an Introduction by Edward Penfield, R.H. Russell, New York, 1896, unnumbered pages.
6. To Beardsley's basic design he brought a flood of decorative elements.
7. It is worth remembering that small bookshop posters were often run off at the same time as the covers and were left to artisan lithographers.
8. With poster-mania at its height, poster shops and dealers spread to every town and city. Posters became big business, without, however, proving successful in the world of advertising; see Nancy Finlay, 'American Posters and Publishing in the 1890s', *American Art Posters of the 1890s*, ed. David W. Kiehl, The Metropolitan Museum of Art, New York, 1988, pp.45–55, esp. p.51.

Louis John Rhead, 1894

Lafayette Maynard Dixon, 1895

Richard Felton Outcault, 1896

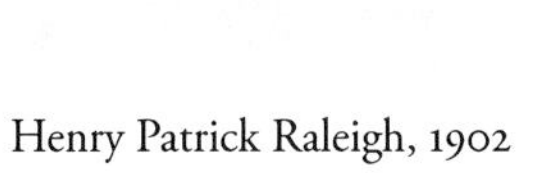

Henry Patrick Raleigh, 1902

S. H. Benson, *c.* 1903

Ferdinand Andri, 1906, detail

AUSTRIA

Koloman Moser, 1908

Gustav Klimt, 1898

Ernst Klimt, 1892

In 1857, in an attempt to underline his status, Emperor Franz Joseph ordered the construction of a ring road – the Ringstraße – around the heart of Vienna. It was to be lined with monumental buildings. Within this circle the commercial poster and the art poster were practically ignored and for a long time were non-existent. In 1897, just before the foundation of the Vienna Secession, Julius Meier-Graefe observed that 'Even more than in Germany, the modern poster is almost entirely missing, and it is very much the exception to the rule when one sees a serious artist apply himself to a task of this kind.' He went on to list Vienna's attractions. Its music, its rich literature, its modern architecture and the Viennese spirit, which he compared to that of Paris, should all have predisposed the Austrian capital to embrace the poster: 'In Berlin the absence of posters is entirely natural, but in Vienna one can only be amazed.' He concluded that 'If Vienna had an art, it would also have Viennese posters.'[1] His prayer was soon to be answered, for in March 1897, the Group of Seven associated with the architect Otto Wagner and including Josef Hoffmann, Joseph Maria Olbrich, Adolf Karpellus, Maximilian Kurzweil and Koloman Moser were joined by dissidents from the Vienna Künstlerhaus. Together with Gustav Klimt, they founded the Secession. In his memoirs, Moser writes that 'In those days the times were not at all favorable for us young people in Austria. Everyone was completely under the spell of the Makart style with its fancy-dress and imitative arts and its dusty bouquets.'[2]

After that, things moved very quickly, and by March 1898 the first exhibition had been held in Vienna that introduced local art lovers to the work of Rodin, Khnopff, Whistler and Puvis de Chavannes. The exhibition poster was the work of Klimt, who, like Franz von Stuck in Munich, found inspiration in Greek mythology, this marking the full extent of his concession to the academicism of the period. His allegorical image depicts Minerva on the right watching over the fight between Theseus and the Minotaur, a symbol easy to decode. Scandal erupted when the censor noticed that Theseus's genitalia were all present and correct, requiring the artist to reposition the trees in order to preserve the Greek hero's modesty. And yet the poster's radically graphic style in general was also found to be shocking, with its uniform background, outlined figures and inventive typography. That same year the Secessionists founded

1. Julius Meier-Graefe, 'Autriche', in Maurice Bauwens and others, *Les Affiches étrangères illustrées*, G. Boudet, Paris, 1897, pp.77–88, esp. pp.77–8.
2. Koloman Moser, 'My Life', in Rudolf Leopold and Gerd Pichler (eds.), *Koloman Moser, 1868–1918*, Prestel, Munich, 2007, pp.14–19, esp. p.14. The piece originally appeared under the title 'Mein Werdegang' in *Velhagen & Klasings Monatshefte*, 31 (1916), 254–62. With his luxurious pictorialism, Hans Makart (1840–84) was the least offensive of the artists associated with the Vienna Künstlerhaus.

Alfred Roller, 1902

Ferdinand Andri, 1906

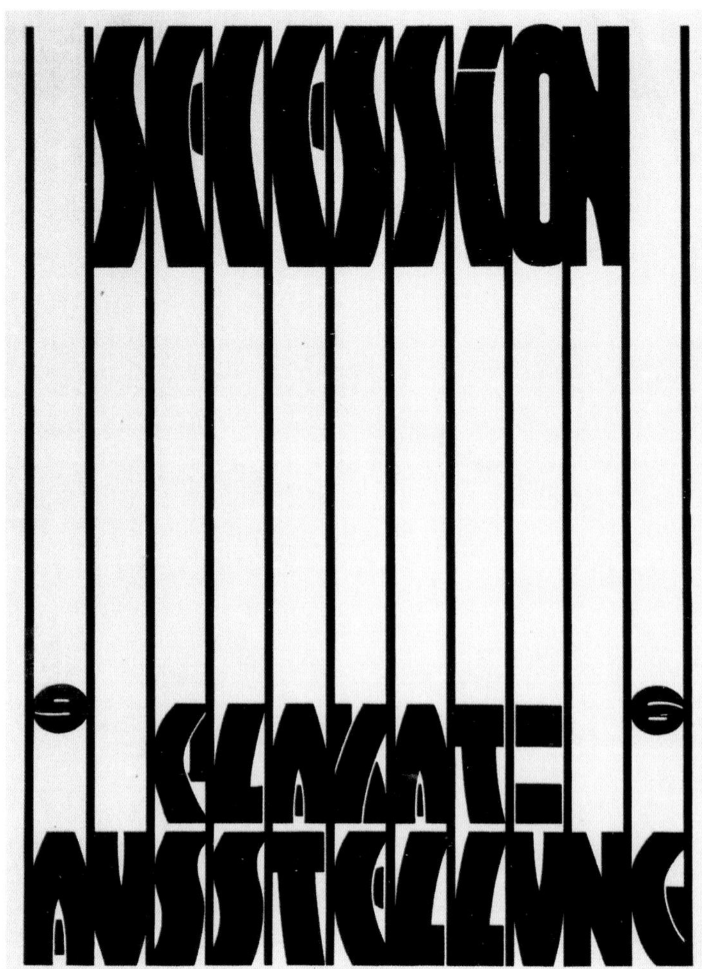

Ernst Eck, 1912

Koloman Moser, 1902

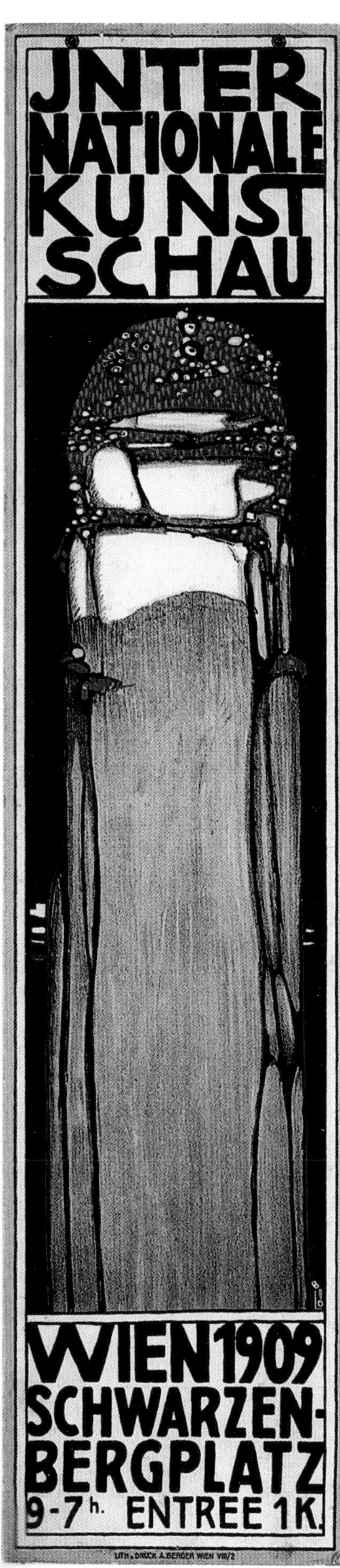

Bertold Löffler, 1909

Ver Sacrum, which contained the first illustration of the movement's geometric tendencies. It was square in format, measuring 29 x 29cm/11.42 x 11.42in. From the outset, it abolished the old hierarchy between the major and minor arts.

It was Olbrich who designed the poster for the Secession's second exhibition, also in 1898. It depicted the Secession building that he himself had designed[3] and where the movement's exhibitions were held, all its members contributing to the installation and to its posters and catalogue as a living example of the total work of art.

3. Miraculously, the building still exists.

The following stage was the creation of the Wiener Werkstätte on which Hoffmann and Moser worked closely together. This was the first time that the ideas associated with the Arts & Crafts movement and of the Glasgow School could be said to have gone into production, with the use of purified geometric forms and of black and white being extended to furniture, to everyday objects, to furnishing fabrics and even to the world of fashion. In this way the Secession played a decisive role in opening up the way to industrial design.

The Secession's influence was all the greater in that Moser, Hoffmann and Alfred Roller all taught at the School of Applied Arts, training generations of students who regarded themselves as decorators or designers first and foremost and whose work was reflected in the pages of publications such as *Die Fläche* and *Die Quelle*.

In the field of the poster, conversely, the Secession was less influential. The curve was soon abandoned. The members of the Secession took turns to design their posters, the most interesting of which predate 1905. Their goal was clearly not to communicate but to display each artist's graphic ingenuity. The distinction between the 'art poster' and the 'poster as such' that was drawn by *Das Plakat* in 1914 could have been devised with the Secession's posters in mind. The Secession chose three tutelary symbols in the form of painting, sculpture and architecture, which are found in Roller's poster for the fourth exhibition and in Moser's for the thirteenth. Elsewhere the geometric stylization increased while the

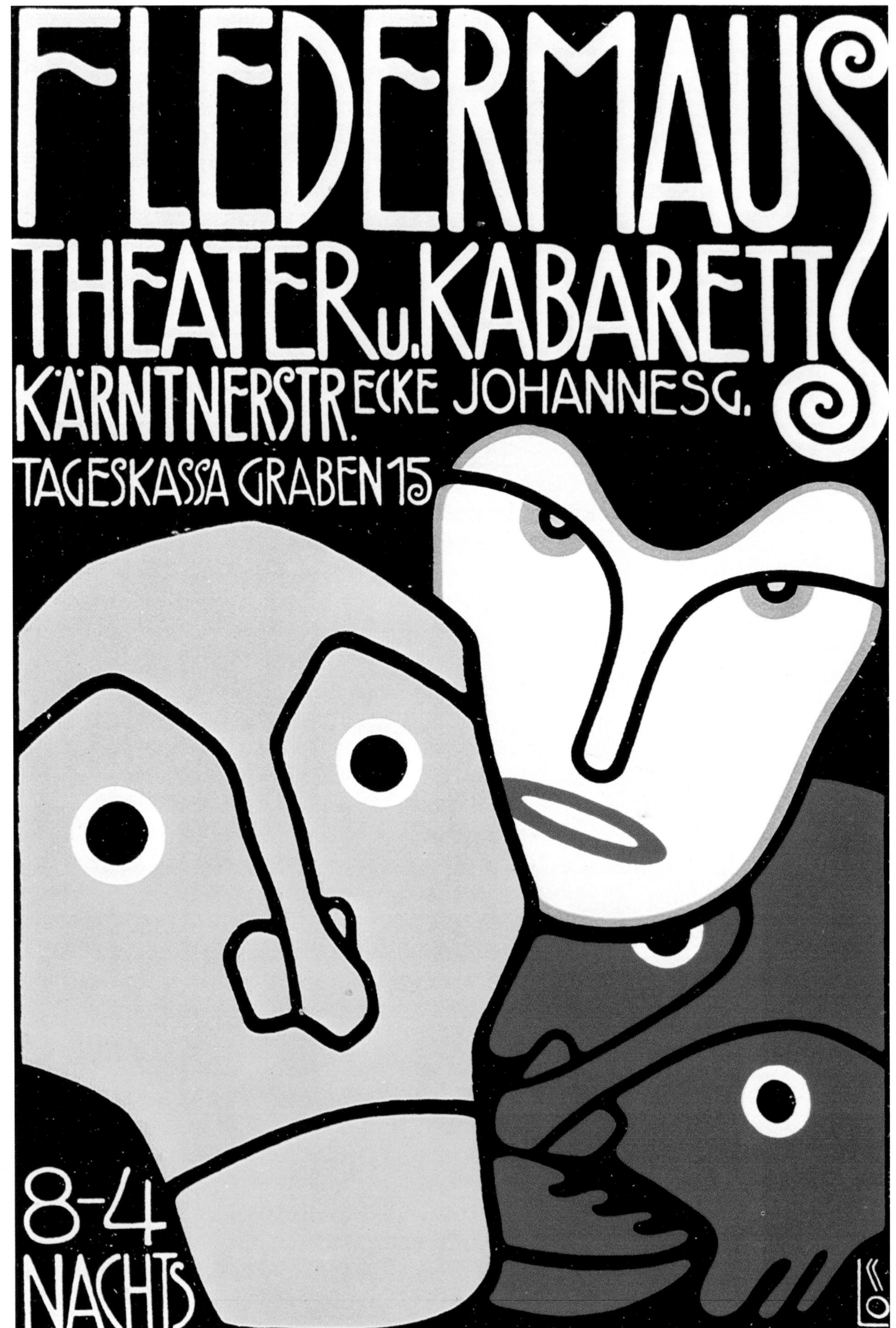

Bertold Löffler, 1907

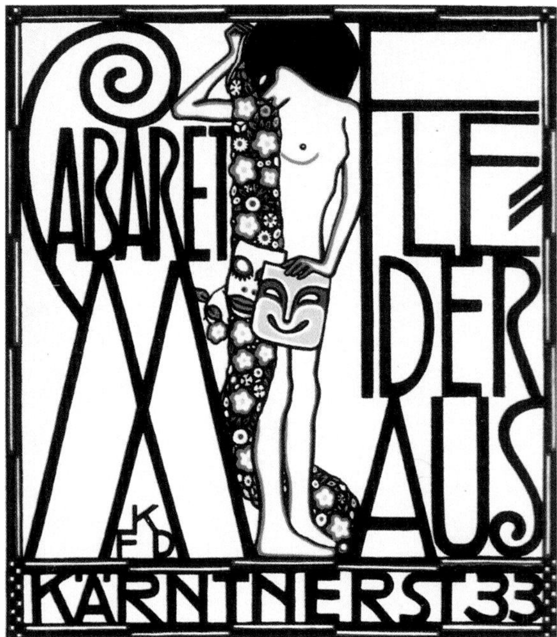

Franz Karl Delavilla, 1907

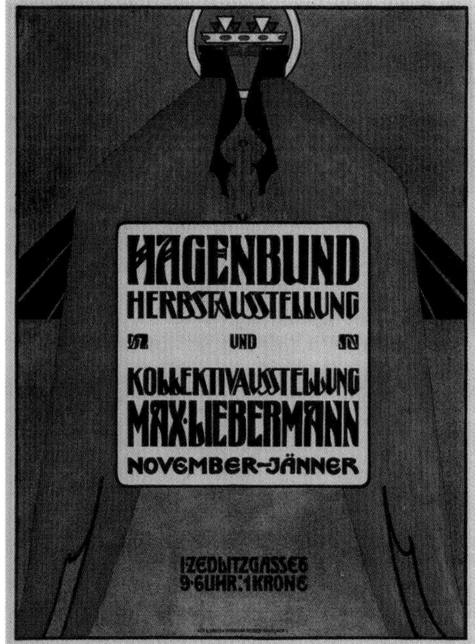

Joseph Urban, 1901

Koloman Moser, 1899

typography became illegible. Esotericism continued to gain ground in the work of both Roller and Ferdinand Andri, both of whom were influenced by the ideas of Rudolf von Larisch, for whom writing was just another decorative element. In spite of this, their posters were – conceptually speaking – the most remarkable. The forty-eighth and last poster was an Expressionist design by Egon Schiele, after which everything fell apart.

For the 1908 exhibition organized to celebrate Franz Joseph's sixtieth jubilee, Bertold Löffler designed a clear and lucid poster notable for its use of bright blue and golden yellow. Rudolf Kalvach designed an Expressionist poster, while that of Oskar Kokoschka was never published. An entire room at the exhibition was devoted to the poster as an art form.

The Hagenbund was a group of moderately modernist artists that was formed at the same time as the Secession, which it survived. The architect Joseph Urban and the painter Heinrich Lefler were two of its driving forces. Lefler's poster for the Auer light fittings was undoubtedly the first and one of the best modernist commercial posters in Vienna.

The Secessionists were certainly able to draw a distinction between 'posters as such', which they designed for their own exhibitions and which were not necessarily easy to decipher, and the ones they intended for a wider public. This was certainly the case with Kolo Moser's 1899 poster for Fromme's Calendar, which is clear and readable, while striking a modern note with its flat tones in heavy outlines. And it was above all the case with the posters intended to promote the Wiener Werkstätte, which were rigorously geometric and a perfect reflection of the product in question. In parallel, the tireless Moser designed sets, costumes and posters for the Jung Wiener Theater. And like all the avant-garde movements of the age, the Secession opened its own cabaret, the Fledermaus, which was decorated by Moser using unmatched ceramic tiles. The programmes were designed by Klimt, Emil Orlík and Kokoschka. Having helped to launch Die Elf Scharfrichter in Munich, its star singer Marya Delvard moved to Vienna in 1907. Löffler designed an extraordinary poster to open the new cabaret: three faces in yellow, white and red. Unfortunately, Franz Karl Delavilla's typography proved to be all but indecipherable. The Viennese spirit lent itself well to the cabaret, and many were opened, most notably the Lucifer, whose poster, designed by Victor Schufinsky, is a masterpiece of its kind.

There were few links between the artists of the Secession and the world of commercial advertising. Kolo

Bertold Löffler, 1908

Oskar Kokoschka, 1908

Egon Schiele, 1918

Josef Maria Auchentaller, 1900

Victor Schufinsky, 1904

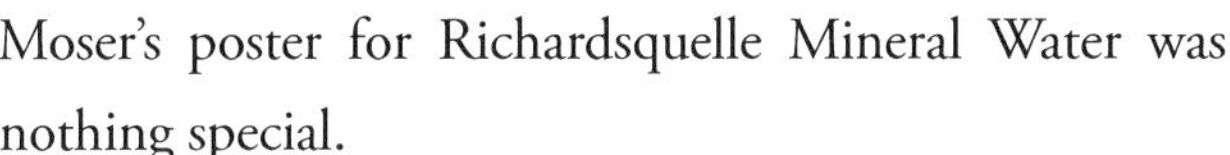

Moser's poster for Richardsquelle Mineral Water was nothing special.

The only member of the Secession to work as a commercial poster artist in Vienna was Josef Maria Auchentaller, who used an understated version of the whiplash curve and demonstrated a perfect mastery of flat tones, heavy outlines and composition. His posters were printed by Weiner, a vast enterprise with offices in London and Paris that held a virtual monopoly of commercial advertising in Vienna, employing numerous lithographic designers who never signed their work. The results could be surprising, as in the case of Vim, which had already established its logo by this date. A handful of poster artists none the less succeeded in making a name for themselves, notably Adolf Karpellus and Emil Ranzenhofer. Two Austrian artists who moved to Berlin, Julius Klinger and Emil Orlík, also designed the occasional poster. ☙

Josef Maria Auchentaller, 1899

Emil Ranzenhofer, 1900

Artur Berger, 1912

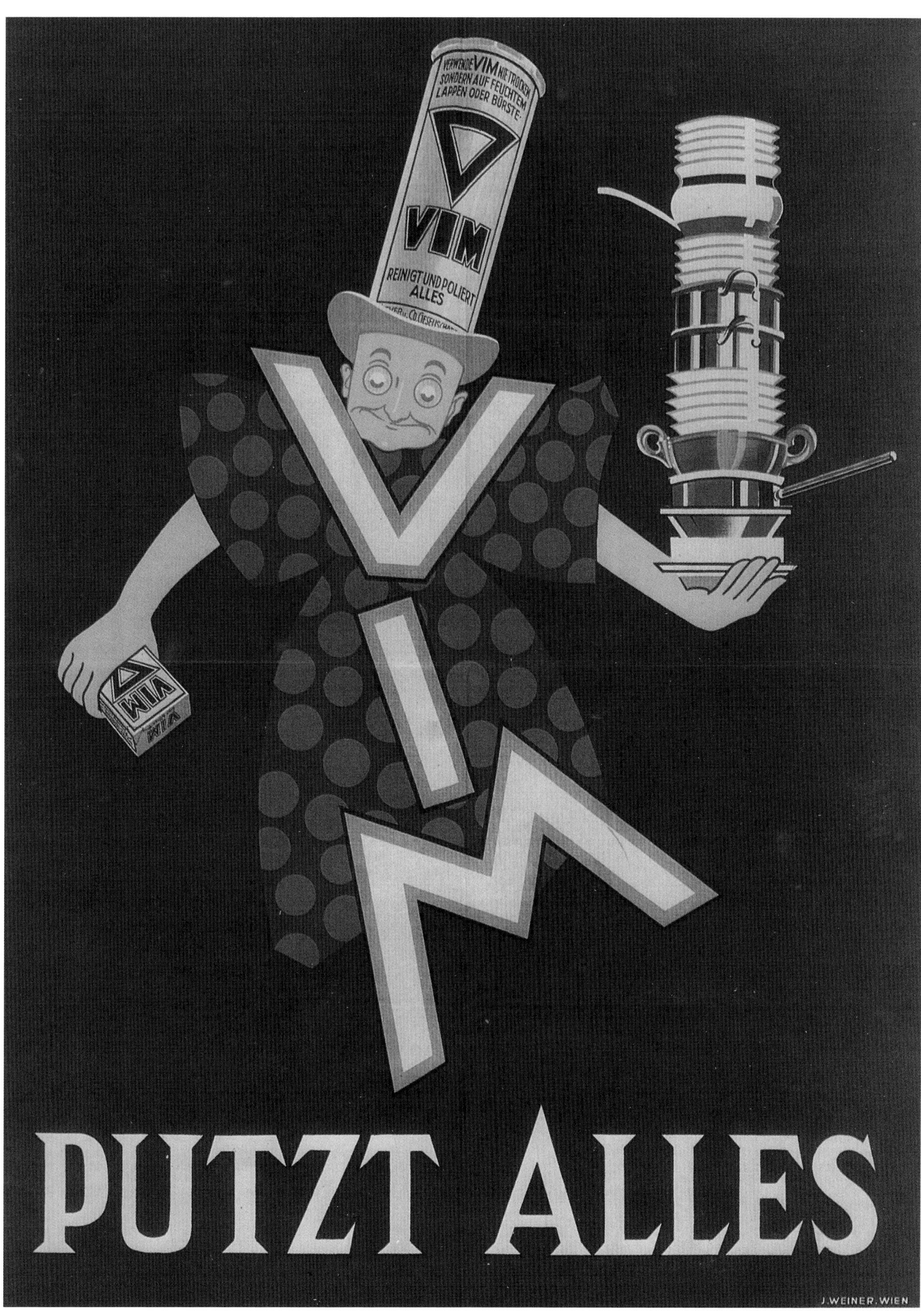

Anonymous, 1904

Julius Klinger, 1913, detail

GERMANY

Julius Klinger, 1911

Posters appeared in Germany relatively late in the development of the medium. This was confirmed by two seminal publications, both dating from 1897: Maurice Bauwens's *Les Affiches étrangères illustrées*, to which Julius Meier-Graefe contributed the chapter on Germany, and Jean Louis Sponsel's *Das moderne Plakat*. For Meier-Graefe, 'It is difficult to speak of the German poster since, strictly speaking, the poster as conceived in France does not exist in Germany.' He went on to deride a poster designed in 1889 by Emil Doepler for the Universal Exhibition for the Prevention of Accidents, noting that 'instead of simple decorative lines we have a mass of trivia, and in place of simple colour contrasts there is a generalized tonality resembling nothing so much as gravy'.[1]

Sponsel offered an apt explanation of the problem, arguing that the Germans, having witnessed the birth of the lithograph and produced a number of major printers, regarded the poster as a simple means of reproduction rather than as a creative medium. The great collector Hans Sachs, who founded the periodical *Das Plakat*, was equally pointed in his criticism: 'Here we still see the old prejudices on the part of the bourgeois against the artist and of the artist against the bourgeois. The bourgeois manufacturer would no more think of having his products promoted by a 'scatter-brained' artist (for a lithographer would certainly work in a finer and more serious way) than an artist of this period would debase his brush by using it for such profane ends.'

Berlin was the city that was the most resistant to the poster. Apart from its advertising columns that were used exclusively to promote spectacles, there was practically no space for commercial advertising, with the result that the earliest moves were made in Dresden, Munich – the 'capital of the arts' – and Hamburg. It was in Hamburg that Adolf Friedländer had made a name for himself designing circus posters since 1872, employing talented draughtsmen such as Christian Bettels who were skilled at drawing animals. Paradoxically, these were undoubtedly the earliest true German posters.

Writing in 1977, Christina Thon pointed out that 'During the 1890s the historicist pastiche was for a long time the general rule, albeit with characteristic distinctions and specializations: for the exhibitions of decorative and artisanal objects, the poster drew for its inspiration on the German Renaissance [...], while for industry, artists had recourse to pseudo-baroque apotheoses capable of being used to highlight the triumph of technology. The posters for the major national and international art exhibitions borrowed their style and thematic language from classical antiquity, this being felt to be a suitable way of underlining the timelessness to which all art should aspire.'[2]

1. Julius Meier-Graefe, 'Allemagne', in Maurice Bauwens and others, *Les Affiches étrangères illustrées*, G. Boudet, Paris, 1897, pp.1–27, esp. p.1 and p.7. As the artistic director of the Berlin-based *Pan* and founder of *Dekorative Kunst* as well as the creator of the Maison Moderne in Paris, Meier-Graefe knew what he was talking about.
2. Christina Thon, 'L'affiche', in Gerhard Bott and Brigitte Tietzel-Hellerforth (eds.), *Jugendstil (Europalia 77)*, Palais des Beaux-Arts, Brussels, 1977, p.274.

Alexander Kips, 1890

F. Döppler, 1889

Thomas Theodor Heine, 1896

Franz von Stuck, 1891

Angelo Jank, 1898

Fritz Dannenberg, 1896

Franz von Stuck's poster for the 1893 Munich Secession exhibition marked a turning point, and while it repeated the Minerva motif – here depicted in profile in mosaic – his treatment was resolutely graphic. This pioneering piece was followed by others by Josef Sattler for *Pan* in 1895, by Fritz Dannenberg for *Jugend* in 1897 and above all by Thomas Theodor Heine for the satirical magazine *Simplicissimus*, also in 1897.

Simplicissimus's publisher, Albert Langen, assembled a team of young artists that included Bruno Paul, Albert Weisgerber, Hans Christiansen, Angelo Jank and Olaf Gulbransson. Heine soon found himself dubbed 'the German Lautrec', which was certainly true of his pre-eminent position within the group. His style was closer to that of the Beggarstaffs: flat tones, often without any outline, to which he added a profoundly German Expressionism. In 1899 he served a six-month prison sentence at Königstein for ridiculing the Kaiser – while there, he briefly overlapped with the dramatist Frank Wedekind, whose work for *Simplicissimus* had likewise caused offence. Thanks not least to the chanteuse Marya Delvard, the cabaret Die Elf Scharfrichter surpassed all of its Gallic models through its sheer expressive vigour.

Otto Fischer, 1896

Hans Unger, 1896

Johann Vincenz Cissarz, 1899

Johann Vincenz Cissarz, 1903

Fritz Rehm, 1896

The commercial poster evolved slowly, and it was in Dresden, where important national and international exhibitions were held, that it took its first and most interesting steps. Otto Fischer started the trend in 1896 with his use of bright colours, bold outlines and a pointillist background to advertise *The Old City*, followed by Wilhelm Hoffmann's *The Art Institute for Modern Posters*, a truly modern poster with its flat tones and bold outlines. Also in Dresden, Fritz Rehm designed an equally modernist poster for Laferme Cigarettes, while Johann Vincenz Cissarz adopted a more synthetic approach in his 1898 poster for Dr Thompson's Laundry Powder. For his 1896 advertisement for Estey Organs, Hans Unger set a Symbolist portrait within a decorative floral frame. These different examples reflect the tremendous creativity that was typical of these independent centres of German art. Last but not least, it was in Dresden that the Expressionist group Die Brücke was founded in 1905.

Ten or so years were to pass before the German poster style found general acceptance, which is to say that Jugendstil was slow to establish itself in a country disinclined to embrace change. The Artists' Colony established by Grand Duke Ernst Ludwig of Hessen in Darmstadt was a step in the right direction. Following the lead taken by the Arts & Crafts movement in Britain, German artists were now resolved to abolish the pastiche and to breathe new life into the decorative arts.

With the exception of the Hanseatic ports that were open to the world, Germany was a petty bourgeois society afraid of things new and foreign. For years, the Wertheim chain of department stores had to contend with a rear-guard action waged by small businesses, quite apart from suffering from the fact that its owners were Jewish. Kaiser Wilhelm was himself an arch-conservative. And yet things took their course. The mother of Grand Duke Ernst Ludwig was daughter of Queen Victoria, and so the anglophile ruler was receptive to the ideas of the Arts & Crafts movement. He invited Joseph Maria Olbrich to help found his Artists' Colony, whose members soon included Peter Behrens and Hans Christiansen. In 1901 its historic exhibition *A Document*

Joseph Maria Olbrich, 1901

Bruno Paul, 1901

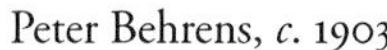
Peter Behrens, *c.* 1903

Fritz Helmuth Ehmcke, 1914

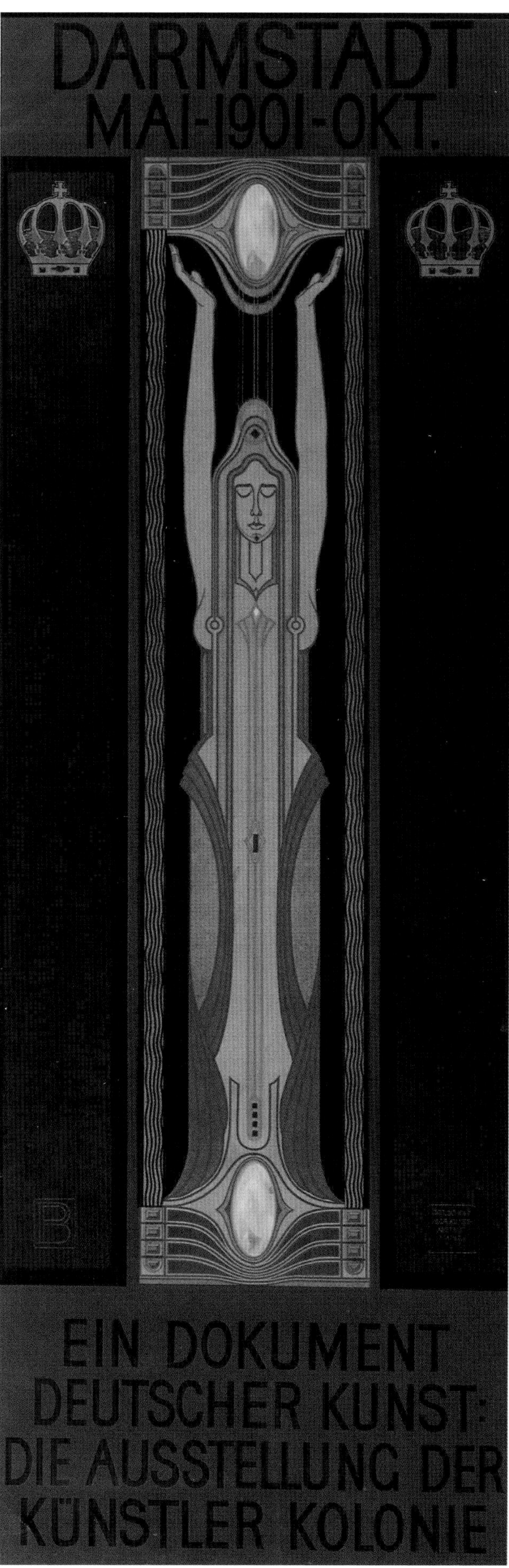

Peter Behrens, 1901

of German Art presented the work of the Colony's artists, work which was clearly modernist in style.

Olbrich based his poster on the one he had designed for the Vienna Secession, while Behrens produced an image in the purest Jugendstil. The local townsfolk would have none of it, but the grand duke ordered a set of new furniture for his official residence. Also in 1901, Bruno Paul designed a poster for the Kunst im Handwerk exhibition in Munich. From then on there were exhibitions in many German towns and cities. The movement had finally been launched.

On the advice of Count Harry Kessler, Wilhelm Ernst of Saxe-Weimar-Eisenach invited Henry van de Velde to Weimar, and although the grand duke withdrew his support for the project in 1908, apparently aghast at his own temerity, van de Velde managed on a shoestring to build a school that prefigured the Bauhaus.

Van de Velde and the architect Hermann Muthesius, who had followed at first hand the growth of the Arts & Crafts movement in England, sprang into action: 'It is clear that machines will one day make good all the misery that they have caused and that they will redress all the wrongs that have been imputed to them. Incapable of choosing, they will give rise to the beautiful as well as to the ugly.' By bringing together the finest artists and architects as well as progressive industrialists, they founded the Deutscher Werkbund in 1907.[3] It was an initiative that was unique in the world and resulted in a number of exemplary partnerships, including Behrens and AEG that was due to the vision of the company's boss, Emil Rathenau. And it allowed Germany industry to be at the cutting edge of design.[4] Much the same was true in the field of advertising, at least as it related to the decorative arts.

Ernst Growald, who ran the printing firm of Hollerbaum & Schmidt, could congratulate himself: 'The applied arts have emphatically understood the advantages that the tasteful decoration of shops can offer, and painters and sculptors likewise know that they can walk hand in hand with commerce and find material advantages without betraying their artistic ideals.'

3. According to the preamble to the Werkbund's statutes, its aim was to 'ennoble industrial work by combining the resources of art, industry and craftmanship'.

4. Equally unique was the formation of the Verein der Plakatfreunde (Association of Poster Lovers) by Hans Sachs in 1905, a development that was to culminate in the launch of the periodical *Das Plakat* in 1910. Unlike the societies formed by poster lovers elsewhere in the world, Sachs's organization brought together collectors, poster artists and museum curators. See Susanne Anna (ed.), *Historische Plakate 1890–1914*, Städtische Kunstsammlungen Chemnitz, Daco, Stuttgart, 1995, pp.18–20.

Lucian Bernhard, 1908

Lucian Bernhard, 1914

Lucian Bernhard, 1909

The times when 'artists' refused to countenance commercial commissions was now well and truly over, and a new generation could devote itself with enthusiasm to the task in hand.[5]

Lucian Bernhard was fifteen years old and self-taught as an artist when in 1903 he entered a competition to design a poster for Priester Matches. His initial design depicted a cigar, an ashtray on a checked tablecloth and two dancing women formed from the cigar smoke, but he was so dissatisfied with the result that on the eve of the competition he removed everything apart from two matches and an enlarged text. Most of the jury could make no sense of it, but one, Growald, was so enthusiastic that he was able to convince the others to accept the design. This heralded the birth of the *Sachplakat*, or 'object poster'. Bernhard immediately signed a seven-year contract to work for Hollerbaum & Schmidt.

5. In his biography of Hohlwein, Hermann Karl Frenzel notes that the man who commissioned the work, the dealer and the captain of industry, was now more important than anyone else. He could be heard saying: 'If art can be of some use to me, I am all in favour of it. Otherwise, I'll be happy to give it a miss.' See Hermann Karl Frenzel, *Ludwig Hohlwein*, Phönix Illustrationsdruck und Verlag, Berlin, 1926.

At a conference in 1908 Growald announced that Bernhard 'was the first to discover the emotional impact of a black background and black shadows' and the first to realize that 'the visual presentation must be simple and succinct, the text as brief and as eye-catching as possible'. Bernhard had a lucky client, Manoli, for whom he designed posters for the company's entire range of products from 1910 onwards, even working on the brand's headquarters.

He literally covered the walls of Berlin. His style was instantly recognizable, invariably depicting the object that was to be sold against a uniform background behind lettering which, although very large, is exceptional in terms of its quality and elegance. The image is completely flat and casts no shadows, thereby emphasizing its presence. Writing in the magazine *Der Sturm* in 1911, Max Brod observed that 'The whole of Berlin is but a

Lucian Bernhard, 1911

Lucian Bernhard, 1912

Julius Gipkens, 1913

Hans Rudi Erdt, 1911

Hans Rudi Erdt, 1912

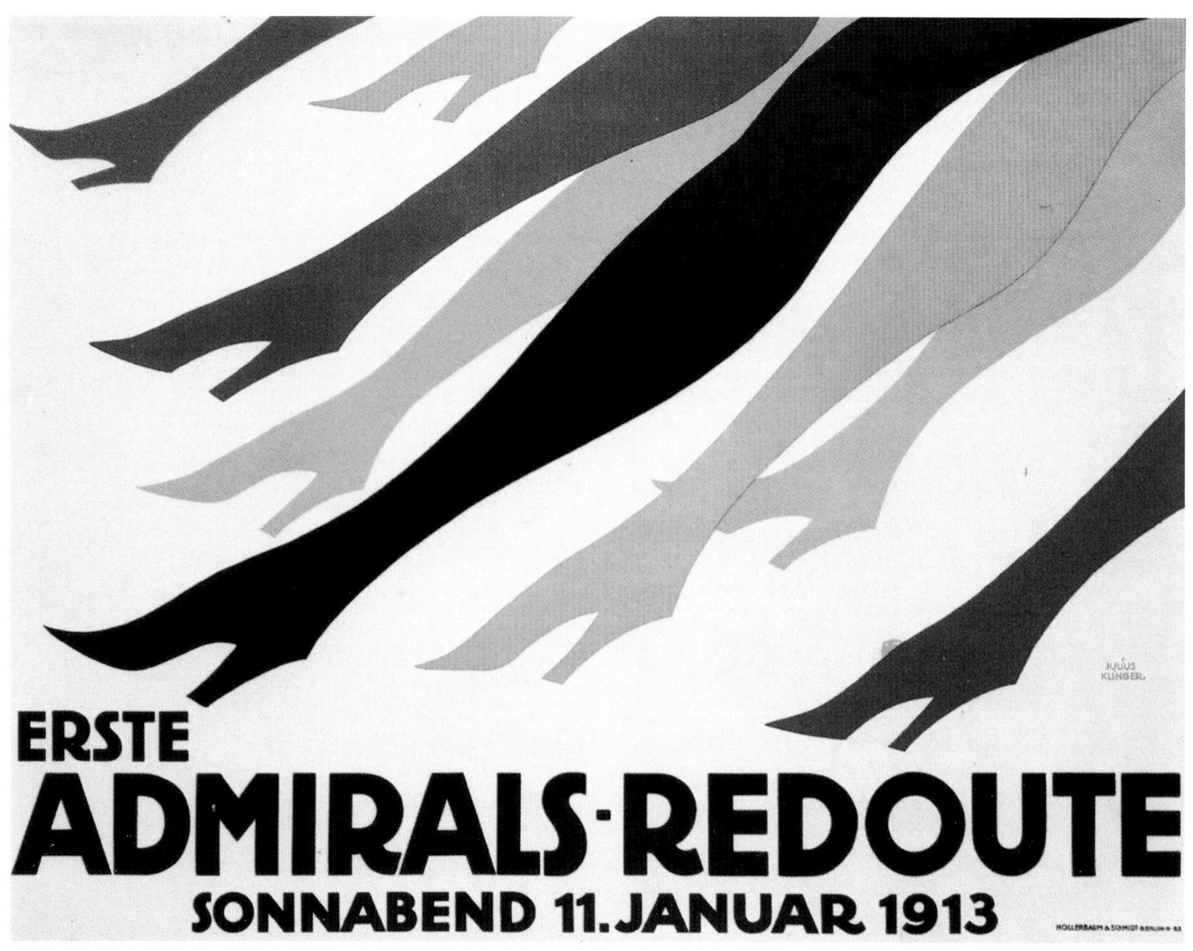

Julius Klinger, 1913

Julius Klinger, 1910-1911

Julius Klinger, 1906

Ernst Deutsch, 1912

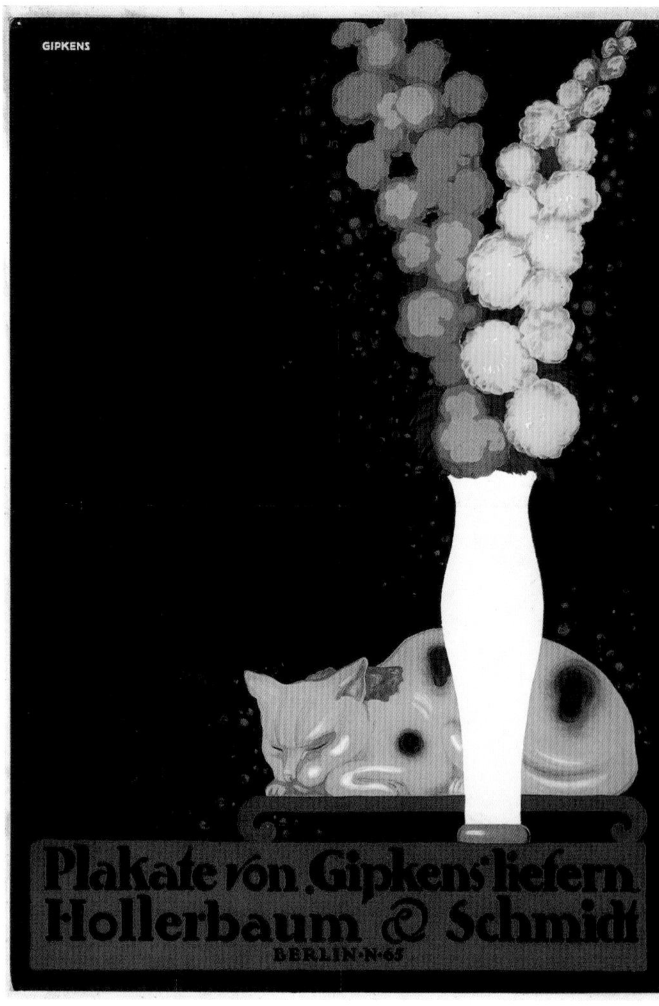

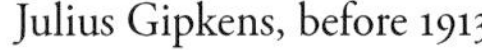

Julius Gipkens, before 1913

Edmund Edel, 1903

Paul Scheurich, 1912

Hans Lindenstaedt, *c.* 1900

Ferdinand Schultz-Wettel, 1904

Knut Hansen, *c.* 1903

Ludwig Hohlwein, 1908

single poster by Bernhard'. It is also worth recalling that even though the poster as an art form may have won the battle, legislation had become no more flexible and that posters were produced in only absurdly small formats.

The troops assembled by Growald included not only Bernhard but also Hans Rudi Erdt, who likewise specialized in boldly outlined areas of colour, while also including figures, and Julius Gipkens, who was at his best when not losing himself in the poster's typography.

To these names must be added three more: Paul Scheurich, an excellent caricaturist of Berlin society; Edmund Edel, one of the pioneers of the Berlin poster who was dragooned into joining Hollerbaum & Schmidt; and Ernst Deutsch who in 1919 changed his name to Dryden and who was a perceptive observer of the world and the demi-monde.

A native of Vienna, Julius Klinger was a special case, so insane was his imagination and so wild his sense of humour, allowing him to produce work of the most extraordinary variety, his human figures and animals sometimes going to the very brink of abstraction in a riot of colours. Klinger was a true genius.

The poster artists of Berlin demonstrated a lightness of touch at odds with the rest of the local scene, following a stylistic model made up of flat tones and boldly outlined figures and proliferating in number in order to meet the demands of business and of the entertainment industry. Chief among them were Fritz Rumpf, Hans Lindenstadt and Louis Oppenheim.

A handful of other artists developed styles that allow us to distinguish between them: Knut Hansen specialized in variety shows and produced posters that are recognizably French in character; Ferdinand Schultz-Wettel applied his Symbolist outlook to advertising; and Jo Steiner created a series of posters of the major figures of the Berlin arts scene and entertainment industry.

We should also mention the excellent typographer Fritz Helmuth Ehmcke of the Steglitz Studio and Peter Behrens, who for AEG worked as an architect and product designer and who created the company's entire graphic line, including all of its posters.

6. Walter von Zur Westen, *Reklamekunst*, 2nd edn, Velhagen & Klasing, Bielefeld and Leipzig, 1914.

7. 'It is impossible to imagine Hohlwein without Munich or Munich without Hohlwein,' wrote *Le Studio* in 1912. 'The most vivid memory I retain of a visit to Munich in 1908 is that of an early Hohlwein poster on the street hoardings, a silhouette of grey on white', Austin Cooper, *Making a Poster*, The Studio Ltd., London, 1938, p.54. It was presumably Hohlwein's Hag Coffee poster that Cooper saw.

The situation in Munich was very different, for in spite of the lead provided by *Simplicissimus*, commerce and industry was unwilling to follow, prompting Walter von Zur Westen to comment that 'the Munich poster has retained its essentially artistic character and has no intrinsic value as a form of advertising'.[6]

When compared with Berlin, however, Munich had one decisive advantage, for in terms of its content, the poster was not considered blasphemous, with the result that large formats were possible.

Incredible though it may seen, it is entirely possible that Hohlwein single-handedly triggered the vogue for the poster in Munich, much as Chéret did in Paris.[7]

Hohlwein was born into a middle-class family in Wiesbaden in 1874 and studied architecture, before visiting Paris and London and embarking on a promising career as an architect in Munich. Like van de Velde and Behrens, he was interested in draughtsmanship as a discipline in its own right. But in this as in other things, he was idiosyncratic – one imagines him at a hunt meeting rather than mixing with Secessionist artists. He loved nature, riding and hunting, which were his earliest sources of inspiration. He never stopped smoking, be it a pipe or cigars, and he sat on a committee that organized beer festivals. Nor was he the sort of man to pass up the chance to devour a plateful of sauerkraut. He was married, with two daughters, and soon developed a paunch. His studio was located on the first floor of his house and had nothing in common with the exquisite furnishings of colleagues such as Leonetto Cappiello and John Hassall; his daughters and his wife might easily be found sitting with him at the table at which he drew.

Hohlwein's biographer, Hermann Karl Frenzel, confirms that he never had an assistant or a disciple and that he did everything himself, believing that he owed it to his clients to offer them an original design.

He began by making small preparatory drawings of the motif, using photographs (he was adept at handling his Leica), before creating the poster itself. He played with only a small number of elements, namely, shade, foreground and background, in compositions that

Ludwig Hohlwein, 1912

Ludwig Hohlwein, 1904-1905

Ludwig Hohlwein, *c.* 1910

were relatively sober. This is presumably how he was led to design first one and then several posters for the gentleman's outfitter Hermann Scherrer. So successful were these designs that he very quickly became a full-time poster artist. It was no doubt during his visit to London that he picked up the Beggarstaffs' lost outline technique, together with a preference for uniform backgrounds. Above all, however, he was an extraordinary draughtsman, juggling with light and shade, having recourse to complex monochromes, instilling a sense of balance in his compositions and arranging his impeccable typography within a square or rectangle.

When we recall that in 1926 Frenzel reckoned that Hohlwein had designed three thousand different works relating to advertising, we can well appreciate that it required an exceptional talent for Hohlwein to avoid repeating himself. What is astonishing is that he designed practically no bad posters, which is all the more remarkable is that he never stressed the object that was intended to be sold.

Hohlwein worked out a number of systems. For everything related to horses and hounds, his sketches were always sufficient – by his own admission, it then amused him to work on the layout and colour. His still lifes were made up of two squares – text and image – included within a rectangle. His scenes in bars and restaurants were never a problem either. By preference they also included a little black boy serving the customers, which in turn led him to add a touch of exoticism to those of his posters that were intended for major clients such as Marco Polo, where his array of characters included Chinese and Indians. He produced a number of masterpieces for the Munich Zoo, and with

Ludwig Hohlwein, 1913

Vassily Kandinsky, 1909

Emil Preetorius, 1911

Walter Schnackenberg, 1910

Emil Pirchan, 1913

the passage of time animals became a part of the cast of characters with which he was fond of peopling his scenes.

In the face of such a *monstre sacré*, Munich's other poster artists were reduced to adopting a practice unique in the history of the graphic arts, when six of their finest – Franz Paul Glass, Friedrich Heubner, Carl Moos, Emil Preetorius, Max Schwarzer and Valentin Zietara – joined forces, guaranteeing that each would provide a project for any potential client who could choose among them.

While Moos specialized in winter sports and Preetorius was an excellent cartoonist, as exemplified by his posters for the weekly magazine *Licht und Schatten*, the others were unable to disturb Hohlwein's routine.

In the cultural domain, the academic artist Julius Diez remained a constant presence, and the same was true of the *Simplicissimus* team of Heine, Angelo Jank, Bruno Paul and Albert Weisgerber.

Two exceptional artists emerged in the run-up to the First World War: originally from Vienna, Emil Pirchan designed a series of strange theatre posters, while Walter Schnackenberg produced a handful of masterpieces for some of the more decadent and even illegal cabarets, posters that included more than the odd wink in the direction of Toulouse-Lautrec. ❧

Marguerite Burnat-Provins, 1905, detail

SWITZERLAND

Emil Cardinaux, 1908

Emil Cardinaux, 1914

Carl Moos, 1907

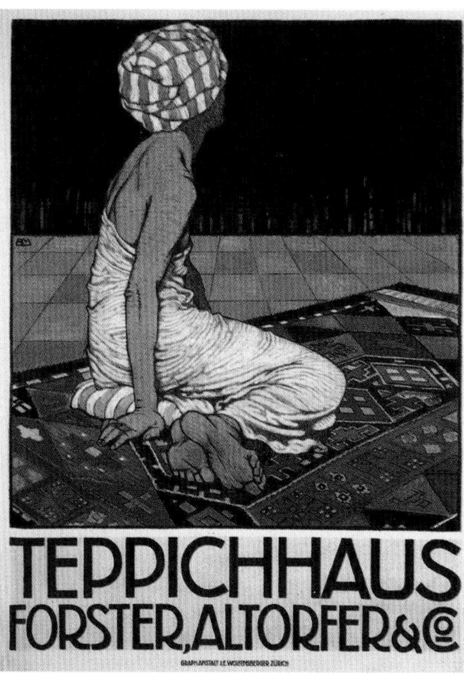

Burkhard Mangold, 1912

Switzerland came late to the poster, approaching the medium from two different directions, one of them Francophone, the other Germanic. But in record time it then became one of the most promising countries in Europe in terms of its espousal of poster art. The impetus came from the painter Ferdinand Hodler, who began by creating a scandal. The stylized vigour of his monumental figures and his crude colours, which received the blessing of the Vienna Secession in 1904, helped to liberate the creative energies of an entire generation.

The first great Swiss poster dates from 1908 and was designed by Emil Cardinaux, who had studied in Munich with Franz von Stuck. It was an advertisement for Zermatt. Until then, there had been few, if any, Swiss posters. The pioneering Karl Bührer had devised the 'monocard' in 1905, small advertising cards that allowed a generation of young artists to familiarize the public with publicity imagery. They included not only Cardinaux himself but also Robert Hardmeyer, Burkhard Mangold and, from further afield, Ludwig Hohlwein and Carl Moos.

Prior to his premature death, Bührer succeeded in gaining acceptance for a standard format for posters, 90.5 x 128cm/36 x 50in, which came into force in 1914.[1]

On the Francophone side, the Société Générale d'Affichage (SGA) was established in 1900 and by 1910 enjoyed an almost complete monopoly of hoardings and advertising pillars throughout the country. One final critical element in the evolution of the Swiss poster was the fact that it remained in the control of the artists themselves and was not left to the devices of lithographers unresponsive to the ideas of art nouveau. In Zurich, the Swiss poster was tirelessly promoted by an altogether exceptional printer, J.E. Wolfensberger.

If *Zermatt* marked the début of the Swiss poster, Cardinaux achieved a second major coup in 1914 with his poster for that year's National Swiss Exhibition in Berne, which depicts a peasant brandishing a yellow flag and mounted on a green horse. It provoked a lively reaction, but the green horse was as instantly identifiable as Leonetto Cappiello's red horse for Klaus Chocolate.

1. Ironically, this *Weltformat* (universal format) was used only in Switzerland.

Auguste Viollier, 1898

Marguerite Burnat-Provins, 1905

Writing in the *Neue Zürcher Zeitung* on 29 May 1911, Alfred Baur expressed the view that 'One of the great needs of capitalist culture is advertising, which, rather than being an environmental nuisance and evidence of a lack of culture, should be transformed into the leaven of every artistic culture.' Tradespeople and tourism supported him and engaged the services not only of Cardinaux but also of Burkhard Mangold, the young Otto Baumberger, Ludwig Hohlwein, Walter Koch and Carl Moos, who specialized in winter sports.

Among Francophone poster artists, the pioneer was Auguste Viollier, who in 1896 became the first president of the Cercle des Arts et des Lettres, a group of Swiss artists that included all the advocates of modernism. He was also the first artist to design a poster worthy of the name and was behind an original initiative: the Swiss Society for Art Posters which, following the necessary recapitalization, acquired a well-equipped printing works able to print posters, much like its rival, Imprimerie Atar.

Viollier was clearly inspired by the French school, whose contours and gradations he used with marked intelligence. Henry-Claudius Forestier used subtle flat tones without outlines, a style reminiscent of British poster artists of the period. We should also mention Louis Dunki, Édouard-Louis Baud and the influential Marguerite Burnat-Provins, who was an excellent painter and a brilliant poster designer. Prior to 1914, two other young hopefuls emerged on the scene: Édouard Elzingre and Jules Courvoisier.

Antoni Utrillo, 1906, detail

SPAIN

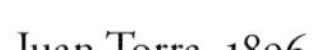

Juan Torra, 1896

Alexandre de Riquer, 1900

Miguel Utrillo and Ramón Casas, 1897

The first Spanish posters date from the eighteenth century, designed to promote bullfights and sporting events. At the end of the nineteenth century, only Catalonia played an active role in the art nouveau movement, Madrid remaining in the grip of the Royal Academy of Fine Arts and bogged down in a kind of academic neoclassicism. But Barcelona was a busy port and quickly developed into a major industrial centre.[1] During the revolution of 1868, the ramparts and citadel were destroyed in order to modernize the city and create the Parc de la Ciutadella, an important symbol of the national revival. It was here that the Barcelona Universal Exhibition was held in 1888, raising the city to the status of a metropolis. The poster was the work of the pioneering Josep Lluís Pellicer.

1. In the 1860s, for example, the city accounted for 80 per cent of the country's textile industry.
2. See the exhibition catalogue *Ramón Casas y el Cartel*, published in 2005 by the Museo Valenciano de la Ilustración y la Modernidad in Valencia.
3. He was the father of Maurice Utrillo, who was the outcome of an affair with Suzanne Valadon.

Barcelona was also the first Spanish city to be connected to Paris by train, contributing to the influence of the French capital on Catalan artists. Ramón Casas[2] and Santiago Rusiñol spent several years in Montmartre in the building that housed the Moulin de la Galette. There they assimilated Impressionist techniques and were members of the group of naturalist artists who lived in this quarter of Paris. They met Miguel Utrillo, the son of a liberal republican lawyer who was living in exile in France.[3] A veritable globetrotter, Rusiñol remained in Paris until 1894, when he returned to Barcelona, as did Casas and Utrillo.

It was this small group of artists that provided the impulse for *modernismo*, a term used for the first time

Miguel Utrillo, 1897

by the Catalan magazine *L'Avenç* (Progress). Eliseu Trenc sums up its spirit as follows: 'Its innovation consisted in adapting the modern art of Paris to the climate of Barcelona and, in doing so, modernizing the whole wide range of Catalan graphic arts.'[4]

Another Catalan artist who for a time lived in exile was Alexandre de Riquer,[5] the son of a family of Carlist aristocrats, who studied at the School of Fine Arts in Bordeaux and who in 1893 founded the Cercle Artistic de Sant Lluc in Barcelona. The Sitges Modernist Festival that was held annually between 1892 and 1899 was modelled on the Brussels Libre Esthétique and provided a forum for all of the arts. The first major exhibition of posters was held at the Sala Pares in 1896 and proved a tremendous success.[6]

Two journals saw the light of day at this period: *Luz* was an artistic and literary journal that was Symbolist in its tendency, with de Riquer as its artistic director; while *Pèl y Ploma*, founded by Casas and Murillo, tended, rather, to adopt the Parisian model. They were joined by de Riquer when *Luz* ceased publication in 1898. Casas, Utrillo, Rusiñol and the dynamic impresario Pere Romeu opened the café and bar Els Quatre Gats in 1897. Inspired by Le Chat Noir, it had its own illustrated magazine, also called *Els Quatre Gats*. Although the bar closed down in 1903, the movement had developed a momentum all of its own, leading to rapid developments in the field of Catalan culture. Two complementary figures dominated the world of the early Spanish poster: Ramón Casas and Alexandre de Riquer, the latter a Symbolist, a follower of both the Arts & Crafts movement and of the Pre-Raphaelites and an admirer of both Eugène Grasset and William H. Bradley.

De Riquer designed the first modernist poster in 1895 for the Fourth Exhibition of Fine Arts, further developing and refining his style later that same year in his poster for the Napoleon Photographic Company.[7] He favoured elongated formats, placing the image within a decorative frieze made up of plant-like ornaments or within a set of motifs related to the product being advertised, most notably in the case of his poster for

Ramón Casas, 1898

4. These links with Paris remained very strong: the only issue of *La Plume* to be devoted to an entire country was about Spain.
5. See Eliseu Trenc Ballester and Pilar Vélez, *Alexandre de Riquer: Obra gràfica*, Marc Marti, Barcelona, 2006; see also Eliseu Trenc Ballester and Alan Yates, *Alexandre de Riquer, 1856–1920: The British Connection in Catalan 'Modernisme'*, The Anglo-Catalan Society, Sheffield, 1988 (also available online).
6. Others included the Lluís Bartina Collection of American posters and the two exhibitions organized by Lluís Plandiura in 1901 and 1903 mentioned in our chapter on poster-mania.
7. The poster was printed by Chaix. De Riquer was in regular contact with printers and poster dealers in Paris. His *Four Seasons* decorative panels were published by Pierrefort.

Lluís Labarta, 1909

HIJO DE S.
COMAS Y RICART
A. COMAS
4 RONDA S. PEDRO
BARCELONA
CASA FUNDADA
EN 1797
NAIPES
COMAS
IMPRESO EN LOS TALLERES DE LA CASA

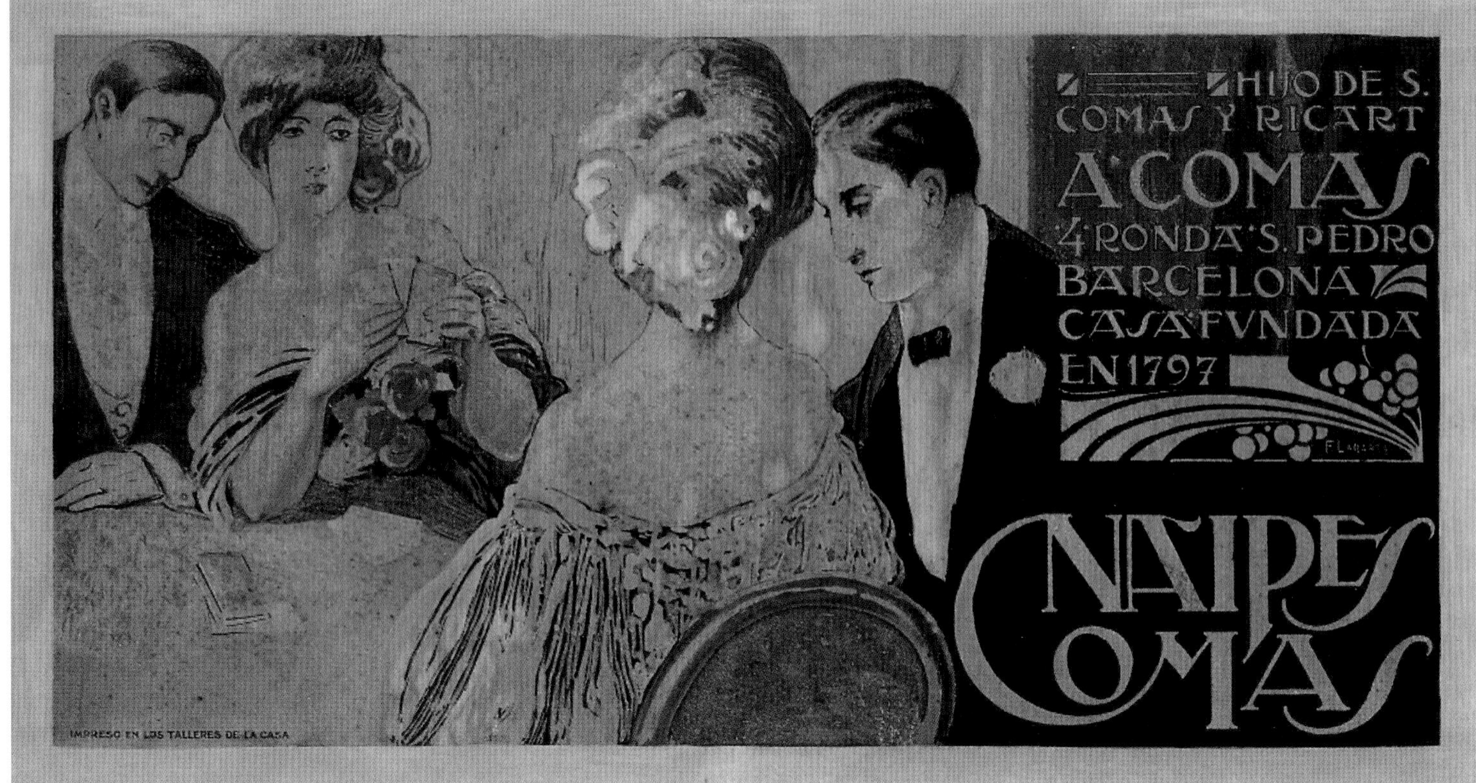

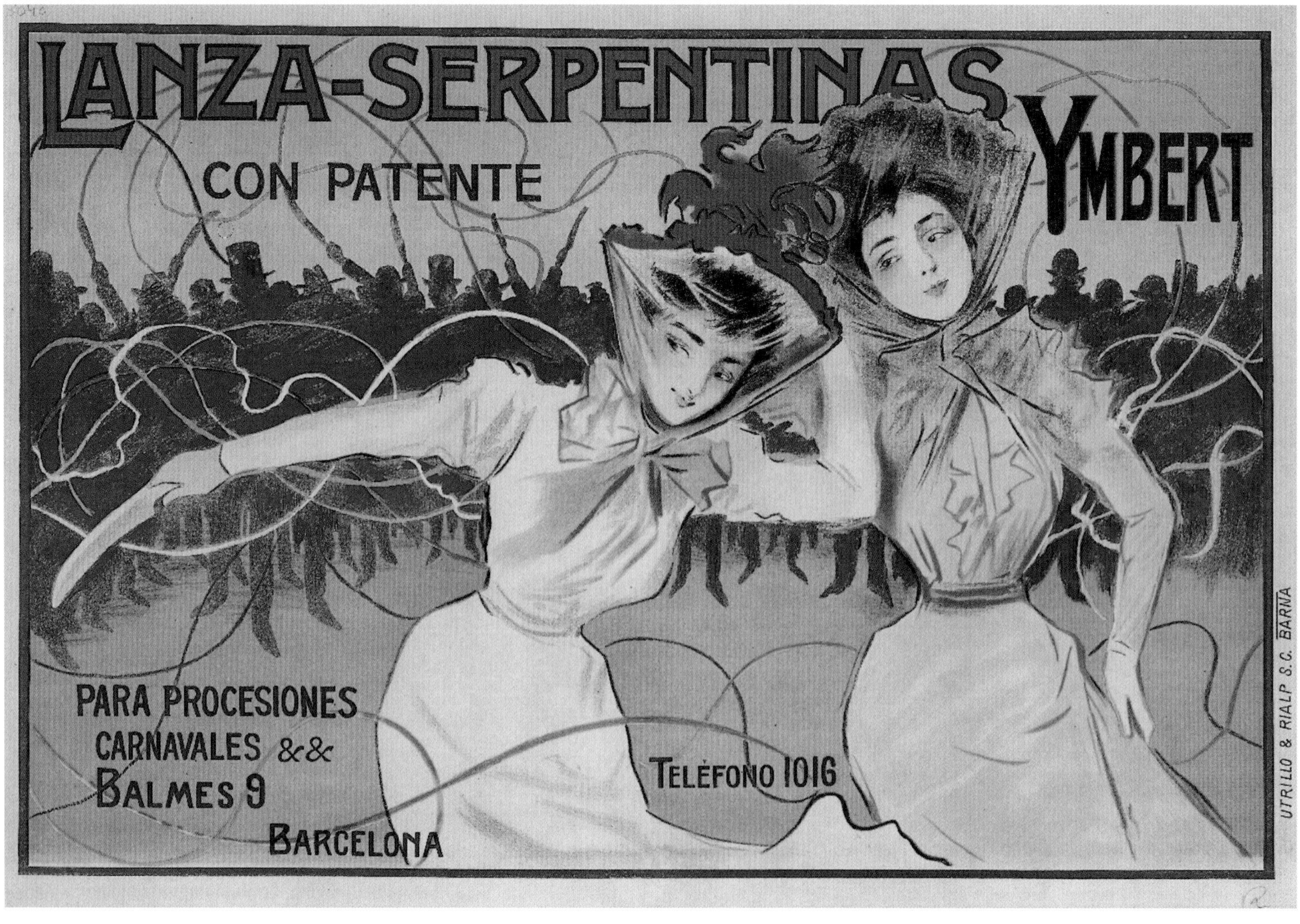
LANZA-SERPENTINAS
YMBERT
CON PATENTE
PARA PROCESIONES
CARNAVALES &&
BALMES 9
BARCELONA
TELÉFONO 1016
UTRILLO & RIALP S.C. BARNA

A Utrillo, 1906

Joan Llimona, 1902

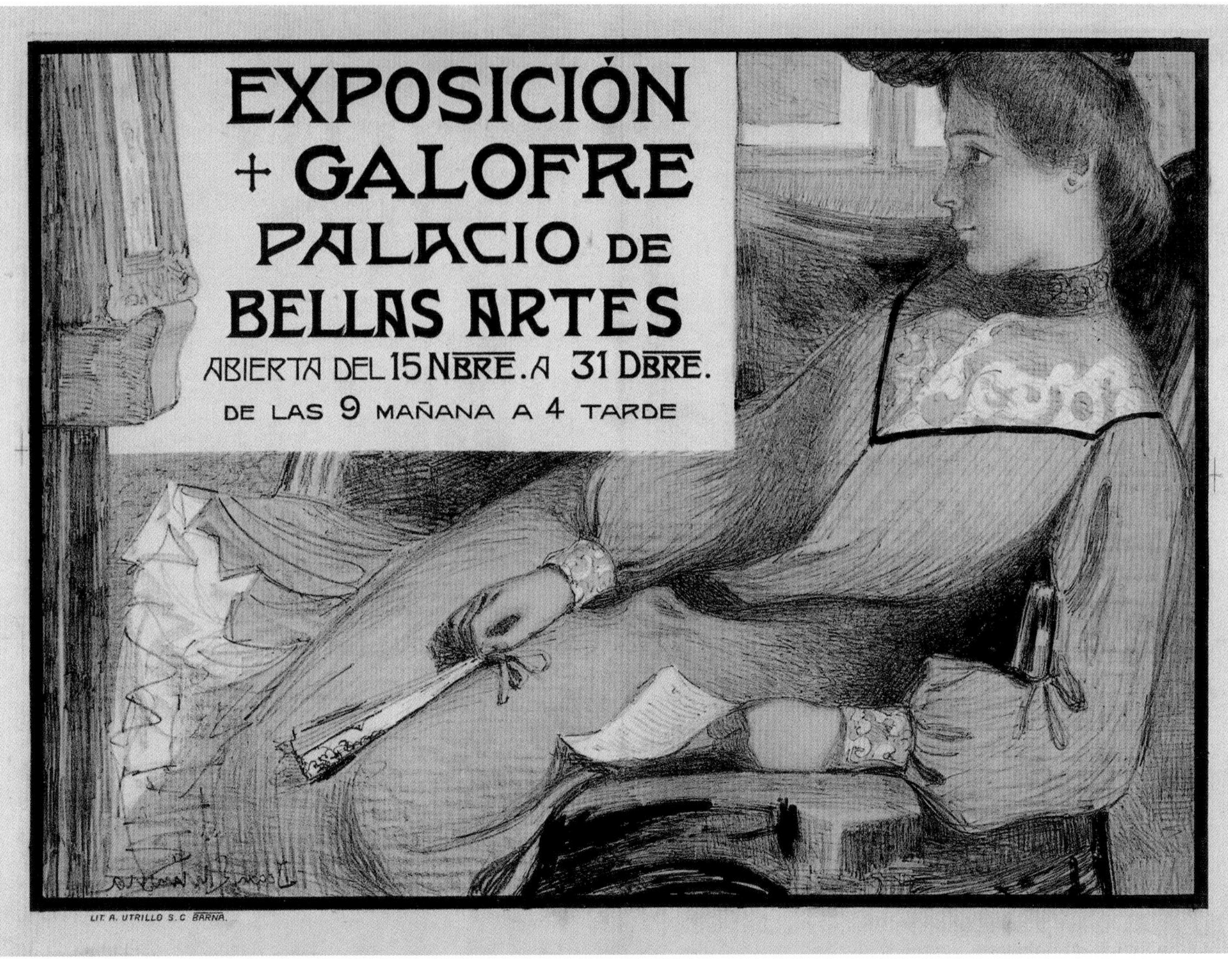

Llorens Brunet, 1900

Gaspar Camps, 1900

Francisco de Cidón Navarro, 1903

sausages, to which he brought an unexpected note of nobility. He suffered from a natural tendency to over-design his posters, his graphic tours de force sometimes rendering the typography almost unreadable.

Ramón Casas represented a synthetic naturalism that was very much in the spirit of Montmartre. As such, he takes his place in a line that can be traced to Steinlen and Ibels. In 1898 he won a competition organized to find a winning poster for Anis del Mono – it proved to be one of his best-known posters. His second prize at the Cava Condoníu Competition led to his being invited to design a further poster. He also designed those for Els Quatre Gats, one of which was co-signed by Miguel Utrillo, in his day an excellent painter, who also designed a series of posters of his own, including a remarkable one for the Teatro Lírico. Some of Joan Llimona's posters also reveal Casas's influence.

Francisco de Cidón adopted a purely graphic approach that ignored the whiplash curve.

Rusiñol designed only a small number of posters, but they are all magnificent expressions of the artist's gifts as a painter – which is what he essentially was.

A playwright, impresario and pioneer of the Catalan cinema, Adrià Gual was a Symbolist artist who left a number of posters of an ephemeral kind, but his design for Cosmopolis Cycles is undoubtedly visually striking.

Antoni Utrillo, who was a cousin of Miguel Utrillo, was another of the founder members of the Cercle Artistic de Sant Lluc. Together with Claudi Rialp, he founded a lithographic workshop and produced countless high-quality posters that tread a fine line between art nouveau and naturalism, while attesting to a clear and effective sense of composition. He worked for commerce and industry as well as for popular shows, for which he designed a series of elegant advertising posters.

Gaspar Camps was rightly known as the 'Barcelona Mucha' on account of his floral style. The most successful of his works was a set of illustrations for the Colección Ambos Mondos that was published in Barcelona from 1900 onwards. Champenois enlisted his services for a series of decorative panels. A ubiquitous presence on the European arts scene, Champenois also managed to sell three posters with Mucha-inspired images to the Barcelona-based chocolatier Amatller, which were all were printed in Italy.

Lluís Labarta was another pioneer, whose 1887 poster for El Vino Amargós is already modernist in style.

Llorens Brunet used the biggest local printer, Henrich, for his posters, which represent an honest attempt to follow in the footsteps of modernism. He evidently felt especially comfortable designing posters for the Teatro Novedades Aurigemma. ♣

Alphonse Mucha, 1899

Georges Privat-Livemont, 1899

Adolfo Hohenstein, 1901, détail

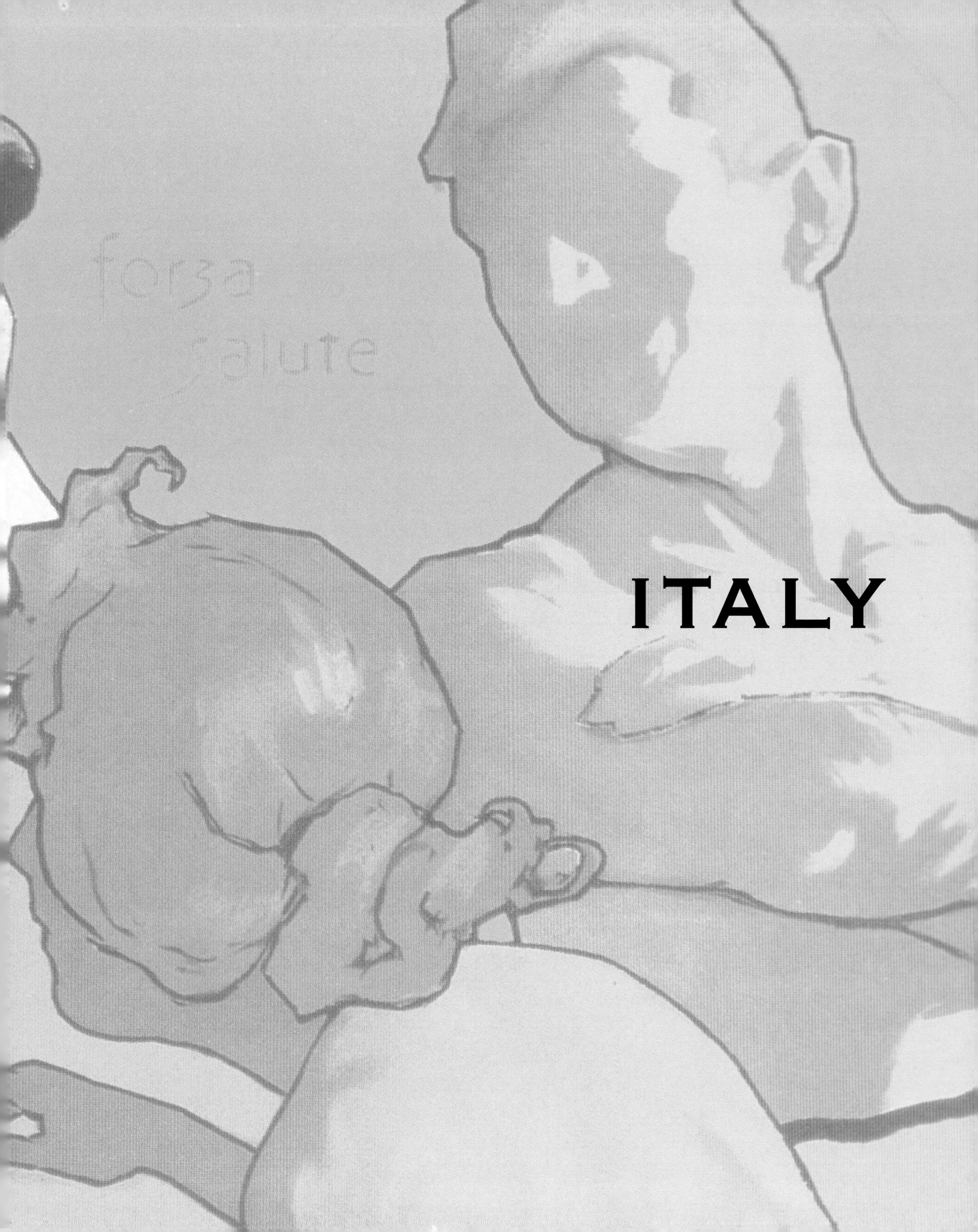

ITALY

Marcello Dudovich, 1908

It was not until the end of the nineteenth century that the poster really began to evolve in Italy. The process of industrialization did not begin until 1870, and then only in the north of Italy, where it led to spectacular urban development and to the emergence of a new middle class. In Milan, the Via Pisacane, which dates from 1906–7, was described as 'showcasing the decorative repertory' of the age as applied to 'current urban architecture'.[1] In other words, it was an example of the 'Stile Liberty', as art nouveau was known in Italy, a style that produced a veritable frenzy of floral exuberance in Ettore De Maria Bergler's murals in the Villa Igeia in Palermo.

Not only did the poster make a late appearance, it was also limited to a handful of printers – Doyen in Turin, Gaffuri e Gatti in Bergamo and, above all, Ricordi in Milan – and a few advertisers, including Mele & Ci. in Naples, Campari in Turin, various other distillers and, of course, opera.

The history of the Italian poster is more or less synonymous with the history of Ricordi[2] and its team of cosmopolitan artists: Adolfo Hohenstein hailed from St Petersburg, Leopoldo Metlicovitz and Marcello Dudovich were cross-border commuters from Trieste, which was then an outpost of the Italian empire, and Franz Laskoff came from Poland. Only Giovanni Mataloni was from Rome, while Leonetto Cappiello, although a native of Livorno, left for France at an early date.

The house of Ricordi, which was founded in Milan in 1808 and which in 1884 opened an in-house lithography shop to promote its opera and sheet music, looked to enhance its standing by publishing opera scores, eventually acquiring an international reputation with its editions of the operas of Verdi and Puccini.

The year 1895 was a turning point for the Italian poster. For *La bohème*, Adolfo Hohenstein designed a poster inspired by Jules Chéret, in which the image takes up the entire plate. Mataloni's style was somewhat rigid but his vocabulary was pure art nouveau,[3] a point well illustrated by his poster for Auer light fittings. 1895 also witnessed the inaugural issue of the magazine *Emporium*, which championed the Liberty style, and the first Venice Biennale was held as an exhibition promoting new art.

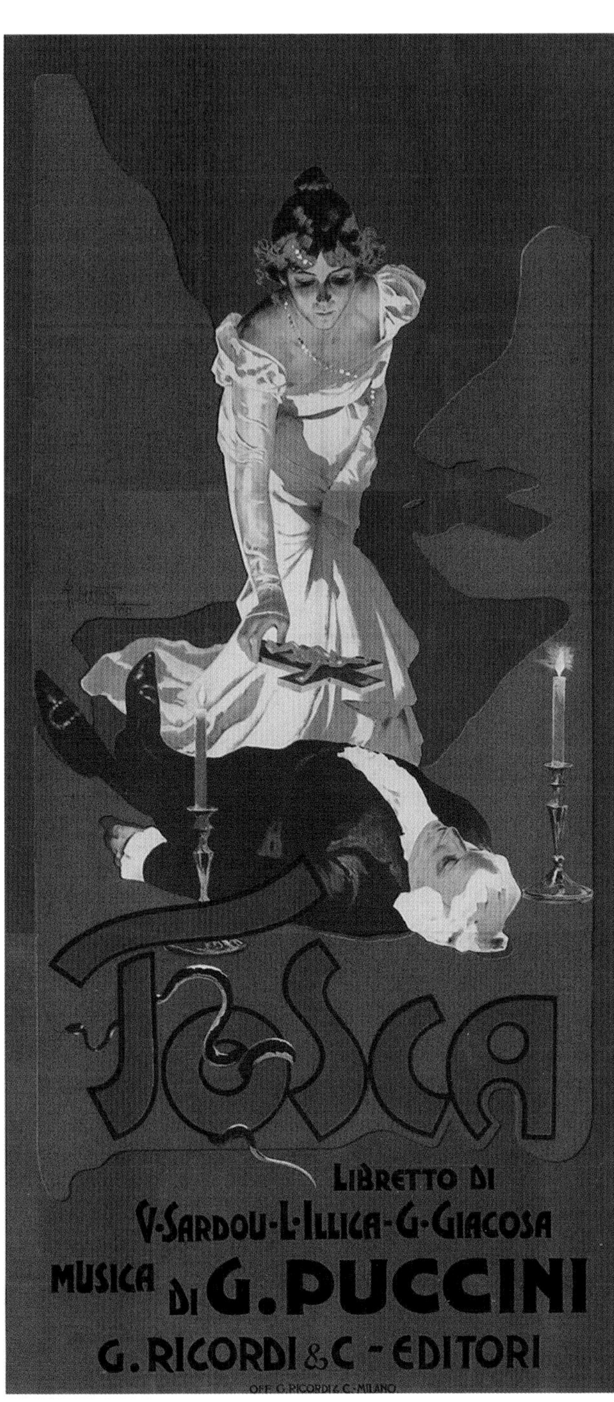

Adolfo Hohenstein, 1899

1. Eléonora Bairati and others (eds.), *La Belle Époque, 1900–1914*, Fernand Nathan, Paris, 1977, p.132.
2. With the exception of Ferdinando Salce's collection at Treviso, no other major holdings were assembled at this time.
3. Mataloni continued to use this over-elaborate style, notably in his posters for Giovanni Buton's Distillery in Bologna and for Grocco's Tonic Pills.

Leopoldo Metlicovitz, 1899

Adolfo Hohenstein, *c.* 1900

Adolfo Hohenstein, *c.* 1895

Aldo Mazza, 1909

Adolfo Hohenstein, 1901

Adolfo Hohenstein, 1906

Giovanni Mataloni, 1900

Adolfo Hohenstein, 1898

In 1898 and again in 1899 Hohenstein revealed great stylistic maturity in two masterpieces that take up the elongated format favoured by Mucha, but there the comparison ends: his poster for Mascagni's opera *Iris* is a low-angle shot suffused with blues, reds and yellows, while his poster for Puccini's *Tosca* – this time a high-angle shot – uses the play of shadow and a frame that surrounds the image against a blood-red background.

Gifted with a febrile imagination, Hohenstein placed his characters within a sinuous decorative framework, playing with light and shade and with a sunny yellow that lends a real iridescence to the figures' bodies – his incredible feminine allegory *Fiammiferi senza Fosforo* (Non-Phosphorous Safety Matches) depicts the Devil making good his escape in the blue shadow of night and could be no more than an example of kitsch if it were not for the artist's remarkable virtuosity. Exactly the same is true of the wild Miss Monowatt, who is wearing a belt made of light bulbs. All of his posters attest to an inimitable grace, whether in his reds and yellows for Campari and Birra Italia or in his two posters for the kingdom of Monaco.

Ricordi's art director would also call on the services of Leopoldo Metlicovitz. Among his opera and operetta posters are those for Puccini's *Madama Butterfly* and for Oscar Straus's *Der Walzertraum*,[4] while his image of an Italian distillery bathed in the glow of reddish flames is a tour de force in terms of its design. His posters for the Superator Stove and for Tricofilina – a tonic against hair loss in men – depict scenes of a more *intimiste* kind. He was fond of playing with classical statuary in his posters advertising automobile and bicycle shows and of creating the sort of allegories that included mythical creatures reminiscent of the centaur that the Futurist Filippo Tommaso Marinetti was to hymn as a way of describing the motorcar. Elsewhere we find hyper-sensual women, as in his poster for Sauzé Frères' perfume Flouvella and for Ramos Pinto port wine. He also designed posters for Mele & Ci., but was clearly not at ease here. The results are a little stiff, and a young artist whom he himself had trained was asked to take over the commission.

4. First performed in Italy at Parma's Teatro Reinach in June 1910 as *Sogno d'un valser*.

Leopoldo Metlicovitz, 1905

Leopoldo Metlicovitz, 1911

Plinio Codognato, 1910

Vespasiano Bignami, 1919

Adolfo Magrini, 1906

Adolfo de Carolis, 1911

Leopoldo Metlicovitz, 1907

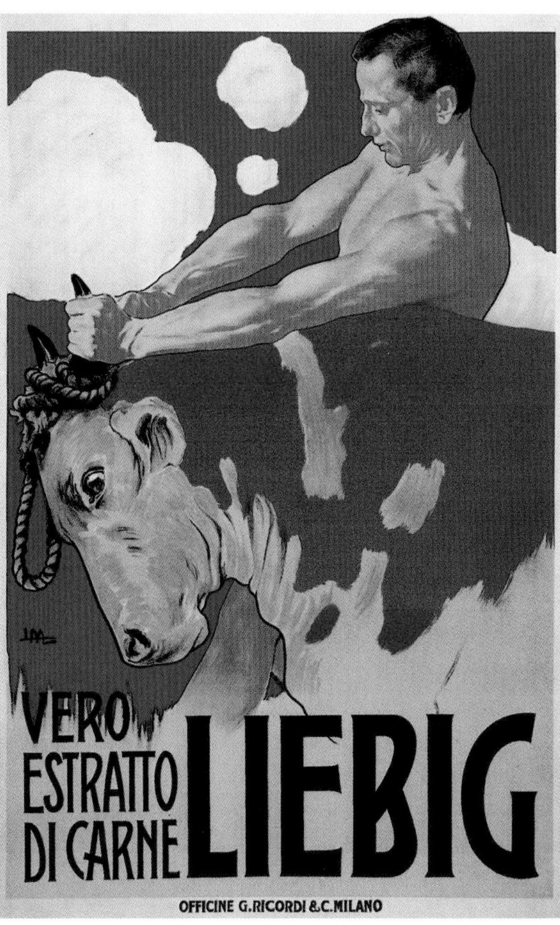

Leopoldo Metlicovitz, 1899

Franz Laskoff, 1900

Marcello Dudovich, 1915

Leonetto Cappiello, 1901

Marcello Dudovich, 1912

Marcello Dudovich was to be Italy's most important and most prolific poster artist of the twentieth century. He was very young when he joined Ricordi and became the favourite of the company's biggest client, Mele & Ci., a chain of shops which clothed middle-class women. Dudovich provided them with exactly what they hankered after. Recalling the Italy of this period, Philippe Jullian has spoken of a type of woman who 'in order to conceal the fact that she has limited means is always a little too elegant'. In his heyday from 1901 to 1911, Dudovich created genre scenes and catalogues of a sophisticated life whose colours changed with the seasons. He would extend his field of action, with the same felicitous results, to motor racing and to brand names such as Dunlop. He created a number of masterpieces, such as his poster for Strega Liqueur. In his poster for the Zenit top hat, the item in question is simply placed on an armchair and bathed in a yellow light.

In the wake of the First World War, Dudovich worked with other leading retail stores, including Rinascente, continuing to design posters until 1945, when he concentrated instead on painting.

In order to satisfy the Fratelli Mele's appetite for publicity, Ricordi was also obliged to call on the services of other artists and developed a gift for choosing wisely.

Aleardo Villa worked for Mele from the outset, his banal realism improving with the passage of time. In 1901 he won a prize for his poster for Paris Cigarillos. Aldo Mazza followed in the footsteps of Metlicovitz, while never quite achieving his standards, while Achille Beltrame was equally assured in his draughtsmanship. Enrico Sacchetti produced his best work for Campari, his earlier designs being weighed down with floral motifs. Aleardo Terzi, finally, followed Cappiello in featuring animals in his posters, notably his monkey for Dental. Cappiello's elegantly outlined caricatures and his colours, which were brighter than in France by way of a genuflection at the shrine of Mediterranean luminosity, proved a triumph for Mele and Campari. He reserved a little gem of a poster for his native Livorno.

Leopoldo Metlicovitz, 1911

Mario Borgoni, 1910

Aleardo Terzi, 1911

Marcello Dudovich, 1911

Mele's team also included a singular artist who was directly inspired by the Beggarstaffs and by John Hassall. This was the Polish artist Franz Laskoff, whose life is largely shrouded in mystery. He used strong colours, sometimes outlined, sometimes not, producing an effect close to that of paper cut-outs, with figures that seem to have been stopped suddenly in their tracks and most often depicted in profile. The resultant effect is strange and arresting. He applied this formula to an oratorio (*S. Petrus* by Paul Eugen Josef von An der Lan-Hochbrunn, who took the name Pater Hartmann when joining the Franciscans), to Mele (for whom he even used techniques reminiscent of the shadow theatre), to Suchard Chocolate and, finally, to Costina's Coffee.

Given the extraordinarily impressive number of posters produced by Ricordi, it is frustrating that so few have been preserved, the main exceptions being in the collection of Ferdinando Salce. Familiar images include a handful of Liberty style posters by Giovanni Battista Carpanetto and by the Pre-Raphaelite Adolfo de Carolis. More consistent in his output was Mario Borgoni for Richter's print works in Naples: his portfolio includes Birra Italia, Verona, De Luca Daimler, numerous exhibitions and even posters for one of Mele's rivals, Finzi. We know next to nothing about Alberto Chappuis, except that he worked for Strega.

Metlicovitz and his followers were fond of allegorical muscle-men, and they were able to indulge this obsession to their heart's content with the arrival of the cinema, a new medium that proved dazzlingly successful. The first epic film, Gabriele D'Annunzio's *Cabiria*, was advertised with a series of astonishing posters designed by Metlicovitz and two newcomers: Luigi Emilio Caldanzano and the young French artist Achille Mauzan, who alone produced several hundred posters for Savoia Films, Halia Films and Cines, often in gigantic formats. The hero of *Cabiria*, Maciste, became a hugely popular Herculean figure, encouraging filmmakers to broach other great classical themes such as Othello and Macbeth and historical figures like Napoleon and Garibaldi.

Feliks Wygrzywalski, 1910, detail

AROUND THE WORLD

Arnošt Hofbauer, 1899

As the seemingly endless reign of Franz Joseph – emperor of Austria and king of Hungary – dragged on and the region's bureaucracy grew ever more ossified, the centrifugal forces unleashed by the rise of nationalism made themselves felt with increasing violence throughout the Austro-Hungarian Empire. Here the word 'Secession' acquired a significance very different from the one that it had in Vienna, and the demands of artists who refused to embrace academicism found expression at the heart of movements that were politically charged.

In Prague, the Mánes Union, named after the Romantic painter Josef Mánes who helped to trigger the nationalist movement, organized the Topičův, a salon whose posters were designed by Arnošt Hofbauer, Jan Preisler, Vojtěch Preissig and František Kysela. Their work could hardly have been more different from that produced in Vienna. Culturally speaking, Prague was a dynamic city that benefited from the presence of artists of the stature of Mucha, Luděk Marold and František Kupka. Mucha accompanied Rodin to the great exhibition that was devoted to the French artist's work in Prague in 1902 and that was advertised by a remarkable poster by Vladimir Zupansky, while Jan Preisler designed the poster for the Edvard Munch Exhibition four years later. More and more exhibitions and conferences were held in Prague: in 1904, for example, the Congress of Slav Students was advertised by a poster by Vratislav Hugo Brunner, while the Fourteenth Congress of Universal Free Thought in 1907 was promoted by a poster by Karel Nejedlý.

Economic conditions were favourable, not least because Prague was a modern city where leading poster artists – always a sign of true cultural richness – were able to express themselves openly: not only Viktor Oliva, whose 1898 poster for *Zlata Praha* was reproduced in *Les Maîtres de l'affiche*, but also Karel Reisner, Karel Šimůnek, Oldrich Homolac and Jaroslav Benda, all of whom succeeded in asserting themselves in the face of the mass of anonymous posters that covered the walls of the whole of Eastern Europe, most of them inept pastiches of the floral style of the period. ♣

Viktor Oliva, 1898

Vladimir Zupansky, 1902

Jan Preisler, 1905

Luděk Marold, 1898

Karel Šimůnek, 1900

Karel Reisner, 1900

Géza Faragó, 1909

In Hungary, the poster failed to present the same degree of diversity, for all that Budapest was a vast metropolis soon awash with publicity.

Árpád Basch's poster for Kühnee Ploughs was reproduced in *Les Maîtres de l'affiche* but is his only known contribution to the medium. On the other hand, he designed countless illustrated postcards in an over-ornate art nouveau style. Several Hungarian artists such as Jozséf Rippl-Rónai and János Vaszary designed a number of exhibition posters but none was capable of exerting any real influence.

Géza Faragó studied at the Académie Colarossi in Paris, where he met Mucha, before returning to Budapest and designing by far the best commercial posters of the period, their elegant and highly personal images never descending into the excesses of an unduly fussy art nouveau style. After the war he pursued a prolific career in the cinema. The young Mihaly Biro had barely started on his career by this date, and it was only with the war that the graphic arts really came in their own in Hungary. ❧

Mihaly Biro, 1911

Géza Faragó, 1913

Karol Frycz, 1919

It is difficult to speak of Poland in this context, since the country had been divided up among Russia, Austria and Germany in the wake of the Congress of Vienna in 1815. Zdzisław Schubert's excellent exhibition catalogue provides a detailed account of the situation in each of the regions in question.[1]

The finest posters adopted the rules that had been established elsewhere in the world, evolving only in those cultural circles where a young generation of artists had taken an interest in lithography. The posters that were designed by workaday lithographers were mediocre in quality. Most of the posters held by the Muzeum Narodowe in Poznan are commercial posters lacking in originality but, at their best, they are simple and effective.

In Galicia – the Austrian part of Poland – it was very different, for Kraków was a university town and a major cultural centre. Journals were founded, cabarets opened their doors, notably the Zielony Balonik in 1907, and artists formed groups such as Sztuka in 1898. It was, of course, the artists themselves who designed the posters for these associations: Teodor Axentowicz produced several in a deliberately extrovert art nouveau style.

At the risk of oversimplification we may divide these artists into two distinct groups: folklorists such as Józef Mehoffer and Eugeniusz Ludwik Dąbrowa-Dąbrowski and Expressionists like Karol Frycz, the undisputed leader of the group. Mehoffer designed the poster for the Public Exhibition of Polish Art at L'viv in 1910, while Dąbrowa-Dąbrowski did the honours for the First Exhibition of Independent Artists in 1911. Frycz was initiated into the world of art in the course of an extended period of travel, during which time he visited Munich, Vienna, Paris, where he studied at the Académie Julian, and London, where he came into contact with William Morris's circle. In the field of the poster, he was a brilliant exception to the rule, designing high-quality commercial posters for products such as tea and cigarettes.

Warsaw, finally, was in Russian-controlled Poland and was economically well developed but culturally backward. It lacked artists, and those that it did produce all tended to emigrate. One such artist was Ferdynand Ruszczyc, a key figure in Polish art of this period, who moved to Kraków in 1907. The only posters worth mentioning here are those by Stanisława Paradowska for a Fishing Exhibition in 1911, by Juliusz Nagórski-Nałęczów for a clinic and by Edward Butrymowicz for a brand of chicory coffee. All reflect the Austro-German style of the period, with few flat tones and graceful outlines. ❧

1. Zdzisław Schubert, *The Poster Must Sing! / Plakat musi spiewac!*, Muzeum Narodowe w Poznaniu, Poznan, 2012.

Józef Mehoffer, 1910

Edward Batrymowics, 1910

Ferdynand Ruszczyc, 1910

Ivan Bilibin, 1903

Like other countries, Russia underwent a process of industrialization and urbanization in the second half of the nineteenth century, and after 1870 posters were a ubiquitous presence in even the smallest towns. By 1895 there were 103 printing shops in St Petersburg alone, a figure that had risen to 242 by 1901.[1]

It was in St Petersburg that Russia's first international poster exhibition was held in 1897. Out of 727 items on display, only twenty-eight were from Russia.

Russia had a tradition of painted signs, and printers were content to copy them.

But, as was the case elsewhere, there were also young artists who had travelled around Europe and, apprised of the modernist movements in the West, took an interest in lithography and especially in books and engravings, an interest that very soon led them to the world of the poster.

The earliest neo-Russian movement took its inspiration from the popular traditional print, or лубок, which was generally engraved on wood.[2] The pioneers of this Slav revival were Viktor Vasnetsov and Elena Polenova, while Ivan Bilibin adapted this colourful imagery to the poster. The styles were highly diverse: the arabesques of art nouveau were fashionable for artists' balls, as in the work of Nikolai Gerardov and Elena Kiseleva, whereas the theatre posters of Nikolai Remizov were clearly indebted to the Secessionist movement.

At the start of the twentieth century, Sergei Diaghilev published the important review *World of Art*, in which he threw open the doors of Russian art to a radically international modernism. With Alexandre Benois and Léon Bakst, he revolutionized the world of dance with his Ballets Russes, before an even more radical revolution overwhelmed Russia in October 1917. ♣

1. See Alla Rosenfeld (ed.), *Defining Russian Graphic Arts: From Diaghilev to Stalin, 1898–1934*, Rutgers University Press, New Brunswick, 1999, pp.16–38, esp. p.18.

2. After the October Revolution, this was also the model for 'Rosta Windows', lithographic posters that served as revolutionary propaganda and provided advice on daily life. Their name derives from the fact that they were displayed in shop windows. Rosta is the abbreviation for the Russian Telegraph Agency.

Nikolai Gerardov, 1899

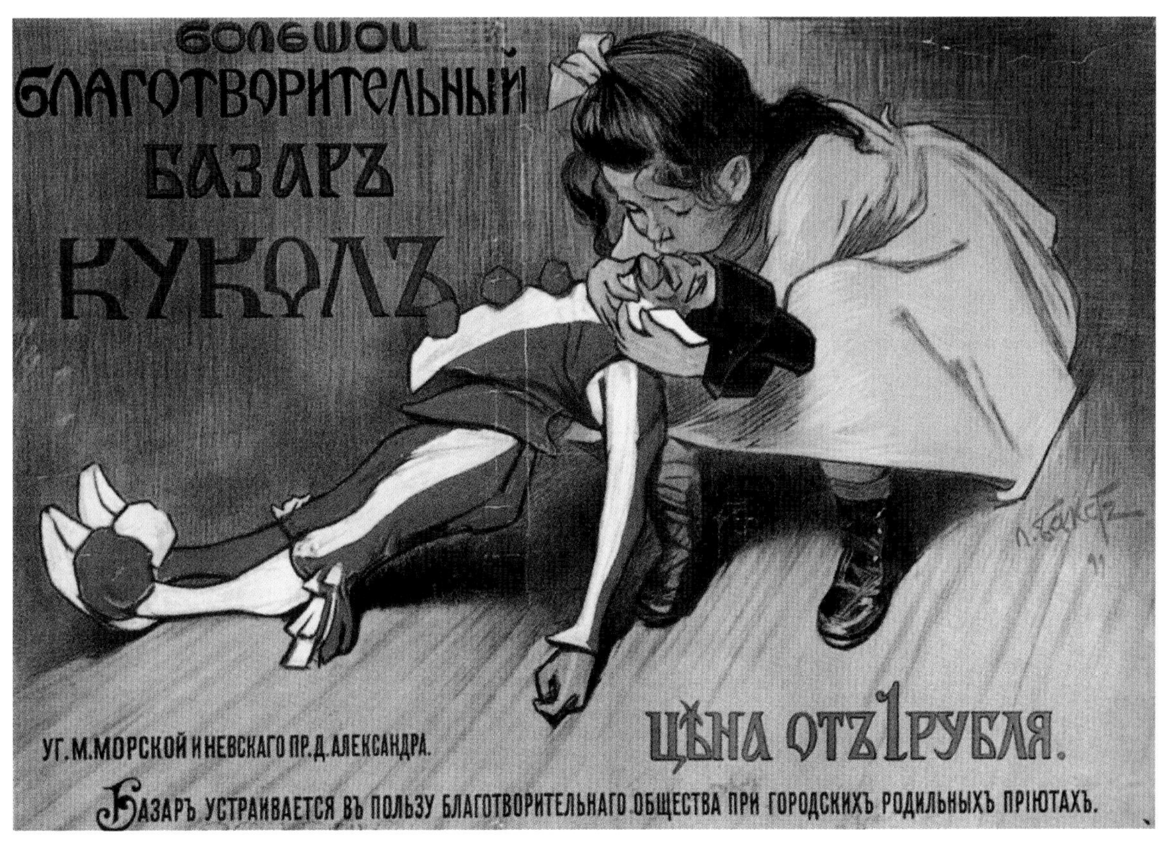

Léon Bakst, 1910-1911

Tsunetomi Kitano, 1911

After 260 years of complete isolation under the Tokugawa dynasty, the Meiji Restoration of 1868 brought with it the return of the emperor. From then on, Japan underwent a rapid process of westernization.

The country's victory over Russia in 1905 helped to reinforce its position, encouraging commerce and industry and fuelling consumerism.

It was an Austrian lithographer, Ottoman Smolik, who initiated the Japanese printer Chokoku-Gaisha, into the art of lithography.

This circumstance no doubt helps to explain why Japanese lithographers used multiple colours to reproduce the designs that were entrusted to them. It is also because Japanese artists never mastered the technique: until the early 1920s posters were no more than reproductions of paintings.

They often depicted *bijin-ga*, beautiful women, which is paradoxical when we recall that it was *ukiyo-e* engravings that influenced the Nabis and, indeed, the whole of Europe. As always, the appeal of all that was new and different proved to be irresistible.

Mitsukoshi sold kimonos and invested a fortune in posters. In 1907 it was a reproduction of an oil painting by Saburosuke Okada that was used. Exactly the same had been the case in the Britain of the 1890s, when advertisers had relied on the services of painters from the Royal Academy. Mitsukoshi organized a competition in 1911. The design that won the first prize was printed as a lithograph requiring no fewer than thirty-five applications of colour.

The vogue for the *bijin-ga* soon spread to brewers, and beer became the newly fashionable drink, leading to an explosion in advertising investment. The same was true of beauty products.

A number of advertisers demanded that their artists take their inspiration from art nouveau, and this was certainly the case with Tsunetomi Kitano for a French-inspired Export Articles Exhibition in 1911 and with Shuzo Ouro for his Anglophone poster for Onoto Fountain Pens. Only after 1914 did a truly graphic approach to the poster begin to develop in Japan thanks to Hisui Sugiura.

Anonymous, 1907

Shuzo Ouro, *c.* 1907-1918

M·S·KOBBS SÖNER
GÖTEBORG
Sedan år 1835 välkända
Importörer af uteslutande
ÄKTA THÉER
BONNIERS LITO·GBG·
FILIALLAGER i STOCKHOLM.
1890

Anonymous

If Jean Louis Sponsel mentions Scandinavia in his book on the modern poster,[1] it was because at the time of writing – 1897 – the whole region was subject to German influence, but he was also keen to point out that posters were to be found in Stockholm, Malmö and Copenhagen. Among examples to which he drew particular attention were ones by the architect Ragnar Östberg for an exhibition in Malmö and by Victor Andreu for a wine merchant and for Pol Roger Champagne, a poster that tapped a notably French vein.

1. Jean Louis Sponsel, *Das moderne Plakat*, Gerhard Kühtmann, Dresden, 1897.

But it was for beer and more specifically the brand Stora Bryggeriet that three artists designed posters, all of them English in style: Carl Westman, Albert Engström and Arthur Sjögren. In general, the Swedish had no misgivings about borrowing from, even plagiarizing, other artists, in particular Chéret's Vin Mariani.

In Denmark, with the exception of Paul Fischer, the images were humourless and lacking in graphic flair, although the situation was to change rapidly after the war. As for Norway and Finland, there was nothing of note.

Anonymous

Axel Erdmann, 1901

Arthur Sjögren, 1895

J. M. Dumontier, 1972, detail

THE ART NOUVEAU REVIVAL

This chapter is a homage to the remarkable exhibition at the Musée d'Orsay in 2009.

Victor Moscoso, 1967

Art nouveau was rendered wholly unfashionable by the Cubist aspirations of the art deco movement and was not welcomed back from the cold until the 1960s, when two seminal exhibitions were curated by Brian Reade at the Victoria & Albert Museum in London: the first was devoted to Alphonse Mucha in 1963, the second to Aubrey Beardsley in 1966.

Both exhibitions were acclaimed, and the Beardsley exhibition even toured the United States. Young and rebellious artists found in Beardsley a prototype for their own revolt against the establishment. Reproductions of his work sold in vast numbers, as did Mucha's *Job*, with its eccentrically coiffured female smoker.

In 1967, George Melly recalled that 'Sometime in the early summer of 1966 I went along to the Victoria & Albert Museum to look at the Beardsley exhibition and was rather surprised to find it packed with people. I was puzzled, not only by the size of the public, but because I found them impossible to place. Many were clearly art students, some were beats, others could have been pop-musicians; most of them were very young, but almost all of them gave the impression of belonging to a secret society which had not yet declared its aims or intentions. I believe now, although I was not to realise it for several months, that I had stumbled for the first time into the presence of the emerging Underground.'[1]

1. George Melly, 'Poster Power', *The Observer Magazine*, 3 Dec. 1967, p.13.

In both London and San Francisco the next two years were to be a colourful, dazzling time that passed with such speed that it could have been an LSD trip.

San Francisco had long been the refuge of numerous beatniks and fringe groups. They included Bill Graham, who ran the Fillmore Auditorium, Stanley 'Mouse' Miller and Alton Kelley, who founded the group The Family Dog that opened the Avalon Ballroom. In this way the ground was prepared for the 'Merry Pranksters' of Ken Kesey and the guru of LSD, Timothy Leary, a defrocked Harvard lecturer. The 'tripfestivals' of the spring of 1966 were the start of a two-year period during which the run-down district of Haight-Ashbury grew from 700 to 10,000 residents and became the capital of

Alton Kelley and Stanley Mouse, 1966

the acid rock culture. Another revolution took place at this time: the concert poster, which until then had been uninspired and stereotypical, became an integral part of the Underground movement that discovered not only music and drugs but also psychedelic art.

There was a good reason for this: the streets of San Francisco permitted a blossoming of poster art which, for lack of space, would have been impossible in Los Angeles or even New York. The poster became the mark of this counterculture. Five individuals – the Big Five – exhibited at the famous Joint Show at the Moore Gallery in 1967. Wes Wilson was closest to Bill Graham, with whom he worked on a regular basis, integrating figures with sinuous art nouveau curves into a typography that almost literally bursts into flames, often acquiring the illegibility of works produced under the influence of acid.[2] His rows with Graham were famous:

Graham: 'Well, it's nice, but I can't read it.'

Wilson: 'Yeah, and that's why people are gonna stop and look at it.'[3]

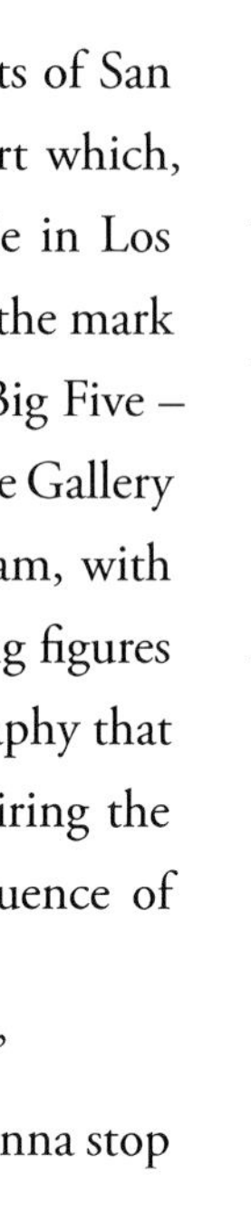
2. In 1966 he saw an exhibition at the University of California at Los Angeles, where he discovered the typography of the Vienna Secession, notably that of Alfred Roller.

3. George Case, *Out of Our Heads: Rock 'n' Roll Before the Drugs Wore Off*, Backbeat Books, New York, 2010, p.56.

It was a dialogue between two men deaf to each other and one, moreover, that came to an end as a result of Graham's greed, when he demanded $100 a poster.

Wilson continued to work for others, most notably Country Joe and The Fish.

He was replaced by Bonnie MacLean, who was Graham's companion and one of his disciples. Graham told another of his successors, David Singer, that he liked his typography. And when David Edward Byrd submitted his work to him, he declared that he liked it precisely because he could read it. Wilson's comment had clearly left him traumatized.

Rick Griffin came from the world of surfing. He was a fantastic illustrator who used saturated colours and a typography that could easily turn to a pixilated neo-gothic: the eye, the insects and the old advertisements were recycled in this baroque magma that could soon become science-fiction. The two founders of The Family Dog, Alton Kelley and Stanley 'Mouse' Miller, were already active in the Bay at this time. Both were

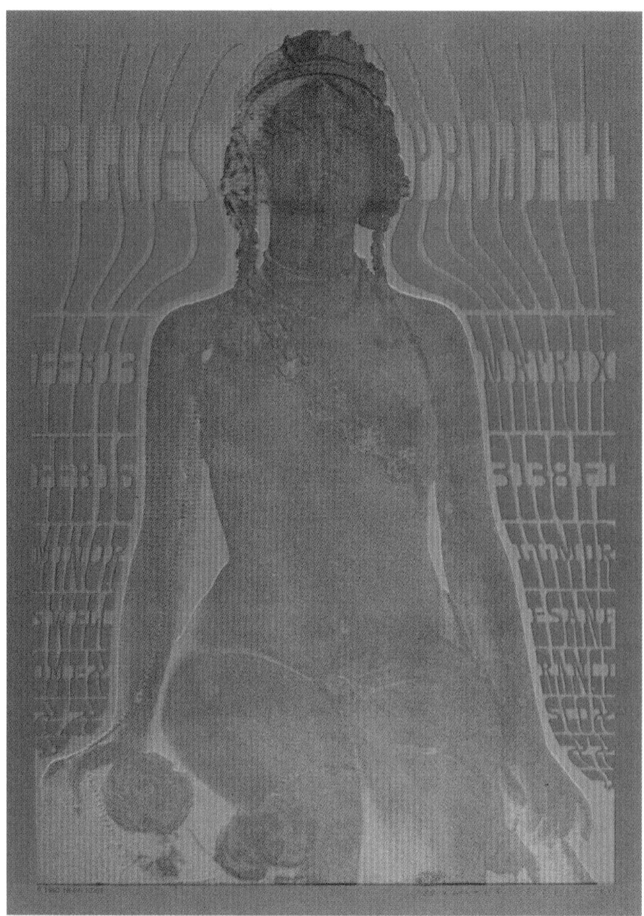

Victor Moscoso, 1967

Victor Moscoso, 1967

Michael McInnerney, 1967

passionate about machinery. Mouse painted hot rods, as he once explained: in 1966 'we were learning how to play with the art-nouveau shapes and to infuse them with our own style and sense of humour'.[4]

Mouse specialized in the lettering, readily admitting to having been inspired by Mucha. In order to come up with ideas, he and Kelley would accumulate a mass of documents that they called their 'image bank' or 'graphic flea market'. Portraits of Native American Indians, stars of the silent cinema and even Edgar Allan Poe were effortlessly integrated into their typographical extravaganzas. And they worked in a joyful spirit of competition in which each of them tried to go further than ever before.

Victor Moscoso was the only member of the group to have had a solid artistic education, having studied at Yale with Josef Albers. From art nouveau to op art, he turned on its head everything that he had learnt at school and found that this worked much better for him. Saturated and vibrant colours and illegible typography – this approach reached its maturity with his poster for The Matrix, a small concert hall, and his series *Neon Rose*, which he produced himself.

We should also mention Lee Conklin, who arrived on the scene at a slightly later date, in 1968, and who drifted between surrealism and the fantastical, and Randy Tuten, who was influenced by Griffin and who is well known for his crazy fruits posters.

But magic is tied to a particular time and place. The stocks of LSD, which became illegal in 1966, were exhausted. Berkeley Bonaparte, the publishing house and distribution company set up by Griffin, Kelley, Mouse, Moscoso and Wilson, shut up shop. The Family Dog was driven from Avalon.[5] The best groups fell under the control of major record labels, a development that merely increased the comings and goings between London and San Francisco.

What happened in London in 1966–7 was in many ways similar to what was going on at this time in San Francisco: LSD, music (and what music!), 'flower people'

4. Stanley Miller and Alton Kelley, *Mouse & Kelley*, Dragon's World, New York, 1979, p.11.

5. Ben Friedman, the astute owner of Postermat, bought up all their stock, together with the surplus copies owned by Bill Graham, which explains why many of his posters are not particularly rare today.

Hapshash and the Coloured Coat
(Michael English and Nigel Waymouth), 1967

Martin Sharp, 1968

refusing to accept the puritan dullness of the day, and a run-down quarter – Notting Hill Gate – where the whole of the underground scene gathered.[6]

It was a far more politicized movement than in San Francisco. There were two important publications: *International Times* (*IT*), whose artistic director was Michael McInnerney, and *OZ*, which first came out in 1967 as a sequel to a magazine founded in Sydney by Richard Neville and Martin Sharp, both of whom escaped prison terms for obscenity. *IT* was the more militant of the two, *OZ* more hedonistic, but they did more than overlap and share the same visions.

In 1966 *IT* found what would be the equivalent of the Fillmore Auditorium in Tottenham Court Road in London's West End: the UFO Club (Underground Freak Out), with Pink Floyd and Procol Harum performing their legendary version of 'A Whiter Shade of Pale'. As Barry Miles has written, 'Perhaps another reason why the UFO became so legendary is that it produced the only English equivalent of the American Family Dog and Bill Graham posters. Most were done by Michael English and Nigel Waymouth.'[7]

6. The hedonism of the Fillmore and the Avalon should not allow us to forget the Berkeley Riots. This, after all, was also the time of the anti-Vietnam War movement and of Martin Luther King.
7. Barry Miles, *London Calling: A Countercultural History of London Since 1945*, Atlantic Books, London, 2010, p.215.

Waymouth soon opened a psychedelic boutique in the King's Road called Granny Takes a Trip. He also became an associate of Michael English, a brilliant student who researched his material in the library of the Victoria & Albert Museum. Together they founded Hapshash and the Coloured Coat and became the UFO Club's official poster designers, while also designing a poster for the Jimi Hendrix Experience at the Saville Theatre (now a cinema, the Odeon Covent Garden). They also published a large number of albums and other posters. Apart from his covers and posters for *OZ*, Martin Sharp pursued similar objectives, including the legalization of cannabis, and founded Big O.

London revived the Paris tradition of the decorative panel and, unlike San Francisco, it was able to provide a clientele. The centre of London became the capital of hippie culture, Biba was transformed into a jungle of art deco, and Carnaby Street simply had to be seen.

Peter Max, 1966

David Edward Byrd, 1970

Tadanori Yokoo, 1968

Tadanori Yokoo, 1968

Tadanori Yokoo, 1966

Keiichi Tanaami, 1968

George Melly summed up the situation at this time: 'The Underground poster is not so much a means of broadcasting information as a way of advertising a trip to an artificial paradise. […] It operated in the gap between life and art'.[8]

After the Summer of Love in 1967, when the Beatles sang 'All You Need is Love', history repeated itself in a rather sordid way. The UFO Club closed. After targeting the Rolling Stones, the police turned their attention to *OZ*, once again charging it with obscenity, and its owners escaped prison only on appeal. It ceased publication in 1973.

If we can speak of a revival of poster art in London and San Francisco, the same was not true of New York. Bill Graham, who opened Fillmore East, produced practically none, while the Push Pin Studios associated with Seymour Chwast, Milton Glaser, Reynold Ruffins and Edward Sorel reflected many different influences but these cannot be reduced to that of art nouveau alone. Even so the fashion for art nouveau was now in full swing. The world abhors a vacuum, and so Peter Max,[9] a skilful artist with a good eye for an opportunity, produced a whole series of decorative images inspired by art nouveau, adding cosmic and tantric elements for good measure. His success, which led him on to wallpaper, was considerable.

In continental Europe the centre of the psychedelic underground was Amsterdam, where the cult's temple was the Paradisio, which for the most part was content to produce typographic posters. It was the most politicized fringe of the younger generation – the 'provos' – who produced posters, in which respect it differed from all that was going on London and New York at this time. These were the same artists as those who set up the popular workshops in Paris in May 1968.

The mere mention of the Summer of Love of 1967 and the events of May 1968 is enough to indicate that we are dealing here with two very different things: serigraphs rushed out to disseminate a powerful message in May 1968, these posters were the opposite of the psychedelic posters of the previous year since they needed to be instantly legible. In Paris, moreover, drugs were practically non-existent – who would entertain the idea of having a trip while standing on top of the barricades?

And yet here, too, art nouveau again became fashionable. The interior decor of the great cafés and bars from around 1900 had in the meantime been destroyed, but were replaced by cheap imitations. Only Wiatscheslav ('Slavik') Vassiliev, who decorated theatres, restaurants and boutiques, brought a modicum of talent to the exercise. French pop music, magazines and advertising were overwhelmed by pitiful pastiches in which the whiplash curve deserved only to be derided and the typefaces were pilfered from much earlier models by second-rate plagiarists. Apart from the images associated with the student revolt of May 1968, two major schools of draughtsmanship dominated the European arts scene at this time: the Poles and the Swiss. Strong personalities with a highly assertive style, they had no need to turn to the past in search of their inspiration. The only artist to stand out was perhaps Jan Lenica, whose opera posters used sensual and boldly outlined curves that sometimes recall the stained-glass windows of art nouveau.

In the end, the surprise came from a quarter where it was least expected.

Tadanori Yokoo had been designing hallucinatory psychedelic posters since 1966. He went further than anyone else, mixing elements from popular Japanese culture, including the Hokusai Great Wave and the rays of the sun found on the Japanese flag, with western references such as Gabriel d'Estrée, Ingres's *The Turkish Bath* and Marilyn Monroe. This was more than a mere extension of the posters for Fillmore and Avalon. In 1968 he designed a poster for the fashionable boutique Jun, creating a Japanese version of Bonnard's *La Revue blanche* and revealing all that he owed to French art nouveau. Using curves in primary colours, Kiyoshi Awazu, who was Tadanori Yokoo's contemporary, also deserves a mention, and the same is true of Keiichi Tanaami, who was more directly inspired by the volutes of art nouveau and by western pop art. ❧

8. Melly, 'Poster Power' (note 2), p.14. The phrase 'the gap between life and art' is one that is associated with Robert Rauschenberg.

9. We have him to thank for a striking portrait of Toulouse-Lautrec.

Lth

Tito Tòpin

Journal de Spirou, unsigned, 1961 © Dargaud – Lombard, 2015

J. M. Dumontier, 1972

INDEX

Louis Abel-Truchet, 1900, detail

Page numbers in **bold** refer to dedicated pages about the artist. Page numbers in *italics* refer to illustrations.

E

F

G

H

I

J

K

L

M

N

O

P

R

S

Eugène Ogé, 1913 (see page 151)

Photo credits

Swann Galleries and Alain Weill for all posters